The Gun That Wasn't There

RUSSELL S. SMITH

THE GUN THAT WASN'T THERE

2007

The Gun That Wasn't There

ACKNOWLEDGMENT

My thanks go out to all those who contributed to <u>The Gun That Wasn't There</u>. Special thanks to Ben Ross, Candace Cooksey Fulton, Henry Beth Hogg and Alfred Allee Jr. who I pestered on a pretty regular basis, to Joe Rivera who led me to three of the main characters, and to Ross McSwain, Areta Robinson and Linda Hermes who proof-read the final drafts. Very special thanks to Elmer Kelton who wrote the introduction and to Anne-Charlotte Patterson (southerncombustion.com) who designed the cover.

Dalton Hogg, The Former Terrell County Deputy Sheriff And Retired Terrell County Sheriff Died On May 28, 1998; Bill C. Cooksey, The Former Terrell County Sheriff, Died On April 27, 2000; And, Retired Texas Ranger Alfred Young Allee Jr. Died On January 12, 2006. Only Allee Was Able To Read A Draft Of The Gun That Wasn't There, But He Said, "It's Pretty Accurate."

The Gun That Wasn't There Is Dedicated To These Men And To All The Law Enforcement Officers And Citizens Who Pursued Alfredo Amador Hernandez. It Is Also Dedicated To All Those Honest Hardworking People, On Both Sides Of The Rio Grande River, Whose Lives Were Affected By This Caveman Bandit.

INTRODUCTION

Texas folklore offers many stories of phantoms, most of which raised questions never answered and left mysteries unsolved. Examples are the legends of the wild woman of the Navidad River, the "murder steer" of the Davis Mountains, and la llorona, the wraith-like mother roaming the banks of Texas and Mexican rivers, crying for her drowned children.

The Dryden Caveman took on dimensions of legend in the 1960s, roaming across the southern edges of the Hill Country and the Big Bend like a will-o-the-wisp. He lived as a coyote would live, hiding in thick brush and caves, burglarizing houses for food, clothing and small comforts. He was regarded as a minor nuisance until he shot a man who caught him stealing from his home, and later shot and seriously wounded Terrell County Sheriff Bill Cooksey, who came upon him unexpectedly while inspecting a cave.

At that point he was no longer a vague, ghostlike figure, but a flesh-and-blood man capable of killing anyone who got in his way. He brought fear to people living along the Rio Grande, but he also aroused a local citizenry determined to end his criminal career.

Legend always demands that some questions remain forever unanswered, and such is the case with the Caveman. After serving a long prison sentence, he walked out of the gates and disappeared as mysteriously as he had lived. After most of forty years, no one knows what happened to him. Or, if they know, they have never told.

Russell Smith did years of research on the Caveman and those who participated in the massive manhunt that finally brought him to ground in a frenzy of gunfire. He also found out much about the wily fugitive and the shadowy life he led. It is indeed the kind of story from which legends are born.

Elmer Kelton

THE PROLOGUE

Every day people cross the Rio Grande River and enter into Texas and the United States illegally. Most of these men and women are hardworking individuals in search of a job and a better way of life.[1] But every so often one of these people is a criminal who preys on their unsuspecting victims; such was the case in the 1960s with Alfredo Amador Hernandez.[2]

Hernandez was a bandit whose burglaries and armed robberies, and at least one attempted murder, brought fear and anger into different areas of Real, Uvalde, Val Verde and Terrell counties. Excerpts of his major crimes were written about within the pages of the Uvalde Leader News,[3] Del Rio News-Herald,[4] the Sanderson Times,[5] Odessa American,[6] Corpus Christi Caller-Times,[7] San Angelo Standard-Times[8] and the San Antonio Express-News,[9] but there is so much more to this part of Texas history.

This story is also about the victims, the people who lived in those counties and the difficulty of the terrain. It is about the law enforcement officers and their posses who pursued the man with their limited resources, and it is about Bill Cooksey, the former Terrell County Sheriff who first told this writer about Hernandez.

Cooksey was a lawman who went to work one day and didn't take the revolver he usually placed in a holster alongside his right hip. Instead he stuck a small semi-automatic pistol inside the waistband of his pants. It was a decision that nearly cost him his life.

This writer's investigation into this Texas history included literally dozens of interviews, thousands of miles traveled and the research of newspapers, photographs, moon and weather data, court and prison records and a file provided by Bill Cooksey. By the conclusion of the investigation, this writer had developed a perception of the criminal's habits and demeanor as he committed his crimes. Even though a few discrepancies were found and memories may not have been as sharp as they were back in the 60s, The Gun That Wasn't There[10] should give the reader an historical account of what some might call the legend of the Caveman Bandit.

CHAPTER ONE
July 1965

A Mexican named Alfredo Amador Hernandez was known to have burglarized many Texas homes and businesses and was suspected of many others. Deadbolt locks and alarms were not the norm in the 1960s and the man basically survived by taking things he didn't own. Through all the interviews and research, this writer developed a perception about how Hernandez went about committing his crimes. This chapter gives the reader a glimpse of the bandit's habits, characteristics and stealth. The location could have been any ranch house and family in West Texas.[11]

Alfredo Hernandez opened his eyes as the Southern Pacific Railroad locomotive started to climb an upward grade. In the midst of the friction of rolling metal wheels upon the tracks he could also hear the jostle, the domino effect that started near the engine and was working its way back toward his open boxcar and the caboose.[12]

As the train slowed, he stood and lifted his morral, his knapsack, with his right hand while holding his hat in the other. He peered out the right side of the car and looked out across the moonlit landscape. Then he looked to his left. The train was almost to a crawl now. He recognized a landmark where the train was leveling off at the top. It was where he would get off.[13]

Hernandez waited for the right time, jumped and his small five-foot six-inch, one hundred twenty-five pound 34-year-old body came to rest on the railroad right-of-way. Within seconds he sat crouched and watched the train move off to the West.[14]

He had used trains for transportation[15] ever since he'd come to the United States from San Luis Potosi, Mexico[16], when he was in his early 20s in the 1950s.[17] The trains were getting harder to catch now; they were getting faster. Of course he never paid for a ride but rather hopped in and out of the open doors of boxcars.[18]

An immigration violation had landed him in the La Tuna federal prison near El Paso[19]. After he'd been deported in 1961, he'd set up hidden camps along the railroad tracks from Sanderson to Uvalde. While most people crossed the border looking for work and a better way of life, this man plied a different trade.[20]

The sounds of the train had faded. He sat there for a moment staring up into the open sky, looking at the stars and at a moon that would soon disappear. He loved the night. It was his time and maybe that was what made him different from most. As he stood and dusted himself off, he felt a hunger in his belly and wanted to satisfy it. Even though he didn't like to enter places when anyone was home, he knew there was a house less than a mile away.

The wood frame, tin roofed house was just like Hernandez remembered, except that it was dark now. The only visible light was a guard light next to a barn that was to the right about fifty yards away. The light cast shadows to the offside of a pickup, a car, two stock trailers and the west and north sides of the house.

He stood there a while looking toward the front door. The guard light exposed it. He knew that the living room area was inside to the left. A bedroom was to the right with a bathroom and another bedroom just beyond. The kitchen, with a back door that was in the shadows, was behind the living room.

He had watched a family leave the last time he was there. A man, woman and teenaged girl—all dressed in Sunday-go-to-meeting clothes—had gotten into a car and driven off. The man had carried what appeared to be a Bible and he assumed they were going to church.

This time was different though because he knew that the people were probably home. He knew he'd have to be quiet and careful, and he worried mostly about the dogs. He worked his way around through senisa, cedar and cactus and made his way to a small shed just west of the house. He stayed in the shadows. Then he froze when he saw something move.

Hernandez felt a slight breeze at the back of his neck and realized the Border Collie had apparently smelled him. It had caused the dog to rise and come toward him. He knew that Collies were great sheep and cattle dogs and that most got along well with strangers. He knelt as the ranch dog drew closer, his tail wagging as though he remembered their last meeting.

He had knelt and rubbed the head of the Collie back then, letting the dog get to know him, while a second dog, a Blue Heeler had kept its distance. Now the Collie was rubbing its head against his leg while he stroked the long hair on top of its back. He sat there with the dog and watched the house. He hoped the dog would not yelp or make any noise when he made his move toward the residence. He finally saw movement again. The Blue Heeler had come out from under the pickup at the front of the house. The dog gave a slight growl, yet quieted as the man walked slowly toward the kitchen door.

He was worried about the Heeler. He knew they normally bonded very closely with their owners. He knew the dogs could be anti-social toward strangers. He stopped a few feet from the kitchen door when the sounds of snoring caught his attention. He looked down at the Collie and over toward the Heeler.

The man felt for a mask in his morral but didn't find it. He made a mental note to replace it later. He moved his hand and brought out a flashlight and a piece of cloth. He covered the lens with the cloth and turned the switch. Only a slight glow emitted the cloth, but it was all he needed. The inside kitchen door appeared to be open. Only the screen door was closed. He knew it was fairly common for the windows and doors to be open because of the heat at this time of year. He reached out and s-l-o-w-l-y pulled on the handle while keeping pressure on the door with the hand holding the light. The door was latched shut.

He turned off the light and put it back in his morral. He felt inside the knapsack and found a piece of metal that he had made for just such occasions.[21] He slid the metal between the screen door and the doorframe. He held the door's handle with his left hand and lifted the homemade tool with his right, lifting the latch off the hook. He was careful not to drop the latch and reached around and grabbed hold of it. Then he slowly opened the screen door and stepped inside.

He slipped off his shoes so he could search the room on his calloused feet. It would be quieter.[22] He wanted to leave his shoes outside but he was afraid one of the dogs might carry them off.

He covered the flashlight once again and turned it on. The glow revealed a pantry to his left. He took a can of refried beans and a can of chili off the shelves and placed them within pockets he'd sewn inside his morral.[23] He knew he didn't want to take too much because he didn't want the people to know he'd ever been there.

He took three flour tortillas from a dozen within a cloth-covered basket and three cookies out of a cookie jar that were on the counter near the sink. Then he put the flashlight away and put his hands on the refrigerator.

Holding the door shut with his left hand, he s-l-o-w-l-y pulled on the handle with his right. Then he let the door open, slightly. If anyone were nearby, the refrigerator's light would have revealed a thin faced, dark complexioned man with jet-black hair[24] that protruded from beneath a black cowboy hat[25]. They would have also seen the morral, a burlap sack tied from both ends with rope that was draped over his shoulder. They would have seen a smile on the man's face.

Hernandez loved grapes[26] and soft drinks[27] and both were on the shelves of the refrigerator. He took a bottle of the soft drink and put it in one of the pockets within his knapsack. The pockets were to keep things quiet, to keep them from clanging together. He broke a sprig of grapes off the cluster and put them in his shirt pocket. Then he shut the door.

Squeak! He had not expected the noise, especially one as loud as it was in the quiet of the night. When he'd stepped back from the refrigerator, his weight on a particular board had caused the sound. Part of the snoring had stopped. He stood perfectly still, slowly reaching for the butt of a revolver that he kept at his side. He listened but could only hear one person.

The woman let out a sigh and propped herself up on her left elbow. She pushed her long auburn hair off the right side of her face. She was sure the noise had come from the kitchen. The woman wanted a cigarette but then realized she'd have to get up and get it out of her purse. She looked over at her husband who was still snoring loudly and decided to go back to sleep. She assumed their teenage daughter was just getting a snack.

Hernandez could feel his heart racing. He kept listening, intently, while part of his mind kept reminding him that he didn't ever want to go back to prison. While in his 20s, he had been arrested and convicted of nighttime burglaries in New Mexico and Texas.[28] When he'd gotten out of La Tuna[29], he told himself he would never go back to prison again.

Alfredo Hernandez. Photo courtesy of Candace Cooksey Fulton.

It was several minutes before he heard the second person snoring again. It was a little different sound, in pitch, but he assumed that it was the person who had moved around. He slowly backed his way toward the screen door. He picked up his shoes and quietly made his way outside. Then he used the tool to place the door latch back into the eye within the doorframe.

As he sat and tied his shoes, he heard the snoring again, but he also heard something else. The wind had picked up and the noise came from clothes hanging on a clothesline, flapping in the wind out behind the house. It took several minutes but he looped out behind the clothes, keeping himself as far away from the bedroom windows as he could. Then he quietly removed two clothespins that held a piece of clothing.

The Collie didn't move past the shed as the man left in pretty much the same way as he'd come. But it was the woman's white nightgown[30] and the grapes that kept his attention until he was a mile away.

He took his time as he ate the grapes. He savored every bite, chew and taste. The freshness of the nightgown reminded him of the woman who was back across the Rio Grande River, the woman who was hundreds of miles to the south in Monterrey.

The last time he'd seen Rosa she'd waved goodbye while standing with her back against the open doorframe of her tan stucco dwelling. She was barefoot, wearing blue jeans and a green button up shirt. She'd pulled her long black hair over her right shoulder and it had fallen beneath the depth of her right breast. She was ten years younger and several inches shorter than he and didn't weigh more than one hundred ten pounds.[31] He regularly sent her money; money she used to help support her family and part of which she'd send to his mother. Or he would take her money when he went to visit her, when he returned from visiting his mother in Tomezunchale.[32]

As daybreak was starting to show itself on the horizon, Hernandez knelt down in front of a thick but familiar clump of brush and cactus. He crawled on his belly, headfirst through a small opening and into an open area that he'd cut out in the past. This was one of his sleeping camps. It was a place that he felt secure in, much like a coyote or fox in its den. He never cooked in his sleeping camp so there was another camp about a hundred yards away. It was designed the same way but with hidden pots and pans that he would use later to heat up the chili and beans.[33]

He laid back and used the morral and his hat as a pillow. He smelled the nightgown. He knew he would cut the sleeves off later to make another mask to cover his face.[34] He felt a slight vibration and heard the increasing sounds of another train, a train that would soon pass within fifty yards of him. As his mind drifted off toward sleep, he thought about another mask, a mask made from a pair of red silk pajamas, pajamas he'd taken from a home in the Texas Hill Country.[35]

CHAPTER TWO
The Hill Country

Alfredo Hernandez had been to prison twice for nighttime burglaries during the 1950s. These previous exploits had taken him to deep South Texas and to the State of New Mexico. In the early 1960s he made his way to Uvalde County and to what is known as the Texas Hill Country.[36]

What drew the man to Uvalde County? The following is only supposition, but this writer wonders if he had not heard about Uvalde and the hills to the north for about as long as he could remember. Had men and women from his native state of San Luis Potosi talked about the rivers, the good climate, the crops grown in irrigated fields and about farmers and ranchers who always had work for them? Or had he heard about Uvalde while he was in prison? Had he hopped into an open boxcar and just gotten off there? Well, for whatever the reason, he made his way there.

The name Uvalde came from the Spaniard Juan de Ugalde. The town of Uvalde,[37] the county seat, is located about halfway between San Antonio and Del Rio. Del Rio is situated on the Texas side of the Texas-Mexico border.[38] Railroad tracks run through Uvalde, and they mostly parallel the pavement of Highway 90. Each connects San Antonio to Uvalde, Brackettville, Del Rio, Dryden, Sanderson and other parts out West.

This writer found no direct evidence as to exactly when Hernandez made his way to Uvalde County. One newspaper article could lead a suspecting person to believe he was in the county seat, with its huge pecan and oak trees that lined the main city streets, in the summer of 1962. It was then that the Uvalde Leader News, the local bi-weekly newspaper, reported a break-in at the Army Navy Surplus store. Five pistols (.22 and .38 caliber) and an assortment of .22 caliber ammunition had been stolen.[39] A presumption could be made because guns were a highly sought after commodity in Mexico and the man used a .38

caliber pistol while committing several crimes, including one in the Hill Country.

Did he follow the Frio River north from a tiny place called Knippa just east of Uvalde or did he follow U.S. Highway 83 north toward the Hill Country? This writer assumes the latter especially since the railroad tracks ran across the north side of town and under the highway. Of course, no matter which way he went, someone might assume that Hernandez built his small hidden camps as he made his way north.

The design of his camp was simple; a small ground level opening that looked more like an animal run than something a man would crawl into, cut into a clump of thick brush, a center area cut out big enough for him to lie down within, then an exit way cut out the other side. The cuttings, tied with twine or wire, secured the entry and exit while he was inside.[40] In the past, similar camps had kept him hidden from Border Patrol agents, hunters and cowboys on horseback.

Alfredo Hernandez had apparently survived by taking things from others for most of his adult life. He seemed to make a practice of leaving the houses pretty much as he had found them. If he took the hinges off of a door or a pane of glass out of a window to gain entry, he would replace them the way they were before he left. He didn't want anyone to know he'd ever been there.[41] But he did leave clues, if only anyone would have known to connect the dots.

Most people who entered the United States illegally were hardworking people looking for work, and they would just take enough food to get them along their way. So did Hernandez, but he also occasionally took other things like a pair of scissors, razor, bar of soap, needle and thread, pots and pans, clothes, paper and pen, envelopes and stamps, gun and ammunition, magazines and books, and, of course, money.[42] Many of his burglary victims did not realize they had been victimized at all. Others just thought or said, "I thought I had another can of beans," or, "a dozen eggs instead of ten." Most just thought they were absentminded about already using or misplacing what was not there.[43]

Hernandez was suspected of spending great amounts of time watching the places that he planned to enter. He must have learned the habits of the people who lived in the houses and worked in the businesses.[44] He made great efforts to not take chances that he didn't have to. He tried not to come face to face with anyone unless he thought the risk was worth the effort.

This was the same method of casing, as they might say in law enforcement lingo, that he seemed to use as he settled into the hills, into the caves along the Frio Canyon area near Concan. It was there along the crystal clear flowing Frio River, with its apron of tall pecan, oak, cypress and sycamore trees, that he found his victims. It was along the power lines and caliche roads and along U.S. Highway 83, the highway that ran the 40 miles from Uvalde to Leakey, with Concan in between, that led him to others.

It was Hernandez's burglaries and thefts that were his very means of survival, with the exception of an occasional deer—hit by a car or caught in a fence—or an errant sheep or goat,[45] whether Angora or Spanish.

All indications are that his crime spree area soon stretched from Reagan Wells, Garner State Park, Happy Hollow and on into the southern part of Real County, not far from the small town of Leakey. While he apparently survived on stolen food and possibly garden vegetables, peaches and pecans, it is easy to assume that he was always looking for money to send home to Rosa and his mother.[46]

It was pretty common knowledge during those times that people who came to the United States to work made a practice of sending money back to their families in Mexico. There is no indication that Hernandez did anything less, only that he stole his money instead of working for it. Of course, he may have sent all his money to Rosa. This assumption was made because Rosa lived in a good-sized city with an organized postal system. His mother lived in what some might call a village, a place where the mail may have been stuck on a nail until it was picked up. Any nail-mail with a United States postmark would probably have been opened or stolen in hopes of finding money. Rosa told investigators years later that she had sent money to his mother on occasion.[47]

Hernandez probably followed another common practice of taking money home with him each time he returned. This may have been on his mind as he watched the Happy Hollow store around the 4th of March 1963.

This writer can just visualize Hernandez hidden in a thicket as he watched the store through binoculars. He was probably sitting on the rise just across Highway 83 and, by then, he was not any stranger to the layout of the Happy Hollow store or the house next door. He had probably been inside each several times before.

In one instance just several months before, the store's owner had taken the day's receipts into his house and hidden them behind some canisters that were high up on a shelf in his kitchen. The next morning, the canisters were sitting on the kitchen cabinet and the money was gone. Otherwise the house was secure. Of course this fit Hernandez's modus operandi, or in layman's terms—his way of doing things.

Hernandez probably sent part of the money back to Mexico via the United States Postal Service, and he'd probably hidden some within the earthen floors of one of the caves that he stayed in on occasion. He also used the caves as a hiding place for many other things.[48]

A passerby might peer into a cave and find a lock or two of his hair, the scissors he used to cut it, a soft drink bottle and a blanket, but nothing else would be visible. Hernandez had learned to hide clothes, non-perishable food, valuables and other things by burying them beneath the place where he slept. His weight on his pallet or blanket packed the earth and made it look natural.[49]

Hernandez probably watched as the outside lights of the Happy Hollow Store were turned off on that March afternoon. Surely he watched owner A.V. Rutherford as he locked the outside door and walked over to his house. He must have searched the man's every movement in hopes he'd see a moneybag or an indication the man had taken the day's receipts to his house.

***

Arthur Vernon Rutherford, known as A.V. to everyone who knew him, was born in Arkansas in 1900. It was there that he met and married his wife Pearl. They had four children, (Harlan Gilbert known as Buster, Bernice, Raymond and Johnie), before they moved to Bronte, Texas in 1926. A.V. had been a barber in his early life.[50]

In 1938 Rutherford moved his family to Happy Hollow, a beautiful little place in the Texas Hill Country just above Garner State Park on U.S. Highway 83. The Frio River lined the back of their new homestead; a homestead that included a house and a small store.[51]

Rutherford family in front of Happy Hollow store. (L-R), A.V. Rutherford, Pearl, Bernice, Ray and Johnie. Photo courtesy of Helen Hillis Gallup.

The area was called Happy Hollow partially because of a large concrete slab that was built between the store and the highway. It had been the site of many an outside dance that had produced a lot of whooping and hollering and a lot of happy people, especially during the time that Garner State Park was being developed by the Civilian Conservation Corps.[52]

The Rutherfords were a product of the depression and had learned to be very frugal. When they opened their small grocery store, that also sold gasoline, A.V. Rutherford only had $20 left to his name.[53]

Travelers and neighbors soon started to do business with the new storeowners. But tragedy also struck the family that year. Their oldest child Buster Rutherford was killed in a car wreck near Knippa just east of Uvalde.[54]

The family persevered and had a surviving business by the mid-1940s, a time when Rutherford thought he'd been made an offer he couldn't refuse. It was an offer that led him to move his family a few miles down U.S. 83 to Garner State Park. A.V. Rutherford was the new Park Manager.[55]

The State of Texas had acquired the park in the mid-1930s and named it after John Nance 'Cactus Jack' Garner. The Uvalde native served as Vice-President of the United States under President Franklin D. Roosevelt from 1933 to 1941.[56]

The new park manager worked to improve the facilities for the park guests. However, by the mid-1950s, conflicts with the higher-ups in Austin moved the Rutherfords back to Happy Hollow.[57]

It wasn't long before the old Happy Hollow store was replaced by a new cinder-block building that was built on the concrete dance floor. It was a bigger store that allowed the Rutherfords to carry more merchandise and increase their business.[58] It was out of this store that A.V. Rutherford had walked on the Monday night of March 4th.

***

If Hernandez was watching that night, it wasn't long before he saw A.V. Rutherford and his wife drive away in their car. He probably couldn't believe his luck as he made his way to their house. While it is suspected that he took the backdoor off to enter their house on the previous occasion, the investigation revealed that he entered through a slightly open window above a flowerbed on the night of March 4th.[59]

He crawled into and through the window and across an old pedal driven sewing machine that was covered with a quilt. It wasn't long before he climbed out of the window again.[60] Contrary to what he normally did, he wasn't careful in going through the house and this writer believes it was because he knew he was going back to Mexico soon.

Hernandez found a moneybag hidden behind a layout mirror high on the kitchen wall, a bag full of silver dollars inside a drawer in the sewing machine stand and money and jewelry in Mrs. Rutherford's purse on the dresser. He also took food from the kitchen and a newspaper clipping that was stuck to the refrigerator door.[61]

Although there is no evidence that he could read or speak much English, something about the clipping must have caught his attention. Maybe he thought it was an account of his earlier theft from the house while it was actually a reporter's account of how Pearl Rutherford had recently returned from visiting relatives in Arkansas. The story had appeared in the Concan Section of a Thursday edition of the Uvalde Leader News.[62]

On March 7, 1963, the newspaper ran another story on its front page, 'The Sheriff's Department is continuing its investigation of the burglary of A.V. Rutherford's house at Happy Hollow on the Leakey Highway

Monday night. Missing is $535 in cash and $100 worth of jewelry. The burglary occurred while Rutherford was gone from the house, only about 25 minutes. Bloodhounds were used by Sheriff Hugh Emsley yesterday in an attempt to track down the burglars.'[63]

***

Sheriff Emsley's wife, Bernice, may have very well answered the phone in their jail-based living quarters that night. She probably turned to the Sheriff and said, "It's A.V. Rutherford; he had another break-in."

By this time the Sheriff should have known that he had a real problem in this area of Frio Canyon. Rutherford had now been broken into twice within the last few months and others, including A.A. Collins the Precinct 3 Justice of the Peace, had reported several break-ins during that same time period.[64]

Collins' burglaries were kind of different though. There was no sign of forced entry and maybe a little food was taken. But whoever did it left their dirty clothes by his wife's washing machine. The JP had commented, "I probably wouldn't even have noticed had the guy not left his dirty clothes and taken one of my favorite shirts."[65]

***

William Hugh Emsley was born in Ranger, Texas on June 5, 1901. His father's family came from England. His mother was of full-blood Indian decent and that probably contributed to the Sheriff's dark complexion. With his black hair, brown eyes and the ability to speak Spanish fluently, he was often thought to be Mexican.[66] The Sheriff was an accomplished horseman and cowboy. For many years he'd worked for the Schwartz Ranch that was east of Uvalde, then moved on into the business of law enforcement as a deputy for the former Sheriff, N.L. 'Hap' Stark. He and his wife never did have children.[67]

Most people didn't give the quiet man much thought until they saw the badge and the German Luger pistol that was holstered on his left side.[68] The pistol seemed out of place with his gray felt hat, white shirt, khaki pants and cowboy boots.[69] Sheriff Emsley was a slender man, about average height whose firm handshake could surprise a person. He was not a man of many words, but he had a look, a look that could stare a hole right through you. Or his eyes could show love and compassion especially when he knelt down, pushed his cowboy hat back on his head and hugged and caressed his dogs.[70]

Sheriff Emsley had not wanted to give up on the search, but his dogs, yelping and howling, had taken off up into a steep sided arroyo that was so thick with trees, brush and cactus that the horses could not follow. There were no trails that led into the place; there were only varied undercuts used by varmints and other animals.[71]

As he and his posse made their way on foot, he'd heard one of his dogs cry out as if in pain. Then the howling stopped. Within a few minutes the dogs had come back to him. He couldn't see anything visibly wrong but they were snorting and sneezing and he knew something had happened.[72]

People would later suspect that Hernandez used cayenne pepper, garlic or an herb from Mexico to dispel the dogs. Others would say he hit them with rocks or sticks, but nonetheless the good-natured dogs did turn around and go back to the Sheriff.[73]

The Sheriff and his posse had eventually made their way out to the back of the arroyo, but they didn't find anyone or anything taken from the burglary. It was getting dark and it was starting to rain so Emsley had called off the search.[74]

Alfredo Hernandez had slipped into the darkness and into the terrain where he felt so comfortable. He had made good his escape from those who chased him. It would not be the last time he was pursued within the Texas Hill Country.

CHAPTER THREE
Search For An Unidentified Bandit

News of the Happy Hollow break-in spread fast among the residents from Leakey to Reagan Wells.[75] With it came more reports of previously unreported burglaries. Within days a car stolen from the Peck Ranch[76] was recovered near the Mexican border at Del Rio. Sheriff Emsley believed there was a connection between the stolen car and the burglary so he decided to ask the Texas Rangers for help.[77]

It was probably a day or two after country music legend Patsy Cline was killed in a plane crash in Tennessee, just a few days after the Happy Hollow burglary,[78] that Sheriff Emsley called Ranger Captain A.Y. Allee.[79]

The Texas Rangers had been a part of Texas' history since it first became a Republic. By 1963 the Texas Rangers had become part of the state police agency known as the Texas Department of Public Safety.[80] The words 'Texas Ranger' evoked a lot of thoughts among the masses by the 1960s. Part of this was due to the advent of television and the movies; part was due to myth or legend and sayings like "One riot, one Ranger." The Rangers were experienced criminal investigators who regularly helped other police agencies with their problems, especially those smaller agencies that had problems that could span across several jurisdictions.[81]

Alfred Young Allee was born on September 14, 1905 in Encinal, La Salle County, Texas. His father and grandfather were both Texas Rangers. He followed their footsteps into law enforcement, first as a special game warden, then Zavala County Deputy Sheriff and finally as a Texas Ranger himself in 1931.[82]

Allee's early Ranger career took him to the Rio Grande border where most of his cases involved cattle rustling and smuggling. By 1963, after he'd been promoted to the rank of Captain in 1947, Captain Alfred Y. Allee managed the Texas Rangers Company D out of his headquarters' office at Carrizo Springs.[83]

Of course, Allee was already a living legend by the 1960s. This was partly due to the national attention of a political corruption investigation that took him to Duval County during the 1950s. He'd also been involved in many other cases, such as the Red River Bridge War near Denison that occurred right after he joined the Ranger Service. He met Pearl Leach during the Red River Bridge case and she became his wife.[84]

The man was a visual image of a Texas lawman. Like most of the Rangers, he wore western-cut suits, cowboy boots and a gray felt hat on his near six foot 200 pound frame. A dark tie, ever-present cigar (in his right hand or set tight in the corner of his mouth) and a pistol hidden beneath his coat were the norm. Piercing black eyes, dark eyebrows and graying hair highlighted his clean-shaven face.[85] The Ranger Captain was not the type of man to mince words. He was direct and probably got right to the point with something like, "Tell those people not to touch anything until I get someone over there."[86]

The Texas Rangers had a system that divided the State of Texas into six areas of responsibilities. The Rangers called these areas Companies, and Company D's area included most of the southern-part of Texas. Captain Allee managed this area that also included Uvalde and Real counties.[87]

The Captain knew that Ranger Levi Duncan was stationed in Uvalde, but he also knew that the big man, who stood head high over most at sixty-seven years of age, was close to retirement. Allee's son, Alfred Jr. on the other hand, had been recently trained in the latest techniques in crime scene investigation. And the car stolen from the Peck Ranch had been recovered in Val Verde County, an area under the jurisdiction of Ranger Company E.[88]

Company E's area reached from El Paso to the lower Texas Plains and down a line through Val Verde and Kinney counties on the Rio Grande. It basically covered the immense area known as West Texas. Protocol would indicate that Captain Allee notified Captain Frank Probst, who managed Ranger Company E out of Midland; he would have related how Border Patrol agents found the vehicle underneath a railroad bridge along U.S. Highway 277 just south of Del Rio. Probst apparently agreed to let Texas Ranger Alfred Allee Jr. process the burglary scene for evidence.[89]

Alfred Young Allee Jr. was born in Beeville, Texas on January 22, 1934. He started grade school in Del Rio and graduated from high school in Carrizo Springs. Like his father before him, he started a law enforcement career at the age of eighteen when he hired on as a dispatcher with the Texas Department of Public Safety.[90]

In 1955, when he was twenty-one, Allee Jr. joined the Texas Highway Patrol and patrolled the highways around San Angelo. He was transferred to San Antonio in 1957. In 1961 he was accepted into the elite group of law enforcement officers known as the Texas Rangers. He was assigned to Ranger Company E and stationed in Del Rio.[91]

Texas Ranger Alfred Allee Jr. Copyright San Angelo Standard-Times.
Reprinted with permission.

A.V. Rutherford was minding his Happy Hollow Store when he noticed the brown Plymouth as it turned off the highway. He saw the two radio antennae and the black-walled tires.[92] He wiped his hands on a rag and got ready to meet the man behind the steering wheel.

Sheriff Emsley had told him that Captain Allee's son would be coming to investigate the burglary. When the man stepped from the car he was much like he'd envisioned; tall, with glasses, dark hair protruding from beneath a cowboy hat and a cigar tucked in the corner of his mouth. A round badge was fastened just above the left pocket on his shirt and a pistol was holstered on his hip; both were hidden when he put his coat on. The light brown coat, matching pants and dark brown cowboy boots completed his Ranger attire.[93]

Rutherford watched as the man walked out to the highway, then turned and looked back toward his house, then his store. He figured the Ranger was getting a fix on things, trying to see what the robber had seen before he broke into the place.

After a short greeting, the storeowner began to show the Ranger how he thought the bandit had gotten into the house. "My wife found them footprints there in the dirt beneath the window," he said as he started to step over into the flowerbed himself.[94]

The Ranger touched Rutherford's arm and held him back. "Just tell me what he did, let's not disturb anything he might have done or left behind," said Allee.[95]

Rutherford guided the man through the house, showing him where money was taken from behind a mirror, jewelry and money were taken from the wife's purse on the dresser and silver dollars were taken from the drawer of an old manual sewing machine. The Ranger developed a mental image of how he thought the bandit had moved through the house. It wasn't long before Rutherford was back minding his store and Allee was getting his equipment out of the trunk of his car.[96]

A.Y. Allee Jr. had learned many things about crime scenes during his training. He'd learned that most criminals do leave some type of evidence at the scene of a crime. He started with the footprints in the flowerbed.[97] He laid a ruler beside one of the depressions in the soft soil and snapped a photograph. The picture could give some indication as to the shoe-size of the burglar. His plaster cast of the footprint might be tied back to a pair of shoes or boots that the criminal was wearing, but it was the black box that contained his fingerprint powders, brushes and tape that he had the most confidence in.[98]

He spent several hours in the house, spreading black and gray powders here and there, looking hard to see if there was any sign of any fingerprint that had been left behind. Then he looked again, using a flashlight to highlight the different areas. He used a special type of tape to lift any visible prints and then placed them on a 3 by 5 card. He initialed each card and wrote where the print was found within the house.[99]

Ranger Allee had a stack of cards by the time he was finished. He knew that most of the prints probably belonged to Mr. Rutherford or his wife. The last part of his assignment would be to collect copies of their fingerprints.[100]

A.V. Rutherford and his wife Pearl had plenty of questions as the Ranger placed and rolled their fingers and hands across a black inkpad; and, then pressed and rolled them onto forms he'd taken out of his briefcase. "We're not the criminals here, why are you booking us?" Pearl Rutherford asked.[101]

"We're not booking you," Allee said with a laugh. "These are elimination prints, so we can take yours out of those that I've collected. Hopefully, we'll have a few left that will belong to the criminal."[102]

The Ranger went on to explain that no two people, even twins, have fingerprints that are alike and that law enforcement had been using them to identify criminals since around the turn of the century. "The prints put the criminal back at the crime scene. Of course, we have to identify him and match his to these before we can make an arrest," said Allee.[103]

(Law enforcement tools were still pretty basic back in the 1960s. This was long before the DNA and fingerprint databases were developed for everyday use. This was long before many of the forensic tools made their way into everyday major crime cases.)[104]

The Ranger didn't have a lot of faith in most of the prints, but two of the prints gave him hope. One was a partial print that he'd lifted from a mirror and another came off the windowsill. Both appeared to be from the palm of the right hand. He knew that a fingerprint expert with the Texas Department of Public Safety would soon eliminate the homeowners' prints from those who might have committed the crime.[105]

A call to his office would later confirm that only the palm prints were not the Rutherfords'. It only left Allee to wonder, "Who left those palm prints and where has he gone?"[106]

* * *

Finding the car at Del Rio led law enforcement officials to believe that the Happy Hollow Bandit was probably in Mexico just a few days after the crime.[107] This writer, based on all the research, concurs with their belief and offers the following account, the following possibility for the reader.

The stolen car probably allowed Hernandez to take stolen property with him, things that he sold before he started his trip south to see his mother and Rosa. It is unknown if he drove the car himself or had someone drive it for him, but later events could lead someone to believe he wasn't an experienced driver.[108]

Alfredo Hernandez more than likely took a bus that led him down the highway that ran between Nuevo Laredo and Matamoros.[109] This trip probably took place about the second week of March 1963.

One could just picture him with his black felt hat and his morral in his lap, the sleeves of his blue shirt rolled up to the elbow and a brown bandana tied around his neck. He probably stared out an open side-window, into the moonlit night and thought about the men who had been chasing him—the Bandit who had robbed the Rutherford's house.

Hernandez definitely met the definition of Bandit, according to the website, TheFreeDictionary.com, that defines bandit as an outlaw, a robber (especially one who robs at gunpoint), armed thief, a criminal who takes property belonging to someone else with intention of keeping it or selling it.

He probably thought about his mother, family and Rosa as he made his trip toward Tomezunchale.[110] His mother was there and he had money for her.

Tomezunchale lies in the lower part of the state of San Luis Potosi in Mexico. Set along the backdrop of the mountains behind the fertile Gulf plain, it is known for sugarcane, tobacco, coffee, cereals, fruit and livestock.[111] Someone could easily surmise that after Hernandez visited with his family that he would then take the highway north to Monterrey.

The highway would take him to his Rosa. He probably couldn't wait to spend time with her or to see the look in her eyes when he gave her the money he had brought her. Rosa was a registered prostitute that Hernandez would visit on the way back from visiting his mother.

However, the woman would lead investigators, years later, to believe that she and the man had more than just a casual relationship.[112]

Hernandez probably had a constant picture of Rosa in his mind; standing there with her back to a doorframe, with her long black hair flowing down along the right side of her chest and one leg bent so her foot rested on the doorframe. Maybe it gave him the incentive to go back to the United States to get more money and to do what he did best.

CHAPTER FOUR
The Red Silk Pajamas

Who would have ever dreamed that a pair of red silk pajamas would play a part in Alfredo Hernandez's life? Surely none of the tourists who drove up and down US Highway 83 near Garner Park in the summer of 1963. Surely none of the area residents whose lives were pretty much back in order after all the burglaries had stopped. Yet a pair of red silk pajamas would come into his possession and he would later design a facemask out of one of the sleeves.[113]

While Texas Ranger Joaquin Jackson would later recall that the pajamas came from a house near Leakey, it is unknown whether the pajamas were stolen out of the house or off of a clothesline. What is known is that Hernandez moved back into the Concan area that year and did come into possession of the red silk pajamas. This writer would like to think they were stolen off of a clothesline beside an occupied house, mostly because this Bandit certainly had the stealth to pull it off. The following paragraphs are offered only as a possibility.

Alfredo Hernandez opened his eyes and immediately realized that a bright red color was now within the landscape, near the house that he had been watching. He picked up his binoculars and gave it a closer look. It appeared as though someone had hung clothes out on the clothesline and a few of the pieces were bright red. He put the binoculars down and closed his eyes again.

He was sitting in a clump of thick Shin oak about half way up a ridge. The tops of the small trees shielded him from the sun. The new runners, the new growth that the white-tailed deer preyed upon, shielded him from anyone down below. He finally felt a chill and opened his eyes again. The sun had set behind the ridge and now he and the Shin oaks were hidden within the mountain's shadow. He looked down below where the sun's rays were still shining on the red garments that were blowing back and forth in the wind.

He stood, stretched and put his morral over his head and shoulder. He put his black cowboy hat on and leaned back against the trunk of one of the small trees. He knew he wouldn't normally go near an occupied house unless there was a good reason, but the red color caught his eye.

This was a time in history when it would not have been uncommon to see kids playing football in the yard during the day, to see a couple sitting in rocking chairs on a porch or men coming back to the house for supper.

More than likely it would have been a large high-ceiling wood-framed house. Maybe with white sides, light brown trim and an A-framed metal roof that had two red brick chimneys protruding through it. A white picket fence might have surrounded large pecan trees within the yard that had a clothesline on the side toward the thief. A clothesline with a pair of red silk pajamas pinned on the wire.

This writer would like to think that Hernandez used the cover of darkness to move across the distance from the ridge to an old wooden barn that was a short distance from the house. Based on the way he committed his crimes, he would have already known the layout of the barn and the house.

But what would he have thought if he had heard laughter and music coming from inside the barn? What if he had peered through a crack and found a blonde-headed girl sitting on a tractor at the back of the barn? What if she was laughing and working her arms back and forth like she was actually driving the tractor. Just what would he have thought if the girl was singing along as John, Paul, George and Ringo, the British rock group known as the Beatles, belted out the words to their hit song, 'I Want To Hold Your Hand.'

This writer would like to think that Hernandez slipped over the white picket fence and stole the garments while people were in the house just a few feet away. There is no evidence as to where the red pajamas came from, only that he would later use a piece of the silk material to cover his face.[114] Of course, the burglaries had stopped and most of the local residents thought things were back to normal that summer.[115]

Tourists were driving up and down the highways, visiting shops and recreational facilities between Concan and Leakey. The clear brisk Frio River was transformed into a playground for those of all ages. Garner Park was full of campers, some hiking up behind the sheer cliff that overlooked the river, others enjoying a good swim or the paddleboats or an inter-tube, and others, including many young people from the surrounding areas, just waited for the weekend dances.[116] The tourists and many locals enjoyed the River Bend's bowling alley that was just up the road from Happy Hollow. The small six-lane bowling alley had brought plenty of excitement to this sparsely populated part of the Texas Hill Country, especially with its fall leagues that pitted couple against couple.[117]

One couple who loved to bowl was Bud and Mary Belle Magers. The Magers lived on a thousand acres of Frio Canyon countryside just below Garner Park. Their land, which spread out along the Frio River crossing and up along both sides of Cherry Creek, had been in their family since the 1850s. Although they ranched the place with the help of their two teenaged sons, they also invited tourists to enjoy the Magers' River Bend Camp.[118]

William Lawrence "Bud" Magers stood six foot and weighed near 200 pounds. His short dishwater blonde hair was slightly visible beneath his cowboy hat. His weathered hands were not unaccustomed to work. Local folks knew he and his wife were people they could depend upon.[119]

Like her husband, Mary Belle Magers was born in the 20s and was a child of the depression. She stood five-foot five-inches tall, weighed 120 pounds and kept her black hair cut short. She'd borne their two boys, Gordon and Gregory, in the 1940s. She also dealt with the tragedy of death in August 1963.[120]

Just about the time of the Happy Hollow burglary, Louise Magers had moved from her home in San Antonio and into one of the Magers' houses just south of the low water crossing known as Magers' Crossing below Garner Park. On August 6th the 86-year-old woman was found floating face down in the Frio River.[121]

The Justice of the Peace, A.A. Collins, wrote 'accidental drowning' in the immediate cause section of the death certificate, but the Magers family had their own thoughts about what had happened. The Aunt had a bump on her head and a ring was missing from a finger on her fully clothed body. The family talked about the possibility that the Happy Hollow bandit might be responsible but no evidence to support it was ever found.[122] However, it wasn't long before that changed.

It was a Sunday afternoon in early November when Mary Belle Magers answered the phone. She listened for a minute, then said, "We'll keep an eye out," and hung up.[123]

The caller was William Hoover who lived up Cherry Creek, between their place and the Dawson family's Cherry Creek Ranch. They had just returned home from church and found several things missing from their home; a few cans of food, sugar, coffee and William's brand new bowling shoes. He hadn't even worn them yet.[124]

A few weeks later the whole nation suffered after President John F. Kennedy was shot and killed while his motorcade moved through the streets of Dallas on November 22, 1963.[125]

The Frio Canyon folks listened to their radios and watched what they could see on their antennae fed televisions. They grasped at every piece of information as reporters revealed the events that also left Texas Governor John Connally severely wounded and Lyndon Baines Johnson sworn in as the next President of the United States.[126]

Within hours and days they learned of the death of Dallas Police Officer J.D. Tippit, the arrest of Lee Harvey Oswald and his subsequent death at the hands of nightclub owner Jack Ruby. Finally, on November 29, 1963, they were made aware that President Johnson had established the Warren Commission to investigate the death of the President.[127] What they didn't know then was that tragedy would strike even closer to home within a few weeks.

Edward and Alice Ruth Niggli had lived in their part-wood, part-rock home for about 10 years. It was located in an area near Concan that was known as Cliff Seven. They had two daughters, Debra Frances and Susan Elizabeth. The husband taught school and on Wednesday, December 11, 1963, he and the girls headed that way just after daylight.[128]

Alice Ruth was thirty-three. She was tall and thin with sandy colored hair that curved down onto her neck. She was supposed to have guests at her house that morning, but as Mrs. Jim Caddel reported in the Uvalde Leader News, Concan section, on December 15, 1963, 'Mrs. William Niggli, Mrs. Larry Hurley and Mrs. John Kennedy were going to meet at the Edwin Niggli home and help Mrs. Edwin Niggli fix table decorations for the Club Banquet, which is an annual thing with the Club Council.

When Mrs. Hurley got in sight of the house, she saw the house was on fire. Every door she opened, the flames met her and some hunters…but there was nothing they could do.'[129]

The morning after the fire the headlines of The Uvalde Leader News read 'Home Fire Explosion Near Concan Claims Life of Young Mother.' The story reported that the explosion and fire apparently began in the bathroom when escaping butane ignited and that Mrs. Niggli was alone in the house at the time of the fire.[130]

After a Mass in the St. Mary's Catholic Church in Uvalde, Mrs. Niggli was buried in the Rio Frio Cemetery. Bud Magers was one of the pallbearers.[131]

Edward Niggli had told authorities that the hose on the heater in the bathroom was old and might have come apart. Justice of the Peace A.A. Collins listed the cause of death as 'gas explosion, home burned, accidental burning.'[132] Many of the Niggli's neighbors didn't believe it and some even thought the Happy Hollow Bandit was responsible.[133]

Even though there was no evidence to support it, people started to talk about the possibility that the death was not an accident. It caused people to start watching out for things and some people started to realize that things were missing from their homes again.[134]

A few weeks later, during Christmas break when the kids were out of school, Bud Magers heard about a man who had been seen on their ranch. A nephew had seen the man while he was hunting in Mary Belle's favorite hunting place, a place where a ranch road crossed Cherry Creek.[135]

The teenager was sitting behind and in the shadows of a really large oak tree growing along the west side of the crossing. The trunk of the huge tree split into three smaller trunks as it branched upward and outward toward the sky. The youngster, with his Winchester 30:30 caliber rifle leaning against the tree, was hoping that a whitetail buck deer would come by when he saw a man suddenly appear across the creek from him. He described the man as a short thin Mexican man, grown but not too old, wearing boots, western clothes and a black cowboy hat. The man had stood by a good-sized cedar bush watching for several minutes. Then he'd quickly walked over to Cherry Creek, dipped up a coffee can full of water and walked back into the brush.[136]

The next morning a search of the area didn't reveal any sign of the man. But the area was full of small brush-laden arroyos that spread like fingers that ran out, up and away from Cherry Creek.[137]

***

On Tuesday, January 14, 1964, Alfredo Hernandez may have very well been up Pecan Creek near a small cave that he slept in from time to time. It was one camp where he'd built a tin porch out over the cave's opening, and if he were there that day, he might have heard the tin rattle as the first breath of an artic cold front screamed into the Texas Hill Country and its Frio River canyons.[138]

The day had dawned with the temperatures in the high teens but had warmed to 47 degrees by midday. It was the first day of the new moon, the wind was picking up and the temperature would drop to 7 degrees by midnight. The chill factor would be well below zero.[139]

"Yes sir, I'll tell my dad as soon as he gets home," said Greg Magers just before he hung up the phone.[140]

Gregory Allen Magers was born in November of 1947. He was sixteen the night he got the call from the Garner State Park Superintendent who thought the Happy Hollow Bandit might be in one of the park bathrooms.[141] The Superintendent wanted Bud Magers to go check it out for him, but Bud and Mary Belle were bowling. So their son Greg had another idea.[142]

The teenager grabbed his heavy coat, a single shot 12-gauge shotgun from a closet and his dad's pickup keys off of a hook by the door. He also took four longneck beers out of the refrigerator. Within just a few minutes he had their tan colored 1962 Chevrolet pickup heading north toward Leakey. Like most people his age, he didn't think there was anything that he couldn't do, but he knew there was strength in numbers so he was going to get his friend Max Guinther and they were going to go capture the Bandit.[143]

It wasn't too long before the two Leakey High School athletes were headed south towards Garner Park. On their way they drank the liquid courage and boasted, much like out-loud daydreaming, about how they were going to bring the bad guy to justice. Finally they turned off U.S. Hwy 83 and headed east into the park.[144]

Except for a light at the entrance, the park looked pretty much like a drive through a dark and empty tunnel to the two boys; a tunnel that started out fairly wide and dwindled down to one about the size of a one-lane roadway at the end.[145] Of course, it would have been a tunnel with trees that were waving back and forth because of the Blue Norther that was setting low temperature records all across Texas.[146]

The San Antonio Express-News newspaper had run front-page stories about the weather on Monday and Tuesday. The boys didn't know it at the time, but the newspaper's Wednesday edition would include headlines that read, '140 Dead In Eastern Snowstorm,' and lower down in the story, 'Fort Worth with 4 degrees at dawn had the coldest Jan. 14 on record. So did Austin with 17. The 11 degrees at Dallas set a record for the date. The cold was tempered by the lack of ice and snow.' However, the boys were not thinking about the 7-degree temperature or the chill factor that was outside the windows of the heated pickup.[147]

Even though they'd seen a light at the Superintendent's house and another one near the concession building near the dance floor, it was the slightly visible light emitting from the park's last bathroom that had finally gotten their attention. With increasing heart rates and voices that had suddenly gotten louder, they finally realized that someone might really be in the bathroom.[148]

Greg Magers finally stopped and parked the pickup about twenty yards away from the building. The tall and thin Max Guinther got out of the right-side door with his own 12-gauge shotgun; the stocky five-foot ten-inch Magers got out of the driver's side door with his. Though the wind and the extreme temperature would have seemed to cut any part of anyone's exposed skin, they didn't even think about the weather. Their eyes and minds were only focused on the bathroom door.[149]

The boys' adrenaline went into overdrive as they walked toward the structure. They didn't hear the howling wind or notice anything outside the realm of right where they were. They had tunnel vision and only heard the sound of any gravel that crunched underneath their feet. When they were four feet from the door, with guns pointing right at it, something happened that is forever etched within their minds. They heard the snap, the sound of someone who turned the light off, and the bathroom went dark right in front of their eyes.[150]

Many times over and even years later, Greg Magers would tell this story. And he would always say, "That guy scared the kazoo out of us. You have never seen two guys get back to a pickup and out of there so fast."[151]

The next morning the bathroom was empty. There was no one there and the light was turned off.[152]

***

On Sunday, February 23, 1964, Alfredo Hernandez was outside the Rutherford's house next to the Happy Hollow Store. His black hat had been left behind in a cave up Cherry Creek where he had apparently been sleeping.[153] He removed a red silk mask from his morral; the mask that he'd made from a large sleeve of the pajama top. He put it over his face and adjusted it so he could see out the two holes in the front.[154]

The temperature had fallen into the low 20's that morning but had risen into the mid-50s during the day. About 9:30 that night it was still around 50 degrees probably because of the clouds that were drifting in and starting to block the image of a partial moon that was high overhead.[155]

The house was dark except for a light that was on in the living room. Hernandez surely heard the sound of the television that the couple was watching. He eased around to the large screened-in porch at the back of the house. You could normally see inside the porch but the Rutherfords placed framed plastic sheets over the porous screens during the winter months. He lifted the latch on the screen door, then popped the pins and took a hardwood door off at the hinges. Then he stepped inside onto the back porch.[156]

A.V. Rutherford and his wife Pearl were sitting in their living room rocking chairs watching television. They didn't get the best reception out of the tall antennae that was outside the house, but it was television and the San Antonio stations did keep their interest. One lamp, on a small table that was between them, was the only light on in the house.[157]

Pearl Rutherford, who was sitting closest to her husband's open bedroom door, suddenly felt a chill on her legs. She got up and went into the unlit bedroom and closed a door that led onto the back porch. She returned and settled back into the rocker. Then she felt the chill again.

Again she went into the room and closed the door, making sure it shut this time before she returned to her chair.[158]

A few minutes later, a combination of surprise, shock and fear gripped the Rutherfords as Alfredo Hernandez appeared within the same doorway that Pearl had just walked through. He was talking loudly, almost yelling and somewhat commanding in Spanish and neither Pearl nor A.V. could understand him.[159]

Rutherford did recognize anger in the man's voice as he spoke. He wasn't sure if one of the words was paper or perro, the Spanish translation for dog. He thought, "Was this the man who had broken into their house before, the one they had chased with the dogs?"[160]

Hernandez peered through the red mask that hid his facial features. He wore western clothes and was brandishing a revolver, moving it back and forth between the husband and wife. He started moving toward Pearl and motioning for A.V. to come over.[161]

A.V. Rutherford's mind went into slow motion. He saw the guy, but at first could not believe that he was there. Then he saw the gun and the huge hole in the end of the barrel. Then he saw the rope, nylon rope that was lapped across the guy's left arm. It was more than enough rope to tie them both up.[162]

He stood when the guy started to motion him toward Pearl. The thought of Alice Ruth Niggli's death raced through Rutherford's head. "Was the man going to tie them up, take what he wanted and burn their house down with them in it too?" he thought as he started to move toward his wife.[163]

The dark headed sixty-five-year-old man was several inches taller and thirty pounds heavier than the man with the gun. He looked at his wife's curly red hair and the look of fear on her face. He thought about their life together and with one motion A.V. Rutherford grabbed the man's gun with his right hand. In what seemed like the same instant, as both men grappled over the gun, it went off sending a bullet right past Rutherford's head and into the living room ceiling.[164]

As the two men's bodies clashed, as primal grunts and words, both in English and Spanish were yelled, the men fell back against the wall next to the open door and Rutherford ripped the gun out of the smaller man's hand.

Then he thrust the gun's barrel into the man's stomach and pulled the trigger. But the gun only snapped. Even though the firing pin fell on the cartridge, it had not gone off.[165] The men fought their way back into the dark bedroom with Rutherford grabbing hold of the top of the man's mask and his hair. He again pushed the gun forward and pulled the trigger. But again the double action revolver only snapped and did not fire. Then the man broke free of his grasp.[166] A.V. Rutherford still had the mask in his hand as the man ran out of the bedroom door.

Alfredo Hernandez had not fallen like an actor in a movie when Mr. Rutherford pulled the trigger twice. This man who seemed to have MORE than nine lives just ran away and disappeared into the darkness of the night.[167]

CHAPTER FIVE
The Uvalde County Search

Alfredo Hernandez had probably never been as scared as he was the night he entered the Rutherford home. He'd probably never been so close to death even though he did have a scar from an apparent knife wound above one eye.[168] As he ran across the highway and headed toward his Pecan Creek camp, he probably didn't realize exactly how close he really came to dying that night.[169]

Rutherford had ripped a Smith and Wesson Model 10 Military and Police .38 caliber revolver out of Hernandez's hand. "I saw the bullets later and there were distinct firing pin impressions on the ones that did not go off," said retired Texas Ranger Joaquin Jackson years later.[170]

The headlines of the Thursday edition of the Uvalde Leader News read, 'Still At-Large. Posse and Dogs Used In Search For Masked Gunman Near Happy Hollow.' The story highlighted how law enforcement officers, tracking dogs and a citizens' posse had been searching for the man who broke into the house at Happy Hollow Sunday night.[171]

It went on to say, 'The man, reportedly wearing a red mask and brandishing a pistol, entered the Rutherford house shortly after 9:30 p.m. Sunday, pointing a pistol at the couple and shouting, "Paper, paper!" Rutherford, according to the report from Uvalde County Sheriff Hugh Emsley, rushed the intruder, forcing his arm into the air, discharging the gun and blowing a hole in the ceiling.'[172]

Law enforcement officers from the Uvalde and Real County Sheriff Departments, Texas Rangers Levi Duncan and L.H. Purvis and Ranger Captain Alfred Allee, Uvalde Game Warden Jim Reeves, United States Border Patrol agents Tom Hupp and Jack Thurman, Utopia Constable Lonnie Schaefer and a group of 25 armed citizens, including Ray Rutherford and his brother-in-law Hudson Hillis, were involved in the search.[173] "My husband and his friend Roy Redden, a rancher from Utopia, used Redden's hunting dogs to try to catch the guy," said Mrs. Ray Rutherford.[174]

Border Patrol airplanes and a private helicopter were also used during the search Tuesday and Wednesday. The newspaper reported, 'Using first a trailing dog owned by Sheriff Emsley and later bringing in a bloodhound from Kenedy, Texas, the men trailed the dogs some two miles from the Happy Hollow area in a southwesterly direction where they came upon a well hidden cave.'[175] "The cave had two pieces of tin above and out front of the entrance. He'd taken the metal from a place across the highway from the store," said Hudson Hillis, years later.[176] Even so, the cave was well hidden.

'Ranger Captain Allee noted that a knife was found among other items in the cave. He also noted that the area in which the camp had been found was in some of the roughest land imaginable for searching purposes and that it would take a lot of tracking and trailing to find anyone who apparently knew his way around the area as well as the man they were pursuing.' The posse also found black hair and scissors in the camp. Unfortunately the dogs lost the man's scent after it started raining Monday afternoon.[177]

'Sheriff Hugh Emsley reported late yesterday (Wednesday) that part of the force of law enforcement officers seeking a masked gunman near Happy Hollow had been directed to an area east of Happy Hollow towards Utopia as a result of a report given by Mrs. H.L. Peck, who lives near Bear Creek, that she had seen a stranger on her property about 7:30 Wednesday morning.'[178]

The incident at Happy Hollow had consummated the fear that had been slowly growing since Mrs. Niggli had died. People were carrying guns and had real concerns about the Bandit not being caught. "People were so concerned that they called my dad, Hap Stark, who had been the sheriff before becoming a Deputy United States Marshal for the Western District. I remember that rancher Woodrow Langford called from Reagan Wells," said daughter Jo Mari Stark Bradley who was 16 at the time.[179]

People were calling the Sheriff's office to see what had been done, to see if they had caught the guy. They were also talking about things missing from their homes, prompting Sheriff Emsley to arrange a meeting at the Concan schoolhouse on Friday night.[180]

Ranger Captain Alfred Allee joined Emsley for the meeting that included about forty area citizens. Most were really upset, complaining to

Emsley that he needed to do something about the man who was stealing and robbing from them. "Before he kills somebody," said one of the citizens.[181]

Emsley told the group that they'd found a footprint of the man that matched one that they'd found at the Bowles' place in Real County. He also heard from many of the residents that many of the burglaries had happened on Sunday, as though the guy was watching and went inside after they left for church.[182]

He knew that Ranger Levi Duncan was spending the night with the Rutherfords, but the group wanted someone special to watch after their area. Emsley and Captain Allee picked two men from the crowd and asked them if they'd be willing to serve as deputies.[183]

Uvalde County Judge Leo Darley swore in the two new deputies the next day. Willard VanPelt was a tall 40-year-old ranch hand with salt and pepper colored hair who lived a few miles south of Garner Park. Fritz Streib was twenty years his senior, average height and weighed about 190 pounds, and his straw hat hid most of his baldhead. He lived just north of the Garner Park entrance.[184]

After the swearing in, Sheriff Emsley gave the men a badge and a pair of handcuffs. Streib already had a pistol, but VanPelt didn't, so the Sheriff gave him a .38 caliber revolver. He also told them to arrest the man and bring him in to the jail. "You mean shoot the SOB, don't you," said Captain Allee.[185]

The next morning, Sunday March 1, 1964, the dark bold type on the front page of the Uvalde Leader News read, 'Manhunt Continues For Happy Hollow Burglar.' The story detailed most of what had happened that week and told about the two new deputies. A picture at the bottom of the page showed the mask, .38 caliber Smith and Wesson model 10 revolver, knife and scabbard, pair of blue jean pants and a piece of rope. The caption detailed how the trousers, knife and scabbard had been found in the cave.[186]

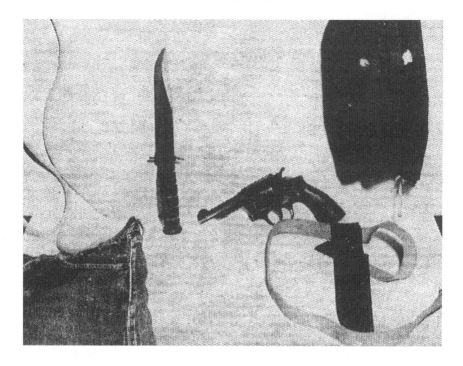

Red mask, gun and rope used at Happy Hollow. Knife, sheath and pants found at cave. Copyright 1964 Uvalde Leader-News, Uvalde, Texas. Reprinted with permission.

The following Sunday the newspaper revealed how officers had released a man, a Mexican national, who had been caught by Border Patrol officers in Medina County. "But the man had been in Mexico at the time of the incident," said Border Patrol agent Tom Hupp.[187]

Hupp had joined the Border Patrol in 1960. He was stationed in Eagle Pass until he was transferred to Uvalde in 1962. He was twenty-six when he and his partner teamed up with Texas Rangers Levi Duncan and Jack VanCleve as the search for the Bandit moved into the second week.[188]

For weeks the men searched an area that moved them from Concan toward Leakey toward Utopia and down south toward Sabinal. "We did find a small hole along Bear Creek (which was east and over a large ridge from Cherry Creek) that opened up into a big cave that had a lot of water in it. But the guy wasn't in it," said Hupp years later.[189]

A few days after VanPelt and Streib were sworn in, Captain Allee brought them a Redbone hound to help them search for the guy. A week later he brought them a horse from the King ranch. Both men were amazed at how the Ranger kept smoking cigars—one after another.[190]

The new deputies were eager to catch the Bandit. They went about their tasks with the fervor of rookie policemen. Early on they searched an area that was south of the cave where the knife and scabbard were found. Then they started moving along Elm Creek that was west of the highway from Garner Park, in a piece-by-piece, draw-by-draw manner.[191]

The Texas Hill Country is full of hills and valleys, creeks and draws, points and gullys, and it was in one gully along Elm Creek that the two men found a glob of black hair, human hair that would become a trademark of the man they were looking for. The men also found two magazines.[192] It is unknown which two but popular issues that could have been around were the one with President Johnson on the cover of the November 29, 1963 issue of Time Magazine and the San Diego Chargers' Rote handing off the football on the cover of the December 16, 1963 issue of Sports Illustrated.

The men also found a large tree that had fallen across and down into the gully. It appeared as though someone had made a habit of defecating in the same place along the tree each time they were there. They were sure the man they were looking for had been there. They turned over the evidence, the hair and the magazines to Sheriff Emsley.[193]

The deputies were diligent in their search. Even after the large search party dissipated, they kept searching and following up any leads, checking out any reported sightings and kept trying to keep an eye on Happy Hollow.[194]

The men had a habit of watching the Rutherford's house at night. They'd take VanPelt's blue pickup and park on a road that ran up beside a steep hill, a hill that was about a hundred yards away and across the highway. It was on one of those stakeouts that they may have gotten close to the Bandit.[195]

Willard VanPelt. Photo courtesy of Greg Magers and Van Pelt family.

It was one of those nights when you could have heard a pecan hit the top of the Happy Hollow store even from so far away. It was just dead calm. No breeze, no bugs and very little traffic moving up and down the highway. The men kept taking turns using binoculars to watch the house and store. By midnight the only sound they heard at all was a periodic light snore out of Gilly Dee, Streib's wife, who was too scared to stay home alone. Then "Bam!"[196]

Everyone came alive when a large rock hit the top of the pickup cab. It rolled off and onto the hood. The men were immediately out with their flashlights and their guns pointing up the hill. They searched for over an hour but never found anyone or heard anyone leave the area. They were sure the Bandit was playing with them.[197]

Bud Magers helped the men work the Redbone hound. Once they let the dog smell one of his son's t-shirts after they'd told the boy to go hide somewhere; they let the dog go and he treed Greg somewhere across the river.[198]

The teenager was tagging along once as the deputies searched an area across the Frio River from A.A. Collins' River View Camp. When they got up just high enough to see the River View area with binoculars, they found a small camp hidden within the underbrush.[199]

It was there that they found a few more magazines, tennis shoes and a metal grill on top of some rocks that were placed in a circle. The rocks and grill were scorched black. They assumed it was where the Bandit watched the Collins' house, where he waited for them to leave so he could slip inside and put his dirty clothes by their washer, where he would return to cook the food he stole from their house. Unfortunately the day they found the camp, the sign was old, months old.[200]

The men were diligent in their quest and at some point they started working their way up Cherry Creek. They finally reached a very dense draw that ran out northeast of the creek, right near the ranch road crossing where the kid had seen the man dip water from the creek. It was a draw that wasn't over forty yards wide at its widest point and was only about a quarter mile in length.[201]

It was about ten that morning when Fritz Streib started slowly working his way through the dense brush and trees in the bottom of the draw. He had his pistol and the taller Willard VanPelt was carrying his own deer rifle as he eased quietly along the top. He was located to Streib's left.[202]

VanPelt stayed a little out front of the shorter man and intermittently peered over the side and down along the flat bluffs that caressed the topsides of the draw. He looked inside and under every bush and inside every opposing crevasse. Streib had to force his way through heavy Shin oak, brush and intermittent cactus along the bottom.[203]

The men came to a place where the draw turned toward the north. The taller man peered over the side and took a double take, a second look. He pointed his rifle straight down and said, "Fritz, we may have something over here. I think I see his hat."[204]

The older man made his way to the top of the other side of the draw. He hoped to see the Bandit across the way, but he couldn't see anything because of the dense Shin oak, buckeye and brush that surrounded the hiding place.[205]

Streib started working his way back down into the bottom, with his revolver at the ready, when VanPelt said, "Be really careful, he's in a cave up here."[206]

Slowly, Streib worked his way up to an area just below and south of the area where the Bandit might be hiding. Each deputy tried to talk the man out of the cave but there was no response. Finally, Streib made his move, keeping a curve in the draw and a tree between him and the cave.[207]

VanPelt dropped off the top into a crevasse just north of the cave and both men closed in. Only the Bandit was not there, but they knew they might have found the last place he stayed the night before he tried to rob the Rutherfords.[208]

Greg Magers sits by the Cherry Creek cave where deputies VanPelt and Streib found the black hat and stolen property. 2005 photo by Russell Smith.

There were actually two small caves, side by side, near the top of the draw. One was blackened and scorched and had rocks stacked in front of it, probably to keep anyone from seeing flames from across the way. It was apparent that the man had cooked there.[209]

In the second cave, that wasn't much bigger in size than one big man could lie down in, they found a black felt western hat, a necklace, a pair of new bowling shoes, a newspaper clipping from the Uvalde Leader News and a few magazines. There were also a few clippings of the man's black hair.[210]

The magazines, necklace and the newspaper clipping had been stolen out of the Rutherford home. The bowling shoes were taken out of the Hoover home. The men turned all the evidence over to Sheriff Emsley and disappointedly reported that the sign was not fresh, but was rather old.[211]

There were a few other disappointments that year too. The King Ranch horse died of colic, and, after most people realized the burglaries had stopped, Captain Allee took the Redbone hound back to wherever he'd gotten it from. Willard VanPelt had really become attached to the hound and felt a real loss when it was gone.[212]

Hugh Emsley had his own disappointment that year too. Six other people ran against him for Sheriff and the voters elected a former policeman named Kenneth Kelley to the county's top law enforcement position.[213]

Kenneth Kelley was born in Coleman County, Texas in July of 1924. He and his family moved to Quemado, then La Pryor, soon after the 1936 flood sent torrents down the Concho River and into Coleman County. Kelley joined the Uvalde Police Department in 1955. He left there and ran for Sheriff.[214]

The forty-year-old Kelley was a man who was easy to talk to and sensitive to the needs of the county residents. So, in the spring of 1965, he was quick to act when someone thought they had seen the Happy Hollow Bandit.[215]

The caller reported a man who matched the Bandit's description on a ranch just off Highway 127 between Concan and Sabinal. Kelley and his Chief Deputy, a big burley man named Morris Barrow, combed the countryside and talked to area ranchers about the suspect in the Happy Hollow crimes.[216]

The officers searched several caves where they found black hair cuttings, scissors, needles and thread and soda pop bottles. However, they found nothing of real value and the evidence appeared to be old, so old that it led them to believe that the Bandit was no longer in their jurisdiction.[217]

CHAPTER SIX
Pumpville, Early 1965

Ted Luce was born in Del Rio, Val Verde County, Texas in October of 1938. His dad died when he was just two years old while they lived on the Peterson Ranch near Brackettville. Afterwards, Luce and his mother moved back to Del Rio to live with his mother's parents. Of course neither knew then that Luce would someday raise livestock on a big ranch at Pumpville.[218]

The youngster learned a lot about ranching from his grandfather, Carnell Hill, who ranched 1,700 acres along Mud Creek. His mother remarried when Ted was nine. His stepfather, Richard Tillman, was a Postman who also had a small ranch. It was only natural that he grew up with a dream of ranching his own place some day.[219]

The dark headed Ted Luce was about five-foot eight-inches tall and weighed about 170 pounds when he graduated from Del Rio High School in 1957. He got a job with the cable-company and married Shirley Harrison, his high school sweetheart. The couple had two blonde-headed boys, Jeff and Scott, who were respectively, seven and five by 1965.[220]

On February 15, 1965, with the help of a 100% government loan, Ted Luce signed a lease so he could ranch 12,996 acres of the J.R. Hamilton Ranch near Pumpville.[221]

Pumpville was a tiny little railroad town located in Val Verde County, about 75 miles west of Del Rio. It was just a few miles off Highway 90 and right beside the railroad tracks. Its closest town-neighbors were Langtry, 15 miles back toward Del Rio, and Dryden, 26 miles toward Sanderson out west.[222] Originally formed in the late 1800s as a water pump station for the railroad steam engines, the town spawned into housing for railroad employees, a general store and post office, a Baptist church and a number of houses and buildings. There were also livestock holding pens and loading chutes that allowed thousands of sheep, goats and other livestock to be shipped all across the country.[223]

At one point, twenty people had actually lived in Pumpville, but by 1965 diesel train engines had replaced the steam engines, and the crews and their families no longer lived there. The railroad houses and their offices were now vacant, except when the railroad crews came up to repair the tracks. The only occupied houses belonged to the Baptist preacher and the man and woman who ran the general store and post office. Luce took possession of the old Hamilton ranch house, located right behind the Pumpville store, when he leased the ranch.[224]

The old ranch house was a wood frame, wood floor structure with a tin roof. The living room and master bedroom were up front; a bedroom, bath and kitchen were in the back. An outside wooden porch that wrapped around the front and east side of the house protected those who entered the living room or kitchen doors. A picket fence set across the back of the property.[225] The front of the house was about fifty yards from the back of the store; however, those who used the house normally drove up out back and parked behind the picket fence. The house had been in the Hamilton family for many, many years.[226]

J.R. Hamilton had come from a pioneer ranching family, but as Luce quickly found out, Pelham Bradford, who ranched 9000 acres and ran the general store and post office with his wife, had a little pioneer story himself. His great-great-great grandfather several times removed, William Bradford, had come to America on the Mayflower. The Postmaster often noted that his descendant's diary was donated to the library in El Paso.[227]

The Luces quickly grew very fond of the Bradfords, the older couple who managed the store. They also learned that the couple had a habit of taking a nap most afternoons. So they, like other ranch families in the area, would just go into the open store, get what they wanted and write the things down on a ledger at the counter. They knew that the Bradfords would add the things to their charge account later.[228]

Ted Luce kept his day job working for the cable company but spent most weekends up at the ranch, managing the 1,000 sheep and goats, and a few cows that he hoped to turn a profit with. The old Hamilton house, which they never locked, was used as a bunkhouse for Luce and those who helped him.[229]

It wasn't too many weeks after they put linens on the beds that the Luces noticed that one of the beds had been slept in. The bed had been remade but it didn't have Shirley's touch to it, and a little food was missing out of the kitchen. They just figured that it was someone making their way from Mexico toward a better life in the United States.[230]

Ted Luce could not afford to have people at the ranch on a daily basis so he enlisted the help of area rancher Ross Foster to check the water troughs during the week. He also asked his teenage brother-in-law, Sammy Harrison, and two other high school kids, Brad Bradley and Robert Glenn Walsh to help him out on a pretty regular basis.[231]

Luce taught his sons how to ride at an early age, just as he himself had been taught. He often told people, "Those kids can really ride and round up just like grown men." Of course, his wife could too.[232]

Shirley Harrison Luce was a good-looking woman who was an inch shorter than Ted, and had also been raised as a country girl. She'd lived for a number of years with Ray Hutto and his wife, her uncle and aunt, on their ranch near Del Rio. Many times she'd tucked her long blonde hair under a cowboy hat and ridden off into the pasture to do ranch work.[233]

Many weekends it was just Ted Luce and his family who worked the ranch at Pumpville. It was on a Friday in March, as he drove his tan pickup down the county road toward the house, that they noticed a group of Angora billies that had gotten out of a trap, a holding pasture.[234]

The couple had planned on cooking supper and getting an early start in the morning, but they knew they needed to get the goats back into the 200-acre trap before dark. "I'll just set the groceries on the back porch, then help you saddle the horses," said Shirley as she got out.[235]

She made her way through the open gate of the picket fence. She placed the two paper sacks on the wooden porch just outside the kitchen. She put a rock on top of each and headed toward the pens to help Ted and the boys with the saddles.[236]

It was just minutes before the family was horseback and riding into the pasture across the road from the house. The goats had found a way out of the trap and were in a 2,500-acre pasture to the west. It wasn't long before the four cowboys, or should I say three and one cowgirl, were pushing the Billies back into the smaller pasture near the road. "Let's get a head count and then we'll go to the house," yelled Ted.[237]

The four wranglers were spread out about a hundred yards apart, Shirley was on one end and Ted on the other, with Scott and Jeff in the middle, slowly pushing the goats, trying to get an accurate count. "One-two-three...eleven-twelve...nineteen, twenty," counted Ted.[238] Then the thin faced blonde-headed seven year old Jeff reined up, stopping his horse cold on the edge of a ravine about a hundred yards from the county road.[239]

Alfredo Hernandez heard a commotion and saw a number of goats moving down toward him. Then he noticed a young boy wearing a cowboy hat just up above him. He ducked and tried to conceal himself just as he saw a man up ahead a short distance away. Both were sitting on horses and both stopped when they noticed him. He kept low to the ground, with the paper sack tight to his chest, and hurried until he was sure he was out of sight.[240]

Ted Luce saw the movement as the Mexican man ducked behind some brush in the bottom of the ravine. He could see the man's eyes peering up toward him from beneath a black felt cowboy hat. He saw the man start to move and saw the paper sack wrapped within the blue sleeve of the man's shirt.[241]

He reined his horse to the left and made his way toward Jeff. "Probably just somebody trying to find a job, or going back to Mexico," said Luce to the boy. The whole family knew it was not uncommon to see illegal aliens in this part of Texas. Of course, they didn't know then that their two paper sacks of groceries were missing from the porch of the ranch house.[242] A case of cold drinks was also missing from the refrigerator.

When they arrived back at the house, Ted got a rifle out of his truck and they rode back out into the pasture looking for the man, but never did find him.[243]

Hernandez didn't move a muscle as the people on horseback moved toward him. He laid still, hidden within his cactus hideaway as one of the horses moved right past him. The sacks of food were right beside him but he didn't dare touch them for fear he might be found out. He kept his right hand on the butt of his revolver.[244]

Summer vacation had just started for the kids when Ted Luce got a call from Val Verde County Deputy Sheriff Calvin Wallen. "Could you come by the office Ted? There's a railroad man here who wants to talk to you."[245]

Wallen was a well-respected deputy, about Ted's size, with dark hair, in his mid-60s. Ted didn't know what they wanted to talk to him about, but he left the cable company office and made his way to the Sheriff's Department.[246]

The deputy introduced the two men, but the Railroad Detective was curt and had a look in his dark eyes that didn't seem inviting. He was dark headed, about Ted's height, but was quite a bit heavier and older. He started right in after both men settled into chairs that were across a table from each other. "We've got a problem, but YOU'RE going to straighten it out," the detective said right off.[247]

Ted Luce didn't have a clue what the man was talking about and told him as much. The detective explained that a flatcar, one of the small hand-driven work cars, had been placed on the railroad tracks at Pumpville and ridden off away from town. He also said the railroad houses had been broken into and some food and Masonic books had been taken.[248]

The Detective went on to say that he thought the high school boys that Ted had helping him at the ranch were committing the crimes. "It's something like young boys would do," said the detective.[249]

"Just when was the flatcar taken?" asked Luce. The date was the weekend that the three high school boys, Shirley and their boys had all been there. They had all been together rounding up that day. He knew the boys could not have done the deed because they were with him. "You're barking up the wrong tree, those boys aren't stealing anything," said Luce.[250]

The Railroad Detective rose about halfway out of his chair. His eyes narrowed as he said in a commanding tone, "You, Mister better see that this stuff stops!"[251]

In an instant, Ted Luce was out of his chair and headed around the end of the table. "Nobody talks to me that way!" said Luce, as Calvin Wallen stepped between the two men.[252]

Wallen kept the men apart and calmed the situation down. "Just keep your eyes out for anybody who doesn't belong up there," said Wallen in an asking, respectful tone as he showed Luce the way out.[253]

Ted Luce had always been able to depend on the three high school kids to help him. He knew that they weren't thieves, no matter what the railroad detective had said. So two weeks later, he asked Brad Bradley to go to the ranch on Friday night. "Take the groceries up and have the horses ready in the morning so we can get right to it when we get there," Luce told the thin five-foot ten-inch Bradley.[254]

Brad Bradley was a junior in high school when Luce first asked him to help with the ranch. His parents were building contractors, but he really wanted to be a cowboy and jumped at the chance to help out. There was just something about being on horseback, with a straw hat over his brown hair, staring up into the stars and experiencing a feeling that most would never understand. He was always ready to go when Luce called.[255]

It was nearly ten p.m. by the time Bradley turned his tan four-wheel-drive pickup onto the road that led up to the back of the Hamilton house. The Bradford's lights were out and he figured they were already asleep. There was not a light on in the ranch house either. He gathered up a box of groceries, out of his front seat, and made his way past the picket fence to the back porch.[256]

In Bradley's mind, as in anyone's, there was something a little spooky about an old abandoned house when it was pitch black out. The feeling made him stop for a moment before he shoved the kitchen door open. He flipped on the light switch and walked across to the kitchen counter. He heard a creak in the kitchen floorboards and the jingle of his spurs with his every step. When he stopped and placed the box on the counter, a chill went up into his back, his chest tightened and he felt real fear.[257]

Bradley could hear the living room floorboards creaking as someone walked toward the front door. He heard the sounds of the door's hinges and heard the spring lengthen as the screen door opened. Then he heard someone walking off of the front porch. He hurried out the kitchen door and made his way toward his pickup. Then he looked past the side of the house.[258]

In the dark of night, Brad Bradley could barely make out the outline of a man walking toward the railroad tracks. He saw the shape of a cowboy hat on the man's head and a bag or something at his side. Then the man stopped walking and turned and looked back.[259]

The two men stared at each other for a few seconds. The darkness obscured any real details that either might have seen, but Brad Bradley did gather enough from the experience to know one thing—even if he could not explain it. It was something he told Ted Luce and the others the next day. "I didn't get a good look at the guy but I saw enough to know that you don't want to mess with him."[260]

CHAPTER SEVEN
The Return to July 1965

Alfredo Hernandez had left the Texas Hill Country and moved into the land west of the Pecos River by the summer of 1965. He moved into a land that was rich in history, partially because of the legendary Judge Roy Bean and partially because of the Chihuahuan Desert that landscapes so much of West Texas.[261] The desert can be harsh and the following is offered only to provide the reader with a little glimpse of what he must have dealt with on a day-to-day basis.[262]

The sound of a train brought him from the state of sleep to full consciousness. As the sound faded off toward Del Rio to the east, he realized that a somewhat light pat-pat-pat sound was coming from right outside his hiding place.

He peered through a tiny opening at the base of a Prickly Pear. A small cloud of dust started to dissipate as the sound stopped. Then he saw the Roadrunner with its wings flared out along the ground and its neck protruding straight ahead. The cloud of dust rose again as the grayish brown long-tailed bird started to flop his wings pat-pat-pat along the ground again. He probably didn't know that this dusting action was a normal occurrence that the birds used to try to remove mites from their torso.[263]

Finally, the Roadrunner stood, retracted its wings and started toward the clump of brush that he was hiding within, but it stopped when its yellow eyes caught sight of the eye looking back at it from beside the base of the cactus. For a few seconds the bird seemed to try to identify what it was looking at. It turned its head from side to side, cocking it with its long beak turned out. Then as if it had made up its mind, it scurried off and away from this intruder.

Hernandez laid there for a few minutes, listening for any sounds and feeling for any trembling along the ground. He heard and felt none, and he finally rolled over, bringing the nightgown toward his face as he started to sit up. It was daylight now and he could see the flowered borders along the bottom, cuffs and neckline of the white nightgown that he had stolen the night before. He ripped the large sleeves off of the garment and stuffed them into one of the pockets within his morral. He would make masks out of them later.[264]

Slowly, he crept to his knees and took his time in looking out across the landscape. He looked close at first, then farther out off in the distance. He didn't want any Border Patrol agent or cowboy on horseback to catch sight of him or his hiding place. After he was sure no one was around, he crawled out of his sleeping camp, then stood and looked across the land again.

He must have felt comfortable in this land. He had apparently used the trains to move around in the area from Pumpville to Sanderson for several years.[265] It was thought that he'd never been in the store at Langtry, right near the river, probably because the Border Patrol had a building right beside it.[266] Langtry had been home to Judge Roy Bean and the land West of the Pecos hadn't changed much since the legendary Judge had lived there.[267]

The Chihuahuan Desert, according to the Chihuahuan Desert Research Institute website, stretches for about 800 miles, from Hernandez's home state of San Luis Potosi in Mexico, up into Texas, including those parts west of the Pecos River, and over into southern New Mexico, a slice of Arizona and then back down through Mexico. It is about 250 miles wide at its widest point.[268]

The desert lies mostly between the Sierra Madre Oriental and Sierra Madre Occidental mountain ranges in Mexico. Elevations vary from 1000 feet along the Rio Grande to nearly 10,000 feet in Mexico. Winters, especially at night, are normally cool, while the summer months are typically hot.[269]

The land West of the Pecos is pretty much what one would think. It is covered with what is called Chihuahaun Desert Scrub that includes Lechugilla, sotol, mesquite, and yucca plants. A diverse variety of cacti grow within the region, as do juniper trees along with a variety of other plants and grasses.[270]

The land is home to lizards, snakes, birds, bats, tarantulas, scorpions and centipedes. Many small and larger mammals, including coyotes, mule deer, whitetail deer, pronghorn antelope and an occasional mountain lion survive within the landscape.[271] Alfredo Hernandez lived among them.

Surely it was the diverse landscape and his desire for money (for his mother and Rosa) that led him to this desolate part of West Texas.[272] Not to mention the rumors of a large treasure that led him to Pumpville in July 1965.[273]

The rumors about a treasure came about because of the holding pens and loading chutes. Vaqueros, the accomplished cowboys and horsemen who helped the ranchers take the livestock there for shipping, had seen thousands of dollars change hands there. The rumor was that the money was kept in a safe in the store.[274]

Hernandez had apparently been in the store several times over the years. He knew there were brooms and mops right inside the front door to the right, with saddle blankets and tack just behind and a small room full of oil products behind them. Feed sacks were in a back storeroom, near the back door; food, clothing and general store merchandise along the middle and left side of the building; and a meat case behind them. A phone booth stood in the corner behind a checkout counter that was along the left wall. A door behind the counter opened into the Post Office.[275]

Hernandez had probably tried the knobs on the safe every time he'd been in the store; but each time he'd been unsuccessful in getting it open. However, as evidenced in July 1965, he apparently believed that the treasure was there.

Pelham Bradford and his wife, Estella Lottie Rose, ran the store and managed the pens at Pumpville. He was also the Postmaster and both had been part-time phone switchboard operators. In 1965, he was sixty-seven and she was ten years younger. The couple had four grown children, Pelham Rose, Marcella, John and Beverly. The later two children had been born respectively, 13 years and 15 years after the second daughter.[276]

Bradford was a solidly built man with gray hair who stood five-foot eight-inches tall. He regularly wore khaki shirts and pants, boots and either a gray felt or white western straw hat depending on the season. He was also a man who had a reputation as a hard worker. One story told was that he'd sent some men to dig post-holes, but when he went to check on their progress he dug the rest of the holes himself while they watched.[277]

1959 photo of Pelham Bradford and son-in-law Felix Harrison in front of Pumpville store. Photo courtesy of Marcella Bradford Harrison.

Stella had been an attractive woman when she was young and she still showed evidence of that at fifty-seven. She had kept a medium build on her five-foot five-inch frame and her hazel eyes had that look about them. She still had long dark hair, though during the day she kept it tied up in a bun.[278]

During the summer of 1965, the Bradfords had stopped restocking many things in the store. They had realized that the time was coming when they would no longer tend it. As his wife would say, "Pelham's getting tired and he's ready to let someone else take over."[279]

Their granddaughter Pam, daughter of Pelham Rose and her husband Ross Stavley, helped them out that summer. On Saturday afternoon, July 10, 1965, their daughter-in-law Ella Ruth, their son's wife, came through Pumpville on her way back to Sanderson. Just before the sun disappeared out west, Pam caught a ride back home with her aunt.[280]

Alfredo Hernandez almost certainly watched the two women leave that day. He'd probably been watching the place for days, just waiting for the right moment to commit his crime. In all likeliness he knew that the only other inhabitant, Brother Price, the preacher at the church, had moved out of his own house a few weeks earlier.[281]

Hernandez seemed to have great likeness for soft drinks and he must have wished he had one of the drinks in the metal box outside the store that very night. The same box he'd broken into several times in the past.[282]

Surely he watched as Pelham Bradford dropped the American flag from a flagpole, removed it from its clasps, took it inside the store and walked over to his house for the night.

The long white wood-framed house had a tin roof and a full-length screened in porch on the side toward the railroad tracks. It was common for people to sleep on such porches during the hot summer months.[283]

Trellises rose from the ground and met the roof at the overhang in all but just a few feet along the length of the porch. A screen door was set just inside the only break in the trellises. Vines rose from the ground and a few even reached up to the rooftop.[284]

Bradford home. Photo courtesy of Marcella Bradford Harrison.

It was just after midnight on Sunday, July 11, 1965 when Alfredo Hernandez placed a mask across his face and entered through the back doorway of the Bradford home. He made his way through the kitchen, living room and front door, turning on the lights as he went. He finally pushed open a screen door and stepped out onto the screened in porch.[285]

Pelham and Stella Bradford were asleep on a bed at the far end of the 34-foot length porch. He slept in his boxer shorts and a t-shirt and she wore a white cotton open-neck nightgown. Over the years each had learned to sleep rather soundly, what with the trains thundering by and blowing their high pitched whistles at the county road railroad crossing right by their home.[286]

The couple understood and spoke Spanish and it was Stella who heard Hernandez first. "Wake up! Do you hear me? Wake up!" he said.[287]

She shook her husband and rose to an elbow and looked at the masked man standing not too far away. "I don't want to hurt anybody, I just want the money," Stella heard the man say, even though she thought to herself, still kind of thinking it might be a dream, 'He's saying something.'[288]

Pelham Bradford was sort of dazed, still partially asleep when he slid out of bed. He shook his head as if to get the cobwebs out of his ears, and started walking toward the man standing near the living room door.[289]

Hernandez must have realized the man was about the size and age of the man from Happy Hollow and he apparently didn't plan on ever letting another man put their hands on him. He lifted his revolver and pulled the trigger—twice.[290]

Pelham Bradford dropped and cried out in pain as one of the bullets tore into his right leg. Stella quickly stepped around the end of the bed and saw blood pooling on the floor.[291]

Hernandez ordered her to go on and used the revolver to motion her toward the store. She looked down at her wounded husband and with a trembling voice asked if she could bandage his leg first. She didn't remember whether he said anything, but she helped Pelham into a chair and started tearing long strips off of the bed sheet. She wrapped the leg and then wrapped it again.[292]

As she finally stood, Hernandez pointed toward a piece of rope that he had thrown on the floor. She looked at it but really didn't understand what he wanted her to do.[293]

"He wants you to tie me up," Pelham Bradford told his wife.[294]

Stella Bradford made a very, very poor attempt to tie her husband to the chair. As she would tell her friends later, "A baby could have done better." She also told her friends, "The Bandit was a modest fellow, you know."[295]

Hernandez had apparently seen the nightgown drop away from her chest. The motions of tending to her husband had caused her to expose herself. He turned his eyes away. Then, as she stood, he pointed at her husband's shirt hung on the edge of the chair and told her to put it on. She just stood there—looking at him for a moment, then he told her to put it on again and she complied.[296]

Stella Bradford made her way through the living room and into the kitchen. She took a bunch of keys off of a nail and started out the back door. She felt the gun and the man's presence at her back as she crossed the short distance between the house and the store.[297]

She opened the back door and turned on the light in the storeroom. Then, as she made her way through the store, she turned on another light by the meat counter, one by the scales and the one by the Post Office door. She unlocked the door, switched on the light and knelt down to open the safe. She wiped her eyes, but couldn't see the numbers on the dial in the shadows. "I can't see," she told Hernandez.[298]

He stepped over her and placed a flashlight on the table above her. She took it in one hand and turned the knobs back and forth with the other. Even though she had seldom opened the safe until her third or fourth try, the safe opened the first time.[299]

She removed a drawer and gave Hernandez the bills. Then she gave him a bag of silver coins that a man named Luce Ramos had brought in to exchange for an $85.00 check. But as she stepped back into the store, behind the counter, she decided not to give him the funds from a green tin box sitting on a shelf. It was the money they took in for money orders.[300]

As she stepped around in front of the counter, Hernandez asked her, "Is that all?" And Stella Bradford responded, "Yes."[301]

Of course, Hernandez had been in the store before. He knew there was a green box that normally had money in it. He stepped up to where she had been and pulled it out. Though he shoved some bills into his pants pocket, there was only four dollars in the money order box. He also tried to open the cash register but couldn't get it to open. So he used the revolver to motion her toward it.[302]

Stella Bradford opened the cash register and watched him take the bills but leave the silver. Then as they started to leave the store, she watched as he backed up and tore the phone lines out of the wall.[303]

Pelham Bradford had loosened the rope and made his way into the house. He found one of his rifles but couldn't find any shells so he moved to a closet in the bedroom. He had just pulled out a gun scabbard, wrapped around a 30:30 lever action rifle, and pitched it on the bed when he heard his wife call out from up front.[304]

"Pelham! Pelham! Come unlock the door!"[305]

He found his wife and the Bandit standing just outside the front porch screen door. He lifted the latch and stepped back. At Hernandez's urging, using the revolver to motion them toward the end of the porch, he and his wife walked to the bed and sat down.[306]

Hernandez went into the house and said in what was nearly plain English, "I'm going to find the treasure," except the word treasure was hard to understand.[307]

Pelham didn't understand what he said and asked three times, "What did you say?"[308]

Stella finally said, "He means treasure, he's going to find the treasure."[309]

"What treasure are you talking about?" Pelham yelled toward the man.[310]

Hernandez came back to the porch and looked at the couple. He said he'd heard there was supposed to be a few thousand dollars in the house. The couple assured him he had everything they had. He made several more trips into the house, looking, but never did find the treasure that wasn't there. He finally asked for their car keys.[311]

Stella Bradford went to the kitchen, got one set of keys out of three and gave them to him. She thought, "I wonder if these are the right ones." She went back to the bed and watched as he tried to start the car, but the keys were not the right ones so she gave him another set.[312]

Again Hernandez did not get the car started. So he returned and motioned for Stella to come outside and start it. When it started she released the parking brake and slowly backed the car away from their pickup. She turned it around so it would be headed out the right way.[313]

As she got out of the car, Hernandez herded her back to the porch and warned the couple not to move. "How long should we wait, my husband's been shot and I want him to get to a doctor as soon as I can?" Stella asked.[314]

Hernandez told them to wait thirty minutes and he left the porch. Before he drove off in their car, he raised the hood on the pickup and pulled the ignition wires from the engine.[315]

Stella Bradford would later say that she didn't remember getting dressed but did remember putting on Pam's loafers which were a size too big. And she didn't wait 30 minutes to try to get help for her husband.[316]

The first thing Stella noticed was that the man had pulled the phone lines out of their house, so after helping get Pelham dressed, she tried to call out on a northeast phone line from the store. These were party lines, telephone lines that connected four houses together, lines that all rang at the same time but with one particular ring for each house. Only no one answered because no one was home.[317]

Pelham Bradford found the wires torn off of his pickup. He turned toward his wife, who was on the porch and said, "Stell, I'm going to use the railroad phone." Then he turned and headed off toward the stock pens and the railroad phone booth.[318]

Stella grabbed an aluminum chair and followed her husband across the dusty tall weeds in front of the stock pens. Any other time no one could have paid her enough money to walk through those weeds at night, what with the rattlesnakes that frequented the area on occasion.[319]

The phone booth was locked when the couple got there. Pelham had been given a key a few years before because they were going to ship hundreds of lambs for Cleve Jones out of Sonora. This allowed him to tell the railroad folks how many lambs they had and when they would be there. Only that night he didn't have the key with him.[320]

Pelham Bradford rested in the chair while his wife went back to the house to get the key. It was on a nail along the kitchen wall. She also grabbed a hammer, saw and screwdriver in case the key had been changed or didn't work for some reason, but the key worked.[321]

Pelham Bradford interrupted the railroad dispatcher from Sanderson. The man was talking railroad talk to someone else in another town but stopped and quickly got Terrell County Sheriff Bill Cooksey on the line. After Bradford gave the Sheriff a nickel picture of what had happened, he said, "I feel sick Bill, please send us some help."[322]

Stella Bradford hurried back to the house to get her husband a pillow so he could lie down next to the phone booth. It was then that she started to realize just how much blood he had lost. It was everywhere, all over the bed, porch, living room, kitchen and out on the front steps.[323]

When she got back with the pillow and helped get her husband comfortable, she heard him say, "I'm thirsty." So she hurried back and brought him some water.[324]

Highway 90 was a busy highway through Sanderson in 1965. It was a major throughway between El Paso and San Antonio, between the East and the West. It was a highway that had plenty of traffic especially on the weekends. It was not uncommon for the Sheriff or his Deputy to patrol the streets late at night.[325]

Deputy Sheriff Dalton Hogg and his passenger had just left the Oasis Café after getting a late night cup of coffee. They were stopped in the driveway at Dudley Harrison's Texaco Service Station when the deputy got the call about the Pumpville shooting. The deputy purposely kept his gas tank filled in the event of such an emergency[326].

The forty-two-year-old lawman put his foot into the accelerator of his personal car; a Buick Skylark station wagon that he used as his patrol car, a car that looked just like the county's ambulance. He even had a stretcher and oxygen tank in the back. There were no lights or siren, but the passenger put a red light out on top as the car sped out of town.[327]

The passenger was a tall, six-foot four-inch 180-pound rancher named W.J. Vaughan. The twenty-seven year old wrangler was the grandson of Joe and Elizabeth Nichols who ranched 8,100 acres out near the airport just west of Dryden. He personally ranched the 12,000-acre Brown Ranch that was about seven miles north of Sanderson, as the crow flies, but it was 20 miles if you had to drive to get to it.[328]

Vaughan had a hobby of shooting guns and reloading ammunition. In fact, he actually had a reloading bench set up in the living room of his cinderblock home. He had a habit of going to town, especially on weekend nights, and riding around with Sheriff Cooksey or Deputy Hogg. He'd even given thoughts to becoming a lawman himself.[329]

It was during one of his weekend excursions, during the summer of 1964, that someone had stolen a nickel Smith and Wesson .357 caliber revolver out of his home. They had also taken a coffee can full of .38 caliber reloads that he'd stuffed with wadcutter-style bullets. He had great hopes that they'd run across the culprit someday.[330]

Vaughan's parents had divorced so his grandparents raised him. It was during a trip to the McKnight's Chevrolet House, with his granddad's pickup, that a much younger Vaughan had first met Dalton Hogg. The year would have been around 1953.[331]

The deputy was formerly a body-man for the car dealership and it was only natural that he'd pull a dent out of the pickup, a dent that Vaughan's granddad didn't want the grandmother to know was ever there in the first place.[332]

It wasn't too long after that first meeting that Hogg started taking Vaughan, Eddie Hanson—whose dad owned the dealership and J.D, his own son, rabbit hunting on a pretty regular basis. That first meeting also led to the friendship that caused Vaughan to be in the patrol car on that early Sunday morning.[333]

Stella Bradford saw the headlights while the car was still a good ways off. She held Pelham's hand and ran the fingers of her other hand through his hair. She was worried about the sick feeling that he said was in the pit of his stomach, not to mention that he'd said several times that he felt light headed. She knew that he'd lost a lot of blood from the leg wound.[334]

She watched as the station wagon slid to a stop in front of the house, but she stood, hollered and waved her arms when Dalton Hogg got out. It was just a few minutes before her husband was on the cot and they were headed toward the hospital in Del Rio.[335]

The older daughters, Pelham Rose Stavley and Marcella Harrison, both lived in Sanderson and worked at the Post Office. It was only natural that Pelham Rose was notified about the shooting just minutes after Dalton Hogg started toward Pumpville. It wasn't too many more minutes before the two sisters were headed that way themselves.[336]

The lights were on in their parent's house when they got there. They were plenty spooked and concerned when they saw all the blood. They didn't find their parents so they turned around and were soon on Highway 90 headed toward Del Rio. They were about to Langtry when they met the patrol car from the Texas Department of Public Safety.[337]

Trooper Buddy Burgess received the call about a 'shooting at the Pumpville Post Office.' He put his foot into the accelerator of his state car and headed toward the tiny town in the northwest part of Val Verde County.[338]

Leland K. 'Buddy' Burgess was born in Mesquite, Texas in 1938. His parents farmed and owned the Dallas-based Burgess Business Machines Company. After high school he went to Baylor for a couple of years then married his wife Carol in 1960. She was going to Texas Women's University and he worked at a bakery. He was drafted in 1961 and wound up in Germany.[339]

When Burgess got out of the military he went back to the bakery while his wife taught school in Gainesville. He would later tell his friends, "It was during a drive from Gainesville to Sherman that I saw a Highway Patrolman asleep under a tree and that's what made me think about joining the Highway Patrol."[340]

Buddy Burgess reported to the state police academy in Austin just a few days before President Kennedy was shot in November 1963. He graduated in March 1964 and was stationed in Del Rio. His coverage area included Kinney, Terrell, Maverick and Val Verde counties.[341]

Burgess had seen the ambulance going the other way somewhere between Comstock and Langtry. He only saw one other car before he turned onto Farm to Market Road 1865 that led to Pumpville.[342]

The Highway Patrolman found the lights on in the Bradford house. The porch looked like it had been painted red but he knew that it was blood. He saw the blood trail that led off toward the pens. He searched the house, room by room, but there was no one there.[343]

Then he realized that if the criminal was still around, that it was he who was standing in the light. It was he that would make a good target. So he backed up into the darkness, with his shotgun tucked into the crook of his left arm, and waited for the other lawmen that he knew would arrive.[344]

It was a 75-mile trip from Pumpville to Del Rio and, as the saying goes Terrell County Deputy Dalton Hogg didn't let any grass grow under his feet in getting there. As the patrol car/ambulance pulled up to the hospital, Stella Bradford said, "You know Dalton, I don't know what scared me the most, the Bandit or your driving."[345]

CHAPTER 8

Trooper Buddy Burgess didn't have to wait too long before he had company at Pumpville. A Val Verde County deputy was about twenty minutes behind him. The deputy told him that he'd stopped and talked to the Terrell County deputy in the ambulance. He'd learned that the Bandit had stolen the Bradford's car and driven away. They figured the Bandit was probably miles away from there.[346]

The deputy went on to say that he might have learned more about what happened except that Mrs. Bradford got upset and hollered, "Let's get on to the hospital, we've got my husband back here!"[347]

The Monday morning edition of the San Angelo Standard-Times read, 'Bradford Shot in Pumpville PO Robbery.' The story laid out how a statewide manhunt had been called off around noon after the Bradford's car was found along a county road about a mile north of Langtry.[348] "The guy couldn't drive. He ran right off the road when he came to a curve," said former Terrell County Sheriff Bill Cooksey years later.[349]

The story highlighted the basic details of the robbery and told that a Postal Inspector had joined Val Verde county officials in a more localized search for a Latin American suspect. The man had only gotten $200 from the store. The reporter was quoting Val Verde County Sheriff H. J. Richter.[350]

Val Verde County Sheriff Herman J. Richter. Photo courtesy of Val Verde County Sheriff's Department and Sheriff D'Wayne Jernigan.

Herman J. Richter was born at Lohn, Texas near Brady in 1901. He and his wife, Elsie L. Rudolph, both grew up there. He left the Brady area to take a Border Patrol job during the war but was laid off when the troops returned home. Afterwards, he became a private game warden, a part-time, then full-time policeman and finally Del Rio's Chief of Police. Then the tall slender lawman was elected Sheriff of Val Verde County. It was a position he would hold for 21 years.[351]

There were a few added details in the Monday afternoon July 12th edition of the Del Rio News-Herald. The Postal Inspector was identified as J.W. Biggers from San Antonio. Two Jeep-loads of United States Border Patrolmen were assisting with the search as was one of their airplanes. The 67 year-old Pelham Bradford was reportedly doing well at the Val Verde County Memorial Hospital. The Del Rio newspaper was also quoting Sheriff Richter who related that the Sheriff's Department was also being assisted in the investigation by Texas Ranger L. H. Purvis.[352]

L.H. Purvis, known as Hardy to a few, was born in East Texas, at Corrigan in Polk County on July 14, 1912. He was an investigator for Humble Oil and Refining Company prior to joining the Texas Rangers on July 22, 1943. Prior to his assignment at Del Rio, he'd been assigned to Kerrville, Alpine and Sonora.[353]

The Ranger was five-foot ten-inches tall, weighed about 180 pounds and had graying hair. He dressed in western suits and hats and holstered either a Smith and Wesson Model 27 .357 magnum revolver or a Colt Commander semi-automatic pistol in 38 Super. Some would also say that he was the last true horseback Texas Ranger.[354]

The Friday July 16, 1965 edition of the Sanderson Times revealed a fairly complete story about what happened during what had become known as the Pumpville Post Office Robbery. It let all those concerned know that Pelham Bradford was recovering satisfactorily. By the time the newspaper was printed, law enforcement officers had their own thoughts about where the Bandit had gone.[355]

The search eventually covered a great part of Val Verde County. Officers looked in every cave, crevice and ravine they could find. They searched along the Pecos and Rio Grande rivers and they asked their Mexican counterparts across the river to do the same.[356] By that following Friday they all assumed that the Bandit had absconded into Mexico, and the evidence might lead someone to believe they were right.

Hernandez may have hyperventilated after he drove off in the Bradford's car and that may have been why he drove it off the road.[357] Or Bill Cooksey may have been right when he said Hernandez really didn't know how to drive.[358] Or he may have just placed it there because he knew that he wasn't too far from the railroad tracks. If Hernandez's pattern was true to form, he probably did return home to see his mother and Rosa after he'd taken the money, but he didn't take them the treasure that he had hoped for...

CHAPTER NINE
Dryden 1965

The tall stocky teenager walked out of his father's house just as a blue Volkswagen drove by and headed up FM 349 toward Sheffield. The driver of the car was Bernice Cooksey, the Sheriff's wife who was delivering the mail to rural residents. He knew the woman wore glasses and had dark hair that fell nearly to her shoulders. With the aid of his own glasses, he watched as the 'Bug' sped North over the railroad tracks and finally disappeared from sight.[359]

The youngster wore his brown hair in what some might call a long burr cut. He wore a plaid shirt, blue jeans and boots. Everyone knew him as Benny Ray Ross.[360]

Ross was born in San Antonio in December of 1946. He spent his early years around Dryden, where his dad, Rufus (R.J.) Ross, ranched until the 50s drought ruined him and many others in the ranching industry. The boy's mother died when he was just eight years old.[361]

Benny Ray spent his first three years of school in the tiny schoolhouse at Dryden. He spent the next three years at Sanderson; then he lived with other relatives and went to school in Grand Prairie and Lometa. He spent his senior year at the Allen Military Academy but needed a half credit to graduate when he left. He graduated from Grand Prairie High School early that summer, after which he moved back to Dryden.[362]

Dryden had been a bustling, busy little community in the early 1950s. There was an active railroad depot, three railroad pump houses, a motel, two mercantile stores, a number of establishments many might call 'beer joints', eating places, a Texas State Highway Department office, Baptist and Methodist churches and plenty of small houses for the railroad employees and the locals. The railroad, ranching and tourism fueled the economy, but things had really changed by 1965.[363]

The 50s drought had taken its toll on the ranching business and the railroad philosophy had changed when the engines moved from steam-power to diesel-power. The railroad didn't need crews in nearly every town and the employees and their families were now gone. The school and the Purple Sage Motel were closed, and the population was down to about fifty.[364]

Benny Ray Ross lived in a wood framed house on FM 349 between the railroad tracks and U.S. Highway 90. He walked to the T-intersection and looked to the left toward Pumpville. He looked beyond Jimmy Merritt's house, past a building that had the words GARAGE painted across the top, and he saw Joe Vasquez waiting on a customer at his service station.[365]

Joe's Chevron station was located on the north side of the highway about a stone's throw from 349. A gas pump out front stood alongside the upper frame of an old wind generator. The frame had been modified with a ringer so you could squeeze water out of a windshield chamois. A small parts room was attached to the west side of Joe's service station/store.[366]

Joe's service station was as much a small general store and grocery, with a grill in the back, as it was a service station and garage. Customers could order a hamburger while Joe fixed their flat tire or changed a thermostat. The business was right across the highway from the closed Purple Sage Motel.[367]

Benny Ray Ross looked to the right, down 90 toward Sanderson. He looked past John Montgomery's building, his few acres of junkyard, and beyond the old cars, out by the railroad tracks he could see the top of the drilling mud (oilfield) warehouse. Farther down 90, on the same side of the highway, he saw an old abandoned rock building and then farther down, the Do Drop Inn.[368]

The youngster let his eyes drift across the highway, where a number of cars were parked in front of Lewis Cash's Cactus Café. Then he let his eyes wander back the hundred yards or so to the intersection and across from where he stood. He saw several cars parked at the Dryden Mercantile and the attached Post Office. He knew that getting the day's mail from Alma Jewel Littleton, the Post Mistress, and getting a cup of coffee at Bill Ten Eyck's Mercantile was a daily ritual for most of the locals. He quickly looked both ways and made his way across the busy highway.[369]

(U.S. Highway 90 was a busy highway during this time in Texas history. Interstate 10 was not completed yet so the traffic and tourists brought plenty of activity to Terrell County, which included Sanderson, the county seat, and Dryden.)

The teenager started to go to the Mercantile Store but decided to go wander around, to explore the countryside instead. After all, he'd already heard all the talk, over and over since June, the talk about the terrible flood that had hit Sanderson and the shooting of Pelham Bradford. The Sheriff had also told him to keep a lookout because of some burglaries that were occurring in the area. The youngster started to make his way up the hill behind the store.[370]

A passerby might have noticed the tops of several houses on the hill just south of Highway 90 behind the Mercantile. The first house up behind the store was the home of Bill and Mary Lois Ten Eyck (His last name is a two-worded name pronounced 'Ten Ike' that many people would spell as one word with two syllables.) and their four children. Just west of the house was the home of George Adams.[371]

George Adams was a retired rancher, who stood about five-foot nine-inches and carried 180 pounds below the shine of his baldhead. He regularly wore western attire and a cowboy hat. In his late fifties, he had a reputation of and was thought to be 'a good guy.'[372]

Just behind the Adams' house, were a few vacant houses, and west of them was the home of Mr. and Mrs. Appellano Vasquez, Joe Vasquez's parents. Joe and his wife, Iva Lee Rogers Vasquez, lived on the western edge of this hilltop part of the community.[373]

Iva Lee stood five-foot two-inches tall, weighed a little over 130 pounds and had red hair that she kept dyed brown. She'd borne seven children during two previous marriages. She had two sons, Virgil and Don, during her first marriage to Kye McElhaney. She had five children, 'Junior', Butch, Wayne and Elaine (twins) and Donna during her marriage to Elton Jessie 'Buddy' Rogers. She and Buddy had managed the Purple Sage Motel, but by 1965 they had been divorced for some time and she was married to a much younger Joe Vasquez.[374] (Donna was five, and Wayne, who was 18, lived in the house with their mother and step-dad in 1965. Elaine had married and moved away.)[375]

Vasquez had previously worked at the Lindsey Hicks Ranch at Independence Creek but moved to Dryden when the school shut down so the kids would be closer to the school at Sanderson. He was six feet tall, weighed 170 pounds and walked with a noticeable limp. Vasquez was a man who had a great love for the game of baseball. He was in his mid to late 40s when he started working on a deal to buy the service station from Jimmy Merritt during the summer of 1965.[376]

Another neighbor who lived in one of the hilltop houses was a man named George 'Woody' Rutledge. His house was closer to Highway 90 and just west of another dirt road that led down to the major thoroughfare.[377]

Woody Rutledge was a simple man who never completed the elementary grades; he didn't do well at adding or subtracting. This tall (about six-feet three-inches though he slumped over a little) thin man in his 40s, who did a multitude of odd jobs and day work, was well liked among his peers.[378]

It was not uncommon for the passerby to see the man, wearing a blue work shirt, blue jeans and Brogan shoes, as he rode his three-wheel bicycle along the 20 miles between Dryden and Sanderson. He was a man who definitely gave you a day's worth of work for the money, although you had to give him specific instructions or he might do more than just what you wanted.[379]

One example is a story about the time he was asked to dig a hole big enough for a septic tank next to a Sanderson residence. When the homeowner went to check on him, hours later, he'd dug the hole much deeper than it needed to be. He was definitely a hard worker.[380]

One other story about adding and subtracting was that he spent some of his time trapping varmints for some of the area ranchers. When an out-of-town fur buyer tried to gyp Rutledge on some of the prices, because he didn't do well with numbers, one of the local ranchers told the buyer to stop cheating him or to not come back to their area.[381] Of course, Rutledge lived in a part of Texas where people took care of each other when it was necessary.

Benny Ray Ross walked up the road and walked past the Ten Eyck and Adams' houses. He eased across the open ground that led him into the land south of Dryden proper. Like so many teenagers his age would do, he was exploring, enjoying the outdoors and looking for anything that might come his way. He was also keeping an eye out like the Sheriff had asked him to.[382]

He stood and looked out across that part of the Chihuahuan Desert that was his world. It was the land that was once inhabited by Apache Indians. He was along the edge of a small ravine, south of the Ten Eyck's home when he saw something that got his attention.[383]

The sun was high in the sky and had just come out from behind a cloud when he'd seen the flicker of a reflection that came from some of the dense brush across the way. It was much like a light hitting a mirror that shines into your eyes, drawing you to it, then away from it.[384]

It didn't take the teenager long to get to the dense brush. Hidden within it he found a few cans of food, a Mason jar and a bayonet; a bayonet that he'd seen before. A bayonet he knew belonged to Jimmy Merritt.[385]

Jimmy Merritt was in his late 40s, not very tall and not heavy, with light brown hair and blue eyes. He had owned the service station and garage that Joe Vasquez was in the process of buying from him. He and his wife Bea, who had been the local Justice of the Peace, lived next door to the station. It was rumored the couple was having trouble.[386]

Merritt was a jack-of-all-trades type of guy who had what some people called 'goofy spells,' though others said he was just epileptic and forgot to take his medicine. There were others who said he just never grew up. He was a good mechanic and that fit in well with his service station duties. The man had a passion for guns and motorcycles. He was also a pilot, as was his wife.[387]

There are many stories about the exploits of Jimmy Merritt, including one incident where he laid down behind his concrete gas pump island and used a .22 caliber rifle to exchange shots with someone who had wronged him. But it is the Game Warden story that showed a picture of his character, grit and demeanor.[388]

Texas Game Warden Cliff Wilson needed to deliver an emergency message to a deer hunter in a camp in Terrell County's San Francisco Canyon. Merritt flew them there and landed his small tail-dragger airplane on a really, really short piece of dry gravel bar. After the message had been delivered, Wilson realized that the plane had taken off in a much greater space at the airport. He didn't know how they would ever get the plane off the ground, he was sure they would wreck it.[389]

"Oh don't worry about that, I'll get it off the ground. Just do what I tell you," said Merritt.[390]

The pair spent some time lining up a stack of rocks until they were about a foot high and in a line that was long enough to be wider than the plane's wheelbase. Then Merritt taxied the short distance back to the other end of the space and turned the plane around. Wilson picked up the tail, as he was instructed to do, as Merritt revved the engine. When the plane stood on its own, Wilson got back inside.[391]

Merritt let go of the brake and pushed the throttle all the way forward. As the plane neared the rocks, with enough speed to push Wilson back into the seat and his cheeks back into his face and with the brush-line coming toward them at what seemed like an amazing rate of speed, it looked to Wilson as though the plane would surely be destroyed. When the tires hit the rocks, the plane popped up into the air and they were off. It was a plane-ride the Warden would never forget, or as he would say, "never ever want to emulate."[392]

Benny Ray Ross gathered up the bayonet, cans and Mason jar and headed back toward the Mercantile Store. The teenager thought about the stories that he'd heard about people missing things from their houses in town and out on the ranches. Most of the people said they were missing just a few eggs, a few pieces of bacon, a can of food here and there. Others said that their minds might be slipping. Now he had proof that someone was stealing things from the people around Dryden. He couldn't wait to tell Sheriff Cooksey. He also wondered, "Who had hidden the things there?"[393]

Dryden area map taken from 'Kerr's Headquarters for Hunters' map, provided by Dudley Harrison. Permission for use provided by family member Tom Kerr. Map designed by Rio Grande-Pecos Soil Conservation District.

CHAPTER TEN
Sheriff Cooksey and Deputy Hogg

Terrell County Sheriff Buster Babb resigned during the summer of 1961. The County Commissioners were left with the dilemma of deciding who would replace him. They offered the job to Texas Highway Patrolman Bill Cooksey.[394]

Bill Cooksey was born at Mullin in Mills County, Texas on September 28, 1925. His parents, Tom and Grace Cooksey, ranched the Sleeping Hollow Ranch. He had three older brothers, James Maxwell, Thomas Denton Jr. and Jack Rutherford Cooksey.[395]

The youngest Cooksey went to school in Mullin but left at seventeen years of age, in his senior year, to join the Merchant Marines. It was the same year that he met the woman who would become the love of his life.[396]

Bill Cooksey and Bernice 'Bennie' Mills from Zephyr met on a blind date the night gasoline rationing started in 1942. They weren't on a date with each other but rather with their best friends. After they met, Bill spent three years on a cargo ship in the Pacific before he returned home.[397]

In 1946, Cooksey went to work at a service station in Goldthwaite before he moved on to work at a Goodyear Tire Store in Brownwood. He and Bennie Mills were married on January 18, 1947. The new husband joined the Texas Department of Public Safety in March 1948.[398]

His first nine months were spent as a driver's license examiner in Houston, after which Cooksey was accepted into the Texas Highway Patrol. He entered their police academy at Austin in February 1949.[399]

He was first stationed in Llano and stayed there until he was transferred to Hamilton in Bosque County in December 1953. After a short stay at Gatesville in December of 1957, Cooksey moved into a new safety education position at Waco in January 1958.[400] In his new job he presented safety classes to the public, performed trick shooting at particular events and was involved in a 30-minute local television show. "It was where I got my first taste of teaching and I really liked it," said Cooksey years later.[401]

By this time he and Bernice had three children. Their first son, Stephen Eric, was born in 1950 and Candace Sue followed in 1952. After they moved from Llano to Hamilton, Billie Kay was born in 1956.[402]

However, regular law enforcement was still in his blood so when he saw the notice of a new substation that would open in Sanderson, in Terrell County, he applied. (One of his brothers also had a flying service.) He moved his family out west in October 1960.[403]

The oil boom made it hard to find a place to stay in Sanderson as the population had stretched to near 3,000. In an effort to give the new Highway Patrolman a place to live, George and Viola Turner, who owned the Turner Hotel, moved out of their apartment and into another area of the hotel.[404]

Game Warden Cliff Wilson and Terrell County Deputy Dalton Hogg helped the Cooksey family move into their upstairs apartment. Years later Wilson would say, "I'll never forget moving the furniture up those stairs; we had to take the refrigerator door off and the stove apart to get them inside."[405]

The dark-headed Cooksey didn't have any problems with the minimum height requirements when he decided to join the Texas Department of Public Safety. He stood six-foot two-inches and, except for his glasses, was what most people thought a Texas lawman should have looked like during those times. He was slim, wiry and deceptively strong. He was also a good listener and a slow talker unless the situation dictated some other behavior.[406]

The residents of Sanderson and Terrell County made their new Highway Patrolman and his family feel right at home. Of course, Cooksey's duties caused him to meet some of the residents out on the highway.[407]

Soon after he arrived, while Cooksey was patrolling the highway toward Valentine, he stopped a truck for speeding. It was the first time he met Bert Bell and his wife Joanne. Bert was a railroad conductor and Joanne was a Carruthers whose family ranched 50 sections of Terrell County land. The couple would become lifelong friends of Cooksey and his wife.[408]

Bert Bell gladly accepted the speeding ticket from their new Highway Patrolman. He was awful glad he didn't look in their ice chest. "We'd been quail hunting and had three times too many birds," Joanne Bell said years later.[409]

It was about two months later that Cooksey saw a vehicle pass him, going the other way and he noticed that the taillights were not working. He turned his patrol car around and turned on his overhead red light.[410]

Rancher Walter G. Downie pulled his pickup over, stopped and got out. He was in a hurry and didn't really plan to make small talk with the new lawman.[411]

Cooksey had already learned that the size of a ranch in Terrell County was not talked about in acres but rather in the number of sections that were within its borders. He knew that Downie had one of the biggest ranches. "I'm Bill Cooksey with the Texas Highway Patrol. I stopped you because your taillights are out," he told Downie who was pulling his license out of his wallet.[412]

"If I got a ticket coming, give it to me," said Downie, who followed with, "And if you plan on being here in an hour, you might as well give me two because I plan on coming back the same way."[413]

It didn't take Cooksey long to learn that most of the ranchers came to town at least once every few weeks. He also learned that many ranchers, especially from the largest ranches, like the Mitchell Family Cattle Ranch, Downie, Monte Corder, Herman Couch, John and Pinky Carruthers, Roy and Jack Deaton, Charlie Turk, Sid Harkins, Reggie Monroe, the Harrisons and others, had houses in town for their families; places where most of the wives and kids stayed during the school year.[414]

Bill Cooksey was a people person and it didn't take the County Commissioners long to realize he had the qualities they wanted in a sheriff.[415] They already had another Highway Patrolman, a new DPS graduate named Carl Davis patrolling the area. However, Cooksey had questions for them before he would accept the appointment. "I already have a good job so why should I consider this," asked Cooksey.[416]

The Commissioners offered him more money than he was already making, but Cooksey said, "My goal would be to make this one of the best sheriff's departments in the country, so if you just want things to remain the same you'll need to appoint someone else." The Commissioners agreed that they would let him upgrade the department.[417]

Cooksey talked with former Terrell County Sheriff Jim Nance, a very much-respected Texas Ranger who was stationed at Sierra Blanca. After their talk, with a broken arm in a cast from fighting a drunk, he made his decision.[418]

Bill Cooksey was formally appointed and sworn in as the Terrell County Sheriff and Tax Collector on October 1, 1961. County Judge Sims Wilkinson gave him a small metal fishing box that contained basically the department's only equipment. It contained a few hot checks that merchants had been given, 2 pairs of handcuffs and the keys to the jail.[419]

Terrell County Sheriff Bill Cooksey. Copyright San Angelo Standard-Times, San Angelo, Texas. Reprinted with permission.

The Judge did give him two radios but the new Sheriff already knew that the county did not supply the patrol cars. He and his deputy would be paid mileage and get a car allowance. Of course, he had to find himself a deputy.[420]

It didn't take Cooksey too long to make his choice. Dalton Hogg had been a deputy under Sheriff Babb. He was a local person who knew everybody and he was very strong physically. As Cooksey would say later, "He had the type of upper body strength that could make one believe that he could bend railroad iron."[421]

Dalton David Hogg was born in Lamesa, Texas on January 4, 1923. His parents were farmers and he was one of five children. He did not graduate from high school and was drafted into the military, but he failed the physical. He was given a certain number of days to get a defense related job.[422]

He went to a machinist school in California, then went to work for Brown and Root at their shipyard near Houston. It was there that he met Henry Beth, the woman who would become the love of his life.[423]

Henry Beth Abbot had been born in Stanton, Texas in July of 1921. When she started dating Dalton Hogg, she was a welder that tacked pieces of metal together for the ship welders. She and others like her took on the nickname of Rosie the Riveter. She had a son by a previous marriage. Hogg quickly took to the woman and the boy.[424]

At some point Hogg went to work in the oilfield and the couple got separated from each other. While they were dating Henry Beth had bought him a Masonic pin because he was studying to be a Master Mason. She sent it to his parents' house about Christmas 1947.[425]

Shortly thereafter he wrote her and went to see her. He told her he'd learned to do automotive bodywork and was working for a car dealer in Sanderson. When he started to leave, her son started to cry and Dalton Hogg asked the boy why?[426]

"Because I don't want you to go and momma don't either," said the boy.[427]

Dalton Hogg married Henry Beth on August 11, 1948. They moved to Sanderson on August 16 so he could work at the McKnight Motor Company. "We moved because Jimmy Hanson gave him a guarantee of $25 a month," said Henry Beth.[428]

Dalton and Henry Beth Hogg. Photo courtesy of Henry Beth Hogg.

There was a short time in January 1949 when the couple moved so Dalton could work at the Chevrolet dealership in Fort Stockton and then for Halliburton, but by April they were back in Sanderson. Hanson had not only made him a better offer but also sent men in a truck to move them. "We never left Sanderson for more than a week after that," said Henry Beth.[429]

Dalton Hogg loved Henry Beth and her son. Not too long after they were married he adopted the boy and they changed his name to John Dalton Hogg.[430]

Henry Beth had a number of jobs prior to settling into a job with the Kerr Mercantile in Sanderson. Dalton finally quit the McKnight Motor Company in 1959 and started doing bodywork in a small shop beside his house. He also started riding around with Sheriff Buster Babb, who finally asked him to be his deputy on January 16, 1960.[431]

Dalton Hogg was five-foot eight-inches tall, was balding (with brown hair around the edges) and brown eyes. He was so conscious about his balding that he would not let anyone take his picture without his hat. Though the man had great upper body strength, probably more strength than he even knew he had, he also had a kind heart and regularly tried to make things better for kids.[432]

He was proud to be Sheriff Bill Cooksey's deputy. "We realized the Cooksey's were good Christian people who were concerned about everybody," said Henry Beth.[433]

Terrell County Sheriff Bill Cooksey quickly settled into his role as the top lawman in the county. He knew it was going to involve a lot more than his previous position of investigating accidents and writing tickets.

CHAPTER ELEVEN
The Early to Mid 60s

Sheriff Bill Cooksey made visible changes to the Terrell County Sheriff's Department as soon as he took office. He and Dalton Hogg started wearing uniforms and drove marked patrol cars, but Cooksey was just getting started meeting the challenges of his new position.[434]

It wasn't long before his deputy had completed a basic police academy course. They started a record management system for the jail and the department, and it wasn't too long before they physically upgraded the jail and started negotiations for and finally installed a radio base station. "We thought that base station was the greatest thing that ever happened to us," said Cooksey years later.[435]

The new Sheriff was quick to recognize the help of the County Commissioners and those who managed the day-to-day duties within the office, deputies Eloise Hahn and Elizabeth Murrah, and jailer and custodian Pilar Rodriguez. He also realized that small town law enforcement involved maintaining a working relationship with other sheriffs' departments within the area.[436]

As one example, he worked with Brewster County Sheriff Carl Williams to help get a teletype-loop installed that connected their sheriff departments with the Texas Department of Public Safety and the Federal Bureau of Investigation. He also developed relationships with local law enforcement officers within Terrell County, officers such as Highway Patrolman Malcolm Bollinger (who transferred in after Carl Davis was lured into the oilfield), Southern Pacific Railroad Investigator H.P. Boyd, Border Patrol Agents, Texas Ranger Forest Gould Hardin, and Game Warden Cliff Wilson.[437]

Sheriff Cooksey and Cliff Wilson, and their families, hit it off right away and became very close friends. "The Cookseys were honest God-fearing Christian people. Both of our families melded together like they belonged together. Neither wife smoked, drank or cussed," said Wilson.[438]

Cliff Kevin Cummings Luke Wilson was born in January of 1932 at Barksdale in Edwards County, Texas. His daddy worked for the highway department and his mother was a nurse. His dad was six-foot two-inches and his mother was five-foot even. He had two older brothers, so he was always known as 'Baby Wilson.'[439]

Baby's dad took his family to Del Rio when he was transferred there in 1939, but he was also drafted into the military and killed during WWII. At the time, Baby Wilson was attending Mount Sacred Heart Military Academy but he returned home to be with his mother. She was killed not too long after in a head-on traffic accident near Brackettville. Baby Wilson graduated from Del Rio High School in 1950.[440]

Baby Wilson's grades were good enough to get him into a well-known university, but his temper sent him packing from Texas A&M University that fall. With a resume that included the ability to speak Spanish and a past that included breaking horses for Del Rio rancher Elvis Stewart, Baby went to work reading meters and climbing poles for the Central Power and Light Company. Then the Korean War broke out.[441]

Baby went to San Antonio and joined the Army. He ended up in the Military Police Investigative Service, but his temper and a quick right hand added a court martial to his resume. It wasn't long before he was back working for the Central Power and Light Company at Campwood. But he was not alone.[442]

Cliff Wilson married Laura Mae Skiles, his high school sweetheart, in 1952. A transfer moved them back to Del Rio where their daughter Karen Lee was born in 1954. Sandra Dawn was born in 1956, after the family had moved to Fort Stockton. After a stint driving test cars at the Firestone Test Track, a question from a game warden changed his life in 1959.[443]

Wilson and a few friends were sitting in a café when Game Warden Ted Wheelis stopped by and asked, "Do you know anybody who might want to be a game warden?"[444]

Baby Wilson was just over six-foot in height, about 210 pounds, with brown hair and blue eyes, and he wasn't scared of hard work. The job question interested him and it wasn't long before he was seated in the 35 student game warden class at Texas A&M. After graduation he was assigned as Game Warden to Terrell County.[445]

Cliff Wilson and Bill Cooksey stood nearly nose-to-nose, yet there were a few times when they didn't see eye-to-eye. When they didn't, the Sheriff had a way of speaking through his gritted teeth; even when he had his pipe in his mouth he'd speak in a manner that kept his thoughts between them. Most of the time he'd start out with something like, "Now Wilson…" Even so, the men grew very close and had many discussions about law enforcement and life in general.[446]

Neither man ever thought about calling a person a snitch. They didn't like the word. People who gave them information about crime were either an informer or an informant. The men had deep discussions about the existence of the human race. Those discussions led them to define people three ways: First, a person is what they think they are; then, a person is what other people think they are; and, finally, a person is what they are in God's eyes. The friends also made their share of memories.[447]

Once, just before midnight, when Cliff Wilson was driving down Highway 90, Sanderson's main throughway, he saw two men who looked familiar walking toward a 'beer joint.' He stopped to get a better look only to realize they were two guys who were supposed to be in jail. The men had worked one of the bars loose, a few days before, and were taking their nightly walk to get a beer. Cooksey was not quite as amused as Wilson.[448]

Wilson learned first hand that Cooksey could keep a secret—even from him. One time the Sheriff sent the Warden and Deputy Hogg out on the highway to set up a roadblock to look for a pink Cadillac supposedly used in a serious crime, then he called them and told them they had a fight call at the Oasis Café. When they arrived, nearly running inside, they saw all their friends and a sign—'Happy Birthday Dalton and Cliff.'[449]

The Sheriff and the Warden both liked a good story, a good analogy. They both got a kick out of the County Judge as they listened to him describe Dryden. "During Noah's time, when it rained for 40 days and 40 nights, it only rained a tenth of an inch in Dryden," said the Judge.[450]

The ever-present traffic along Highway 90 and the small West Texas town atmosphere caused each law enforcement officer to take their turn at checking on things or answering a few calls for service, sometimes way into the night. The violent calls caused them to occasionally back each other up.

Baby Wilson and Bill Cooksey answered their share of calls that involved heated tempers and upset people. "I was always amazed at how Bill could calm things down just by talking to people. He was a person who treated people like he would want to be treated. Of course, if they did get out of hand, he knew how to take care of business too," said Wilson years later.[451]

Yes, the new Sheriff was a people person. He quickly began making relationships that would last a lifetime. He also worked with the Chamber of Commerce on any number of things, including a law enforcement training class in March 1962.[452]

The vast amount of traffic along Highway 90 and the trains brought many kinds of people through Terrell County, and unfortunately, some of those people were criminals who stole and committed burglaries along their way. In an effort to combat the problem, Sheriff Cooksey worked with the Terrell County Chamber of Commerce to host a burglary seminar for area law enforcement officers.[453]

The March 9th edition of the Sanderson Times reported that 35 officers from Fort Stockton, Alpine, Monahans, Kermit, Pecos, Midland, Sonora, Ozona, Del Rio and Laughlin AFB had attended the seminar. The Sheriff had introduced Texas Ranger Captain Frank Probst who showed two films and led a discussion about criminal investigation and interrogation. Chamber of Commerce members provided a noon meal, after which the discussion focused on the laws pertaining to enforcement and apprehension of the criminal element.[454]

Most of the Terrell County burglaries were crimes of opportunity. No one was home and many times the doors were not even locked. Many of the ranch house burglaries were committed by people traveling across the Rio Grande, those who came from Mexico to the United States looking for work. Most just took food because they were hungry. (Remember, this was before the regular use of deadbolt locks and crime prevention was just on the horizon.) Other burglaries were a 'crash and dash' type of crime at a business. Many times the criminal was long gone down the road before the crime was even discovered. This was what most of the burglaries entailed, until the Orchid Café and Roadside Inn were burglarized.

It was February 28, 1964, when the Sanderson Times reported a different kind of Terrell County burglar. The criminal was someone who had a different modus operandi; a different way of doing things that included removing the glass from a window, and then replacing it, just like they found it. They had even taken the pieces of the old molding and stuck it back around the glass. Sheriff Cooksey knew it was evidence that a different kind of burglar had entered Terrell County.[455]

This was the type of thing that Bill Cooksey might have told his family as they met for supper each night. It was their family time when they each told about the good and bad things of the day. It was a time when he said the prayer and asked God to bless their food. By November of 1965, he'd had plenty of things to report since they first moved to Sanderson.[456]

The Cooksey's really enjoyed the annual Terrell County 4th of July Celebration, an event that has always been special to those who lived in the area. The birth of two more children, Terrell Denton in October of 1963, and Leslie Arnette in October of 1965, were very special events in their lives too. He moved his family to a house on Cargile Street, a house where neighborhood get-togethers were the norm. "But it was the people, the many dear friends, who made such an impact on our lives. Terrell County is the type of place where people take care of each other when the need arises, and sometimes they do special things for each other when it doesn't," said Bill Cooksey in 1990.[457]

The Sheriff's Department had been given the responsibility of handling the ambulance duties for area residents in 1964. The county bought a Buick station wagon to serve as their first ambulance. Troy Druse, Albert Gilbreath, Carol Fitzgerald, Slim Mueller and others were Texas A&M trained volunteers. Most would say that birth in the back of the ambulance was quite a blessing. Dalton Hogg bought another station wagon that he used as a patrol car and backup ambulance.[458] But Terrell County had suffered its share of setbacks during those years too.

Railroad jobs were abolished at Dryden (summer 1962), and Sanderson (switch engine crew pulled August 1964); the Kerr Mercantile was burglarized (April 1964 and January 1965), a money sack was stolen from the Cooke Food Market (February 1965) and the Sheriff's close friend, Cliff Wilson, had decided to leave his state job and went to work for the United States Customs Service in the Big Bend. But the greatest tragedy of the time struck in June 1965 when a flood hit Sanderson and took the lives of 26 people. A month later, Pelham Bradford was shot at Pumpville, Cooksey's sheriff's office was burglarized and so was the home of Lewis Hill.[459]

Weather and crime continued into August and September 1965. The Riggins Jewel and Gift Shop was burglarized and a tornado hit the Lee Dudley Ranch. Another tornado brought heavy wind and hail to Dryden, took the roofs off of several buildings, destroyed the drilling mud warehouse, Vic Littleton's windmill and the home of Appellano Vasquez. A series of ranch burglaries and break-ins at the Dryden Mercantile, that didn't fit the normal pattern, were still taking place. "The criminal was basically taking food, clothes, guns, ammo and binoculars. But he was real smooth, he'd take the hinges off the doors, then put them back," said Cooksey.[460]

The Sheriff told everyone he came across to keep an eye out, to report anything they saw. Since most of the burglaries were occurring around Dryden, he also told Benny Ray Ross to keep an ear to the ground, to try to find the guy. "Ross had a strong desire to be a policeman and I thought he might run onto something," said Cooksey.[461]

Benny Ray had found some of Jimmy Merritt's property just south of Dryden. A few months later, a ranch hand found what he thought might be some of the stolen property from the burglaries.[462]

Roberto 'Indio' Calzada was a self-made businessman and rancher who was well respected by most of his Terrell County peers. He'd developed a successful business by trading furs and buying and selling livestock. He also ranched a number of the smaller ranches, around 1,000 acres each, in the fall of 1965.[463] It was near the end of October when he told two of his cowboys, Alfredo Gallegos and his brother Jose Gallegos, to go check on the sheep that he grazed on the Goodwin place east of Dryden.[464]

Alfredo Gallegos was born in Ciudad Acuna in the state of Coahuilla, Mexico. He, two sisters and seven brothers grew up on ranches where his father was an experienced Vaquero, a cowboy with many talents. He followed in his father's footsteps and that led him to Terrell County when he was in his early 30s in 1965.[465]

It was late summer when Alfredo Gallegos and his brother Jose received the legal papers that allowed them to live and work in the United States. They moved their families to the Dryden area and went to work for Indio Calzada.[466]

Alfredo was much the picture of a cowboy. He stood five-foot ten-inches tall, weighed 170 pounds, wore chaps (leggings) over his blue jeans, spurs around the heel of his boots, a long-sleeved western shirt, a cowboy hat and leather gloves that protected his hands. It was about midday when he slipped his right boot out of the stirrup and stepped down off the horse he was riding.[467]

The pasture, in this part of the Chihuahuan Desert that ran along Thurston Canyon, had just seemed to gobble up the sheep that Senor Calzada had put there. Alfredo knew that the flock could be just over the next rise, nestled within a small ravine, or, as he was checking on now, hidden within the coolness of a cave along the canyon wall.[468]

He'd nearly missed the cave. The opening was partially hidden by a big Juniper tree, on the first shelf above the gravel bar. Horseback, he'd been able to see the entrance.[469]

Cave and area crime scene photo taken by Texas Department of Public Safety, photographic section, Midland, Texas. Photo courtesy of Candace Cooksey Fulton.

The sheep were not in the cave, but Alfredo did see a blanket, some clothes and other things on the earthen floor. He didn't enter the cave but rather stepped away and made note of the location so he could report it later.[470]

'Later' proved to be the afternoon of Wednesday, November 3, 1965. Alfredo stopped by Joe Vasquez's Chevron station and told the owner about the things in the cave. [471] He also stopped by the Do Drop Inn, his sister-in-law's place, and walked across the highway to tell Lewis Cash.

Cash cast a critical eye toward Gallegos as the man entered the Cactus café and headed toward the long bar that Cash was standing behind. It was just seconds before he and the ranch hand were speaking Spanish, talking about the things that were in the cave on the Goodwin place.[472]

Moments later, the owner of the Cactus Cafe asked Benny Ray Ross, who was sitting nearby on one of the stools, to call the Sheriff.[473]

Terrell County Sheriff Bill Cooksey in uniform with patrol car. Copyright San Angelo Standard-Times, San Angelo, Texas. Reprinted with permission.

CHAPTER 12
Thursday, November 4, 1965

Bill Cooksey normally wore his sheriff's department uniform when he went to work. He normally wrapped his gun belt around his waist and secured the buckle, then slid his Smith and Wesson N-frame .357 magnum revolver, with modified sights and grips, into its leather holster along his right hip. But on November 4, 1965, the Terrell County Sheriff dressed in shirt and jeans and didn't wear the revolver; instead he slid a Browning .380 caliber semi-automatic pistol inside the waistband along the backside of his right hip. It was the proper attire for what he thought he had to do that day.[474]

First, he planned to run his wife's mail route. His wife had borne Leslie Arnette, their third daughter just weeks before in October of 1965. He had taken over the postal duties so Bennie could stay home to nurse their fifth child. His next stop had to do with a phone call he got from Benny Ray Ross.[475]

Ross had told the Sheriff that Alfredo Gallegos had seen some property in a cave on the Goodwin place. They all suspected that it might be property from a series of burglaries that had been ongoing and were yet unsolved. They planned to meet at the Cactus Café.[476]

Cooksey completed the mail run up Highway 349 and stopped by the Café about noon. The restaurant was owned and operated by Lewis Cash and his wife, a couple in their late fifties who were known to cook one of the best steaks in all of Terrell County. "I had lunch and asked Lewis to go with us to check out the cave," said Cooksey.[477]

Cash agreed to go and left the café duties to his wife Minnie Dee. She was the epitome of what many might consider a true frontier woman. She was tall with salt and pepper hair, naturally frizzy hair, and she was not afraid of hard work or long hours. She regularly wore flowered dresses like those worn decades before.[478]

Lewis Cash was a big man whose height brought him eye-to-eye with the Sheriff. He regularly wore a khaki shirt and pants, baseball cap and low-top shoes. He spoke Spanish and had served with the Immigration Service as a Border Patrol agent during World War II, but he lost the position when the regular officers returned home. He also had a reputation as a curt, 'his way or the highway' type of guy.[479]

It was about 12:30 when the group left and headed toward the cave. Lewis Cash, Bill Cooksey and Benny Ray Ross took Cash's pickup and followed Alfredo Gallegos in his ranch pickup. They drove out Highway 90 East for about two miles before they turned off at a gate to the Goodwin Ranch.[480]

The men drove in a northeasterly direction, driving around and past a windmill, a set of livestock pens and finally came to a stop on top of a ridge that defined the south-side top of that part of Thurston Canyon. The Southern Pacific Railroad tracks, with a wide expanse of gravel bar between them, ran parallel to the ridge a few hundred yards farther to the north.[481]

Benny Ray had brought along a Winchester 30:30 lever-action-rifle. It was a gift from Cliff and Babe Sinclair, an aunt and uncle who lived on the Willoughby Ranch south of Alpine. It was an old gun with the ring gone from the latch screw but otherwise it was in good shape.[482]

The teenager chambered a cartridge into the carbine as he got out of the pickup. Cash, who was getting out of his own truck responded by saying, "Boy, don't put one in the chamber, you might shoot one of us." So Ross levered the gun until it was empty and then pushed the shells back into the magazine.[483]

Gallegos explained that they would have to go on foot from there, that the cave was not too far away but along the cliff below the ridge. He and Benny Ray Ross jumped off the edge of the ridge, dropping onto a trail that led downward from where they had parked. The Sheriff followed suit, then waited for Cash who found an easier place to get down.[484]

The men followed the trail single file, with Gallegos first, then Cooksey, Cash and finally Ross. The trail led them towards a large Juniper tree about a hundred yards away. "We didn't try to be quiet," said Cooksey.[485]

Alfredo Hernandez sat comfortably in the cave that offered him comfort from the elements. Although the temperatures had been fairly mild in recent days, with lows in the high 40s and highs in the mid-70s,[486] the Chihuahuan Desert still had a way of bringing a chill upon a person. He'd rocked up much of the opening that left only a small hole to crawl into for an entrance.[487]

Light emitted through the leaves of a Soto bush that he'd cut and pulled up against the passageway. It allowed him to see a green grape that he took from a sprig that he held in his left hand. He popped it into his mouth. He had just started to chew the final grape when he heard someone's voice and his senses went on full alert.[488]

Alfredo Gallegos stepped between the Juniper bush and the cliff, which was to his right, and then stepped back away from the entrance of the cave. He knew the Soto plant had not been there before and he said, "You need to come out of there," in Spanish.[489]

Bill Cooksey had stepped beyond the Juniper and Lewis Cash stood between the Juniper and the cliff. Both were surprised when a thin-faced Mexican man who was grinning from ear to ear stuck his head out of the small opening. Ross stood behind Cash and the Juniper and could only hear Gallegos and the man talking.[490]

Gallegos explained, with Cash translating for the Sheriff, that the man said he had come over from Mexico and that he was working for a local rancher. When asked, the man couldn't tell them who for, so Lewis Cash asked the man to tell them what type of house the rancher lived in, rock, adobe or lumber. The man told them the man had a wooden house.[491]

Alfredo Gallegos told the man that Cooksey was the Sheriff and that he needed to come out of the cave, he was going to have to go with him.[492]

Hernandez pitched out a small radio, an old blanket, quilt, work shoes, coat and an old felt hat that had the crown painted green. He, Gallegos and Cash were conversing in a pretty cordial manner as he slid out of the cave on his belly.[493]

Cooksey started looking through the coat and found the name Silman written on it.[494]

Hernandez, who appeared to be in his late 20s or early 30s to the other men, was wearing a blue shirt and gray pants[495] and had something that looked like an apron tied across his waist. He sat on his haunches and put the hat squarely on his head. Then he rose and started quickly walking down the trail away from the men and toward a little camp where he had apparently been cooking on the gravel bar. "I think he's going to run Bill," said Cash.[496]

Bill Cooksey took off after him and had thoughts that he might bulldog the man.[497] They had covered about twenty yards when Hernandez whirled and he wasn't smiling anymore.

Though the Sheriff did not see it, Hernandez had a gun in his right hand, a gun that he fired twice. The first bullet hit the Sheriff in the left leg. As he twisted and fell, the second bullet entered his back a little above waist high.[498]

Lewis Cash was standing not too far away when the man whirled and the shots rang out. His mind had moved into what would later be described as slow motion and with each of the Bandit's shots, he'd seen Bill Cooksey reach for the gun that wasn't there. He'd distinctly seen the Sheriff slap (leather) on the outside of his right hip, the place were he regularly kept his revolver, while the small semi-auto pistol was in his waistband just inches away.[499]

Immediate unexpected stress and violence can lead a human being to do what they have been trained to do, even when it happens so fast that their mind doesn't have enough time to allow them to make a decision to do so. This condition is what some might call the fight or flight condition. The Sheriff had responded to his training of drawing and firing his service revolver over and over.[500]

How the mind perceives such events may cause people to see things in what they later describe as slow motion, even though the events themselves happen in a very, very short period of time. Lewis Cash didn't see Hernandez's gun and only heard the shots, but he saw his friend reach for and try to draw the gun that wasn't there—twice.[501]

Benny Ray Ross was behind the Juniper bush and had not seen what had taken place. He assumed that the Sheriff had fired up into the air in an attempt to keep the man from running away. He thought they were warning shots. Cash was in his way to the right, so he moved down and around the Juniper so he could see. What he saw was a screaming mad Alfredo Hernandez standing not too far away.[502]

"The Mexican called to Ross, telling him to throw him the gun, a 30-30, instead Ross pitched the gun to me...I pulled the trigger, but it snapped on an empty chamber," Lewis Cash told Texas Rangers J.S. Nance and Arthur Hill on November 11, 1965.[503]

Alfredo Hernandez moved closer to the men and had the drop on them. He motioned for the carbine to be thrown down, and Cash complied. He picked it up and moved back toward the fallen Sheriff. He kept moving the revolver back and forth across the three men who were still standing. He kept telling the three, in part Spanish and English, to not look at his face.[504]

The Sheriff was lying on his side with his head turned toward the cliff. Hernandez knelt down and took the Sheriff's wallet and pistol. He was yelling at the Sheriff in both Spanish and English. Finally he put the barrel of the Winchester against the Sheriff's neck, turned him over and said, "I'm going to kill the son-of-bitchie."[505]

"Why shoot a dead man?" Cash said in hopes of keeping him from pulling the trigger.[506]

Hernandez kicked Cooksey and somewhat screamed in a low tone, "You Gringo son-of-a-bitchie, you think you take me in!"[507]

He suddenly turned and told Benny Ray Ross to go get his knapsack (his morral) and his binoculars from the small camp about twenty yards away on the gravel bar. The teenager understood the broken communication and retrieved the two items. He ordered Lewis Cash to pick up the old radio. And he did.[508]

Hernandez motioned for the men to start moving back up the trail toward the pickups. He marched them along, holding both the rifle and the revolver on them. "I was afraid that the guy was going to kill us all," said Cash afterwards.[509]

When they got to the top of the cliff where the pickups were, he told Alfredo Gallegos to tie the hands of the other two men behind their backs. The ranch-hand took a small piece of rope off of his pickup's sideboards and tied Benny Ray Ross' hands behind his back. He used bailing wire to do the same to Lewis Cash. Then, after the men were told to lie down and cross their legs, Gallegos tied each of their ankles with bailing wire. The men were about fifteen feet apart on the ground. They listened as Hernandez instructed Alfredo Gallegos to get the keys to Lewis Cash's pickup out of Lewis' pocket.[510]

He kept his revolver trained on Alfredo Gallegos as he retrieved the keys out of the ranch-hand's truck. He then told Gallegos that he wanted him to drive him away in Cash's pickup. Before they left, he turned and looked at the two men tied up on the ground. He lowered his pants just low enough to reveal a scar where a bullet had creased him on the upper thigh. He pointed at it and said, just before he and Gallegos drove away, "A Gringo did this."[511]

CHAPTER THIRTEEN
Thursday Afternoon

The Chihuahuan Desert is one of those places where nearly everything you walk by can stick, prick or grab you. It is the type of place where you have to be careful where you walk and what you touch,[512] but Benny Ray Ross rolled his body through fifteen feet of stick, prick and grab, after Lewis Cash said, "Roll over here so we can untie ourselves." Cash worked the rope loose from the teenager's wrists.[513]

Bill Cooksey was conscious but would later say he was stunned and paralyzed after the shooting. "I played dead while he took my pistol and my pocketbook," said Cooksey.[514]

While Hernandez led the three men up the hill, Cooksey tried to stand up but couldn't. At one point he thought he was going to die and prayed he'd at least have a chance to tell his family how much he loved them. He tried to write on a tiny chewing gum wrapper that he had in his shirt pocket, but he was dazed and a gust of wind took the wrapper away.[515] It was about 20 minutes later when Benny Ray Ross came back down the trail to him.[516]

Ross found the Sheriff lying on his back. Some blood was on the ground, mostly from the bullet that had entered the back, but there wasn't a lot. "Are you hurt bad?" Ross asked. The Sheriff responded, "I'm hit twice."[517]

While the teenager tended to his friend, Lewis Cash stripped wire from the taillights on the ranch pickup and tried to get it hot-wired. Finally, he accomplished the task and drove toward the highway, cutting one fence in the process as a matter of saving time.[518]

The Southern Pacific Railroad had long been a part of Terrell County and West Texas. It was the sound of a train coming that caused the Sheriff and his teenage friend to look back toward Del Rio. It didn't take the teenager long to get to the railroad tracks.[519]

The engine and its trailing caboose made up a special train that was taking some executives to the mines at El Paso. A man wearing a suit and tie stuck his head out of the window of the caboose. "What the hell do you think you are doing?" he yelled at Ross who was standing by the tracks waving his arms back and forth.[520]

The radio system in the caboose was not able to reach the Sanderson Depot so the emergency message was relayed through the train engine. 'Benny Ray Ross reports Sheriff shot. Need ambulance to come to the second Goodwin gate east of Dryden on Highway 90.'[521]

The Rio Grande River, the Texas-Mexico border, was about 20 miles away from where the Sheriff was shot. Hernandez told Alfredo Gallegos that he was not going to hurt him as long as he did what he was told— because he wasn't a Gringo. His orders were to take him down Bootlegger Road, the road that led to ranches owned by the Deaton's, Harrison's and others.[522] The same road that led to Agua Verdes, a popular river crossing where people regularly came and went from the United States.[523]

They were about half way to the border when Alfredo Hernandez started to breathe differently, started rocking back and forth, and asked, "Do you think I killed him?"[524]

"He looked dead to me," Gallegos responded to the question from this bearded man who had very bad body odor and ragged shoes.[525]

Still holding the revolver on his driver, Hernandez said, "I don't think so. He still had his cigar in his mouth." It was shortly thereafter that the outlaw doubled over and threw up phlegm, green grapes and vomit all over the floorboard of Cash's pickup. Then he yelled, "Alto, alto!" (Stop, Stop!)[526]

Alfredo Gallegos stopped the pickup about eight miles from the border. He was really worried that Hernandez might kill him, but the Bandit just got out and motioned for Gallegos to drive away.[527]

It was sometime around 2:30 p.m. when the phone rang at the Kerr Mercantile. Henry Beth Hogg was working the checkout counter and she answered. It was Elizabeth Murrah calling from the Sheriff's Office. She was looking for Dalton. Henry Beth knew her husband was in the hardware section looking at tile for their house. "Dalton, the phone is for you!"[528]

Dalton Hogg listened for a moment, then turned and handed his wife two pieces of tile. "This goes in the den and bedroom and this one goes in the kitchen," said the Deputy as he turned and left the store. He didn't tell his wife where he was going or that the Sheriff had been shot.[529]

Bernice Cooksey was taking a nap when the phone rang about 3:00 p.m. Fifteen minutes earlier she'd been going about her duties of keeping house, chasing around two-year-old Terrell and dealing with a new baby. "Mrs. Cooksey, they need an ambulance at the second Goodwin Gate east of Dryden," said Jimmy Merritt. After a slight pause, he added, "I don't think I'm supposed to tell you this, but it's Bill who's been shot."[530]

She immediately called the Sheriff's Office to make sure the ambulance was on its way. Not knowing anything more, the call only left a multitude of questions in her mind. What had happened? How bad was he hurt? She gathered her thoughts in the shock of the moment and started praying. She didn't know what to do, but looked at their round oak dining room table—with its lace lined cloth covered with stacks of mail, diapers that needed to be folded, socks that needed to be matched, a rack of sterilized baby bottles, typewriter, sewing machine and, centered in the middle, a bowl of artificial fruit. She started to clean off the dining room table. As her daughter Candace would write 40 years later, "I could say it was fine therapy—to do something, anything, instead of waiting paralyzed for the other shoe to drop."[531]

Dalton Hogg had the gas pedal pushed down to the floorboard as he drove his patrol car, his own Buick station wagon that he'd stocked with a stretcher and oxygen, out Highway 90 toward Dryden and the Goodwin place.[532]

Lewis Cash had left the gate open and drove straight to a phone at Dryden. He dialed the number to the Sheriff's Office, but the line was busy, so he called Kerr's Mercantile. He was starting to tell Henry Beth Hogg that he would be waiting at the Goodwin's gate, when he saw Dalton's station wagon go by.[533]

Lewis Cash led Dalton Hogg down the ranch road to the ridge top. Alfredo Gallegos was already back. Ross and a railroad man named Reynolds were there with the Sheriff.[534]

Bill Cooksey was loaded on a stretcher and carried along, over and up to the patrol car/ambulance. The men took great care as they loaded him in the back of the station wagon. It was nearly 4:00 p.m. when Deputy Hogg, with Ross there to assist, turned his car onto Highway 90 and headed east toward the hospital—nearly a hundred miles away in Del Rio.[535]

Dr. Hi Newby's receptionist took the call and told the doctor that Herman Richter, the Val Verde County Sheriff, would be by to get him at any minute. She told him the Terrell County Sheriff had been shot near Dryden.[536]

Hi Newby was born in 1929. He grew up in Del Rio where his dad was a rancher and his mother was a schoolteacher. He attended Sul Ross and Baylor Universities, graduating from Baylor in 1951. He graduated from their medical school in 1957. He interned at Robert B. Green Hospital in San Antonio before settling into a practice at Del Rio.[537]

The doctor was six-foot tall and of thin-build with dark hair and blue eyes. Wearing a shirt, tie and slacks, he quickly gathered up a few things that he thought he might need and headed for the office door. The Sheriff was just pulling up outside.[538]

There is something about living in a small town. News seems to travel faster than the speed of light and some people just know that certain things need to be done. Such was the case that afternoon when Mary Beth Turner showed up at Sanderson's Junior High School and appeared at the door of Mrs. Grigsby's eighth-grade geography class. "Something has happened and I need to take Candace and Elizabeth (Mrs. Turner's daughter) with me," she said.[539]

The trio had an obstacle to pass before they left the school. The principal, Carroll B. Card, stopped them before they got out the door, but he stepped aside after Mary Beth, with her lips quivering and her eyes full of tears, told the man, "There's been an accident. It's important for Candace to come with me."[540]

When the three were seated in her Corvair, Mary Beth turned in the driver's seat and took hold of Candace Cooksey's shoulders. "Candy we don't know the details but your dad was making an arrest and he's been shot. Dalton has taken the ambulance out there and he's called a doctor from Del Rio who's going to meet them."[541]

The Cooksey's eldest daughter held her composure until, as she would write years later, 'I remember the moment as if it were happening to another person. I held my cool façade until we got out at the elementary school and I started to go in and get my sister. Without warning, my legs turned to Jell-O and huge shoulder-shaking sobs made me stop."[542]

There was a flurry of activity at the Cooksey house when the daughters got home. Friends and neighbors were helping do all kinds of things, things like cleaning, folding clothes, cooking and mixing baby formula. Three of those present were the wives of three Border Patrol agents who were headed out to the scene. The wives were Carol Fitzgerald, Fonda Epperson and Francis Kline. There were others who also helped out that day.[543]

It wasn't long before former neighbors and great friends Nell and Buddy Sudduth showed up at the house. (Buddy was the chief of the volunteer fire department.) They took Bernice Cooksey to the hospital in Del Rio. Of course, no one realized that when Bernice went to Del Rio to be with Bill, that the new baby, little Leslie, would not take a bottle.[544]

By midnight, the baby was wailing really loud. She did so until Mrs. Joe Hill, who was known as Butch but called M's by the kids, an 80-year-old neighbor who lived two doors down, fixed sugar in a white dishcloth that the baby took to and finally went to sleep. The next day a next-door neighbor named Lana Black took the baby to Del Rio to be with her mother.[545]

Bill Cooksey told Dalton the details as they sped toward Del Rio. "He was a little bully son of a bitch with a long narrow face and a long mouth. But I do have some news for him; there isn't much money in that billfold." The Sheriff also related how he thought it was the same man who shot Pelham Bradford.[546]

Dalton Hogg had notified the Val Verde County Sheriff Herman Richter. He did this to make him aware of the situation and to get a doctor started their way. They were about half way to Del Rio when they met Richter's patrol car. Doctor Newby got in the ambulance and they were on the way again. They had a police escort but Dalton passed the officer right away and kept speeding toward Del Rio.[547] He wasn't letting any grass grow under his feet, probably spurned on by the fact the Sheriff was growing very weak. At one point when the doctor was tending to the Sheriff, the doctor turned to Dalton and said, "You know Deputy, if you'll slow this thing down a little, I'll give this man a shot," The deputy let the speedometer fall back to around 100.[548]

It was just after 5:00 p.m. when the ambulance sped into Del Rio. They easily made their way to the hospital because the intersections were held open by police officers and deputies. Law enforcement officers representing a number of police agencies were waiting at the hospital, as well as a number of doctors and nurses. It wasn't long before Bill Cooksey was in the operating room.[549]

Years later Doctor Hi Newby would credit Dalton Hogg with saving Bill Cooksey's life. Even if the doctor's wife did get a little mad that the deputy drove so fast, the doctor knew that the deputy's sense to call ahead and then getting there fast had made a difference. In the doctor's mind, every second had counted.[550] Of course, he may not have known that two tires on the Buick station wagon went flat in the parking lot after they got there.[551]

It wasn't too long after the ambulance left the Goodwin's gate that Border Patrol Agent Ray Fitzgerald and others headed toward the scene of the shooting. When they arrived, Alfredo Gallegos led them back to the place where he had let the outlaw out on Bootlegger Road.[552]

Thirty-four year old Ray Fitzgerald had grown up in Oregon and was an honest to goodness real cowboy when he decided to join the United States Border Patrol in 1960. First stationed at Tucson, Arizona, he and his wife Carole and their two kids moved to Sanderson in 1963. By 1965 he was well acquainted with the Chihuahuan Desert and the Terrell County ranches that bordered the Rio Grande River.[553]

Border Patrolmen of the 60s were experienced trackers of human beings. It was an art developed by following and catching people who entered the United States illegally. "It wasn't quite dark yet and I could still see a few tracks where the Bandit got out of the pickup, where he started toward the border, but the ground was so hard that we couldn't follow them. So, we just backed off until dogs could be brought in the next morning," said Fitzgerald.[554]

While Fitzgerald studied the human footprints, Benny Ray Ross was getting talked to at the Val Verde County Memorial Hospital. "They put me in an empty room and different lawmen came in and out, asking me a few questions, but none seemed to really care about what I had to say," said Ross. "At least until Texas Ranger Arthur Hill and a railroad detective (H.P. Boyd) talked to me when I got back to Dryden later that night."[555]

Ranger Hill grew up in Santa Anna in Coleman County. He joined the Texas Highway Patrol when he was 32. He was assigned to Seymour in Baylor County until he was transferred to Alpine in 1947. It was in Brewster County where he was appointed as a Texas Ranger. He was 56 years of age when he interviewed the teenager.[556]

Hill had a way of talking to people, a way of listening and a way of learning what he needed to know. The Ranger and Railroad Detective H.P. Boyd spent time talking and listening to the youngster that night.[557]

Boyd, known as Hinkle to his close friends and family, had gotten out of the military and joined the San Angelo Police Department in 1945. He left his Assistant Police Chief position in 1952 to take the job of special agent with the Southern Pacific Railroad.[558]

It was probably about the time that he and the Ranger interviewed the teenager that Mrs. Cooksey learned about the condition of her husband. Family members and close friends soon learned that the first gunshot had been a straight-through shot to the left leg. It was not a wound that would have incapacitated the Sheriff for very long. But as he had twisted and fallen after the first shot, the second bullet had entered his back, down low on the right side near the backbone. As it traveled up through the body it damaged the sciatic nerve, the left lung and the spleen before lodging underneath his arm.[559]

By daylight the next day, the written word would tell many more people about the shooting and the condition of the Terrell County Sheriff. It would list his condition as serious but stable.[560]

CHAPTER FOURTEEN
Friday

Mexican Shoots Terrell Sheriff—Gunman Flees; Cooksey Hurt.' The bold black letters on the top of the front page of the San Angelo Standard-Times on Friday, November 5, 1965 sent word of the shooting to readers all across West Texas. That same afternoon the Del Rio News-Herald led with 'Alien Wounds Officer, Escapes, Bloodhounds Being Used in Chase.' The stories were mixed within other stories about the Vietnam War.[561] News of the shooting had already spread across the law enforcement community and to most residents in and around Terrell County before those stories were in print.

There is something of an anomaly that happens when a law enforcement officer is killed or injured. It is something that happened each time the 145 peace officers were killed in the line of duty across the United States during 1964. Police officers from all over immediately want to help catch the suspect; they may come from miles around and it is something they feel that they need to do when one of their own is killed or injured.[562] But in the harshness of this part of the Chihuahuan Desert most residents felt the same way. It is what they would call 'taking care of their own', and that is how residents felt when their Sheriff was shot.

Austin Chriesman saddled several horses and loaded them into a stock trailer early that Friday morning. The dark headed, blue-eyed Terrell County rancher stood just over six-feet tall and weighed just under 200 pounds. He was an easy-going man who most would say had never met a stranger. He and his family ranched northeast of Dryden. "I'm going to take horses over there where that guy was last seen," he'd told his wife Dorothy the night before.[563]

The Chriesmans were not unaccustomed to burglaries where food was taken from their ranch house. It was common when you lived near the border, near where people crossed the river to find a better way of life, but they had known for some time that they had a different kind of burglar in their midst. "This guy took blankets, razors, tooth brushes and toothpaste, shampoo, soap, scissors, food—including frozen orange juice, and a Winchester Model 94 30:30 caliber rifle from our house," said Blain Chriesman who was eleven when Bill Cooksey was shot.[564]

Austin Chriesman was just one of several ranchers who loaned extra horses to law enforcement officers that morning, others brought Jeeps, and all were armed as they assisted with the manhunt.[565] Of course, some of the law enforcement officers had their own horses.

Deputy Dalton Hogg, who brought along his son's 3-year-old mare, found he had plenty of help for the hunt for the outlaw.[566] There were law enforcement officers from Val Verde, Sutton, Crockett, Brewster and Pecos counties, Border Patrol agents, including Station Chief Bill Binegar, Ray Fitzgerald, Ken Epperson, Bill Burke and Gene Kline, as well as a Border Patrol plane from the Marfa Sector, Highway Patrolman Malcolm Bollinger and others from Del Rio and Fort Stockton and several Texas Rangers.[567]

One Ranger was Forest 'Gould' Hardin who was known as Gould to all the locals. He'd been born in Coleman County on January 11, 1896. His law enforcement career started when he was 44, when he served as a deputy with the Bexar County Sheriff's Office, then as a deputy in Hudspeth County. He spent a few years as a Border Patrolman before he was appointed as a Texas Ranger on September 3, 1948. Gould was 69 when Bill Cooksey was shot.[568] Texas Ranger L.H. Purvis was dispatched from Del Rio to assist him with the investigation.[569]

Texas Rangers Arthur Hill from Alpine, Alfred Allee Jr. who had recently been transferred to Midland, Jim Nance—a former and much respected Terrell County Sheriff who was stationed in Sierra Blanca, (and possibly other Rangers) and Purvis made their way to the Terrell County site.[570] Because he'd been stationed in Sonora for years, Purvis probably knew best that the dogs of Alfred Cooper might just be the best tool to use to catch the Bandit.

Alfred Cooper and one of his tracking dogs. Photo courtesy of Donna Cooper Mikeska.

Alfred Cooper was a long-tenured Sutton County Justice of the Peace. He stood six-foot tall, weighed about 180 pounds and regularly dressed in khaki pants, white western shirt and cowboy boots. His salt and peppered hair and blue-green eyes were visible below the gray felt hat he normally kept on his head. He and his wife Clara had been blessed with five children, three boys and two girls. It was Cooper's hounds that caused him to get the call after the shooting of Bill Cooksey.[571]

The story is told that a two-year-old child walked away from a Sutton County ranch house and they couldn't locate the toddler. They tried to use several of the local dogs, but to no avail until they asked for prison dogs. Because of this, Alfred Cooper decided it was time that someone had a good set of tracking dogs around Sonora; so he set about researching, studying and learning about dogs and which breed would be best for finding people. In the end he decided that bloodhounds would best serve his purpose.[572]

He built pens behind their house and started training dogs when they were just pups. He had his own children and local athletes make trails for the dogs to follow. He'd tell the kids to go hide and let the dogs loose to go find them. Little by little the dogs got smarter and smarter and better and better at finding their quarry.[573] His favorite dog was a bloodhound that came out of Virginia, back east. He named the dog Hutch after the Sutton County Sheriff. Another dog was named Lude, pronounced Lu-Dee, and another named Alex. His first hounds were trained like prison dogs, and the dogs had built quite a reputation by 1965.[574]

Their reputation was built around two major cases. In one, a man who robbed the Sonora Bank was chased toward Eldorado. At some point the man jumped out of his car and ran off into a pasture. Cooper and his dogs were brought to the scene and it didn't take the dogs too long to catch the robber. The robber was more than surprised. "I know that running in a circle confuses dogs but those dogs still found me. Man, those dogs are good," the robber told Cooper that afternoon.[575]

In another case, Cooper set about finding a jail escapee who was wanted out of Kerrville. He got onto the guy's trail and finally turned his dogs loose. He followed on his favorite white horse, leading a pack mule behind them. A short time later he drove back into town with the guy chained in the back of his green step-side Chevrolet pickup, in the back with the hounds that had found him.[576]

Those two cases and others were the reason that Ranger Purvis and many of the law enforcement officers had great faith in those dogs that Friday morning as Alfred Cooper let the hounds smell the tracks left behind by Hernandez the day before.

Ray Fitzgerald, the tall lanky cowboy turned Border Patrolman, and his partner Ken Epperson sat astride borrowed horses as the dogs took to the scent and started to pull on their harnesses, striving, howling and barking as they wanted their handler to let them go.[577] Dalton Hogg, Ranger Purvis and others were ready to bring the outlaw to justice. Cooper looked back at the officers on horseback, nodded, unhitched the dogs and let them go.

Cooper immediately heard the sound of his dogs on the hunt, howling as they followed the trail toward the southeast. "Dad always said that the most beautiful music in the world was the dogs howling as they followed a trail," said Cooper's son Phillip.[578] However, it wasn't long before the howling turned into an intense yelping, then into a magnified whimpering, as the dogs hit a patch of what the local folks called dog cactus or dog pear.[579]

Dog Pear Cactus. 2004 photo by Russell Smith.

The officers found the injured dogs stuck many times over with spines, shivering in the midst of a patch of Graham's Prickly Pear.[580] "The low lying dog pear can paralyze you in just a moment. It is not uncommon to find single plants, a cluster or areas as big as a football field in different parts of Terrell County," said Ellis Helmers, retired Terrell County Extension Agent.[581]

The cactus is about the size of the pear shaped fruit that blooms on the prickly pear cactus. Yet the dog pear sits right on the ground about an inch to two inches high, with cross-grown spines which emulate the size, shape and sharpness of those on the regular prickly pear cactus. "Non-scientifically, it is considered sort of pesky. It is low to the ground and if you're not paying attention, it is easy to stumble into," said Jennifer Baur from the Chihuahuan Desert Research Institute.[582]

According to the University of Texas at El Paso Museum website, the common English names for the plant are Dog Cholla and Devil's Cholla.

The scientific name is Opuntia Schottii, which comes from the cactus family.[583] "Like all Opuntias it has glochids, tiny little spines (about an inch to an inch and a half long) that get stuck in your skin, are hard to remove and are most irritating," said Baur.[584]

Cooper's two dogs had never been around the dog cactus, they'd never seen it before, and they were running all out with their noses low to the ground as they ran into a patch of the stuff. Just like that, the advantage of the dogs was gone.

Ray Fitzgerald gently removed one of the dogs from the brier patch and removed the spines that he could from its body. Another officer did the same and both dogs were placed on the officers' horses and taken back to Alfred Cooper.[585] But as the saying goes, it didn't stop the hunt.

Dalton Hogg and those within the posse spread out across the countryside. They slowly started making their way, following the tracks that came and went within the varied and sometimes very hard landscape, tracks that were heading toward the Rio Grande River and the Texas-Mexico Border.[586]

A very similar search was also underway across the border in Mexico. In what was not a common occurrence, Val Verde County Deputy Sheriff Samuel Perez was in Mexico too, searching for the Bandit alongside a group of Mexican law enforcement officers.[587]

Samuel C. Perez was born in Del Rio on May 27, 1911. His parents were Severiano and Juana Perez. His father worked for the railroad and became quite a property holder in the border city. Perez attended the San Felipe schools. He and his wife Petra raised two sons, Ricardo and David, and helped raise their nephew Tino Flores. Samuel Perez joined the Val Verde County Sheriff's Department in June 1942.[588]

Perez stood five-foot eight-inches tall and weighed 210 pounds. His badge set above the left chest pocket of his western cut uniform shirt, a tie was clasp at his neck, while western boots and a gray felt hat rounded out his attire. A gun belt wrapped around his waist, holding handcuffs and extra clips for the Colt 1911 model, .45-caliber semi-auto pistol that set in his holster. "My dad was a good listener and he was very law enforcement minded," said Richard Perez.[589]

Perez kept a short barreled 30:30 carbine in the trunk of his patrol car.[590] The day the search began, that Friday, one could bet that the rifle was in a leather scabbard that was attached to the saddle of the horse he was riding.

During his career, Deputy Perez had made a point to develop contacts and to network with law enforcement officials on both sides of the border. "My dad had many contacts in Mexico. The Governor of Coahuilla had made him a special officer," said Richard Perez.[591] So on that Friday he and another officer were in Mexico, armed with just a description of Hernandez, helping the Mexican officers search for the man who shot the Terrell County Sheriff.[592]

As the two groups started their search, Alfred Cooper started the drive home with his injured hounds. He made a mental note to have small leather boots made for his precious dogs just in case they were ever needed in that part of West Texas again.[593]

Customs Agent Cliff Wilson was in Del Rio when Bill Cooksey was shot. The next morning, he made his way to the Goodwin place and the cave where the man had been hidden. He found the outside of the hiding place was rocked up, leaving just a small hole big enough for the man to climb through. Wilson barely fit inside himself. He assumed the outlaw had rocked it up himself, to protect himself from the elements and to make it less visible. "The floor was like loose powder, with feed sacks over it," said Wilson.[594]

Texas Department of Public Safety photograph of cave after it was processed for evidence. Photo courtesy of Candace Cooksey Fulton.

Baby Wilson realized the guy lived like an animal, like a coyote that lives off the land. He knew the guy was animal smart and definitely a survivor. He left the cave and headed south to join the search party. "Dalton had officers spread out everywhere, there were people on foot, people on horses—officers and ranchers and airplanes overhead, and they each looked in one area and then another," said Wilson.[595]

The search party had followed the tracks, tracks that came and went within the changing soft and hard landscape. "My dad said the last place they saw the man's tracks was near a windmill and stock tank. They just seemed to stop there, didn't go anywhere," said Blain Chriesman.[596]

Alfredo Hernandez presumably kept low to the ground and kept his eyes peeled for anyone on the horizon or for planes up in the sky. He kept off the tops of the ridges and stayed close to heavy cover. He finally heard the posse off in the distance. He made his way toward the heaviest clump of brush and cactus that he could find. He laid down on his belly and crawled inside.

Hernandez heard his pursuers getting closer and closer. Finally they were right on top of him. He didn't dare move. At one point, he would later tell investigators that one horse and rider passed within just a few feet of where he laid.[597]

This writer's perception of what Hernandez went through follows. His heart had to have picked up speed as he heard the clop, clop, clop of the horses hoofs as they got closer and closer. He surely strained to hear any noise, any sign that he might be found out. Then he must have heard a horse whinny off in the distance, possibly followed by a nicker from the one that had just passed. He must have heard the friction of a human body against leather as a rider adjusted his position in his seat. Then he must have heard the horses and their riders as they slowly moved off toward the Rio Grande River.

Roy Deaton, his wife Nell and his son Roy 'Hoot' were home when four men came walking out of the pasture. "What are all the Chote, Border Patrol doing out there?" one of the men asked Deaton.[598]

Forty-eight year old Roy Deaton was a tall, six-foot three-inch, lanky man who had brown hair and blue eyes. He regularly wore a pair of Levi's, western shirt, cowboy hat and boots. He, along with his brother Jack, ranched 45 sections around Dryden, 50 sections at Sheffield and 50 sections just west of Sanderson.[599]

Nell Deaton was two years his junior. She had blondish brown hair, blue eyes and stood about five foot seven on a medium frame. She'd borne their son in 1947 and he'd just graduated from high school in 1965.[600]

Roy Deaton was accustomed to having visitors from his neighboring Mexico. In fact, he regularly called and had people come work for him, a practice that was common back then. "But the funny thing was there were all these officers and ranchers out there, walking and riding on horseback, and these four guys walk up after coming right through them and asked what's going on," said the son.[601]

Lil' Roy's statement was an example of just how rugged the terrain is in that part of West Texas. There were so many places where a person could hide, almost everywhere, even though it was called the Chihuahuan Desert.

"I'm going to leave this alone. We have to live here, that guy could slip up here anytime and kill any one of us," said Roy Deaton out of fear for his family.[602]

By daylight's end, the search on both sides of the border had failed to turn up even an inkling of the man who shot Bill Cooksey. "We felt like we had to go after him, that we had to do something, but it was really an exercise in futility. The terrain was the fugitive's best ally," said Fitzgerald.[603]

The media wanted information and even though Dalton Hogg had talked to a Del Rio reporter the night before, he left the media chores to Highway Patrolman Malcolm Bollinger and Val Verde County Sheriff Herman Richter. "My husband mostly stayed in the background when it came to talking to the media. Bill Cooksey had normally taken care of those things," said Henry Beth Hogg.[604]

Alfredo Hernandez had given the deputy and his posse the slip. The officers speculated that he'd already slipped across the border, across the river into Mexico or headed a different way and was still out there. They made plans to continue the search on Saturday morning.[605]

CHAPTER FIFTEEN
Death As A Partner

The glow of the moon, a moon that was just three days shy of full, spread across the desert landscape near Dryden.[606] The law enforcement officers and their posses on both sides of the Rio Grande River were set to begin the second day's search for the man who shot Bill Cooksey. Several hundred miles away, the Corpus Christi Caller newspaper ran a story about the Sheriff. The paper's bold black type read, 'Border Lawman Often Had Death as Partner.'[607]

The law enforcement profession is sometimes portrayed as a constant array of cops chasing robbers, shoot 'em up bang bangs, high speed chases and always getting the bad guy. But the actual profession, especially for those who patrol our streets, neighborhoods and highways, involves a lot of tedious and at times boring work. Of course, there are also exciting times, interesting cases and dangerous situations, yet most officers may realize a whole career and never use deadly force against anyone.[608] Bill Cooksey was not one of those.

Texas Highway Patrolman Bill Cooksey's first duty station was at Llano in Llano County. It was there in 1949 that he first met Ross McSwain, a young man who would later become a reporter for the San Angelo Standard-Times, a man who would forever become his friend.[609]

McSwain was twenty when he first met Cooksey. The Highway Patrolman was in a café on the east side of the Llano square. Cooksey and his partner Bill Shipp were the only other customers in the place, which was just before daybreak, when McSwain entered the cafe.[610] He had been up most of the night due to a storm, helping his dad with his feed and hatchery business. "We just got to talking that morning, then I saw him at the barber shop and at dances, when he was there to keep the peace. We just kind of hit it off," said McSwain.[611]

In 1953 Cooksey transferred and moved his young family to Hamilton in Bosque County. His first deadly force experience came on April 6, 1956, just days after his wife Bernice gave birth to their third child, Billie Kay.[612]

It was not uncommon for the Highway Patrolman to stop by the Bosque County Jail at Meridian. Sheriff Royal Clark always had a hot cup of coffee and plenty of pleasant conversation for a visit. It was about 9 p.m. when Cooksey sat down with a cup of hot brew in his hands.[613]

The jail was like a lot of small county jails back then; a combination of Sheriff's living quarters, Sheriff's office and jail cells. In this case the living quarters and office were downstairs and the cells were upstairs. Cooksey and the Sheriff were visiting when they heard a scraping noise coming from somewhere up above them. "I better go check on that," said Sheriff Clark.[614]

Upstairs there were two large side-by-side cellblocks that were set inside the outer walls and below the ceiling. This left a walkway all the way around them. There was also space for someone to get up on top so they could maintain the overhead lights. There was also a shower and inmate runway for the two large cells. The Sheriff's only two prisoners, two burglary suspects, were supposed to be in those cells.[615] But as they wrote in the Clifton Record days later, the prisoners were not in their cells.[616]

Twenty-one-year-old Andrew Howard had taken a piece of wire off of an old broom handle that he'd found in one of the cells. He used the wire to open the cell door. He and the other man then tried to dig out of the jail wall but they were unsuccessful. "They also used the broomstick to break out the backside light bulbs," said Cooksey.[617]

Once up the stairs, the Sheriff opened an outside steel door and immediately realized the prisoners were not in the cells. "They're gone!" He yelled to Cooksey.[618]

The Sheriff rushed inside the cellblock and into the darkness, a darkness that increased as you moved down the path on the right side of the cells. Then there was a thud, a grunt and the sound of someone falling. (They learned later that Howard had found an old window pulley that he put inside a sock, a sock that he swung with such force that it put the Sheriff down.)[619]

Cooksey stood at the other end of the pathway, between the violent man and his freedom. The burglar started towards him. Cooksey told him to stop but the man didn't. He only raised the sock as if getting ready to hit the Highway Patrolman. Blam! Blam![620]

The two bullets hit their mark. The man would never burglarize homes again or do anything else for that matter. The second man, who was hidden up on top of one of the cells, surrendered to Cooksey. The Sheriff was taken to the hospital and quickly recovered.[621]

It wasn't long before Cooksey was transferred and moved his family to Gatesville in December 1957. It was the place where one of the Cooksey traits would develop, a trait that would forever stay with the family and those close to them.[622]

It began with Bernice Cooksey yelling for Eric to come back to them. Only there were a number of Erics in the park that day. So Bill Cooksey started to whistle a particular melody when they got ready to go home. "It was sort of like the old 'Label, Black Label, Calling Black Label' beer commercial," said Candace Cooksey Fulton.[623]

The best way I know to explain it was in the words of retired San Angelo police officer Bobby Berrie. "Cooksey and his family were at my house visiting us, when Cooksey said, "Well, we better get on home." He started whistling and the kids came into the living room."[624]

Or maybe Terrell County Commissioner Sid Harkins had a better way of explaining it. "Cooksey would whistle and all of his kids and every dog in Terrell County would come running."[625]

The Cookseys were hardly settled when just two months later, January 1958, he moved into a safety education job with the Department of Public Safety at Waco. "I got my first taste of teaching there and really liked it. I had a 30 minute television show," said Cooksey.[626] But it was also there that he dealt with tragedy and death again.

Quoting the Corpus Christi Caller, 'In September 1959, Cooksey handled press information when a jet liner crashed into a sweet potato patch near Buffalo in East Texas, killing all 34 persons on board.' The following year, Cooksey transferred back to the Highway Patrol and to the new station they'd opened at Sanderson.[627]

Ross McSwain and Cooksey started to rekindle their friendship just before Cooksey was appointed Terrell County Sheriff. By then McSwain was a reporter for the San Angelo Standard-Times and Terrell County was part of their coverage area. It would be a few more years, as McSwain recounted, "that our friendship really solidified during the Sanderson Flood, when I was the first newspaper person that got into Sanderson through Sheffield."[628]

From the Corpus Christi Caller, 'About 7 a.m. last June 11, (1965), a wall of water roared down Sanderson Creek (Canyon) from the hills like a tidal-like wave. It jumped out of the creek banks and tore at homes, stores, motels, cars and people.'[629] And from personal accounts—

It was raining as Aurora Galvan put her three girls to bed on the night of June 10, 1965. She lived on 4th street with W.L. Babb; both were in their twenties. "It was still raining when we went to bed, but rain here is always a good thing so we didn't think anything about it," said Galvan.[630]

The next morning, about 6:30, Aurora's sister and mom came to the house and woke them up. They were very excited and said the town was being washed away and that people were missing.[631]

The water had roared down Sanderson Canyon and ran smack dab into the columns of a railroad bridge on the west side of the town. "The columns were turned at an angle so they impeded the flow of the fast moving water. It surged out over the banks spreading out across the area from the railroad tracks and over past the main street (Highway 90) as it headed toward the east side of town," said Dudley Harrison who owned Dudley's Texaco Service Station.[632]

The National Weather Service recorded 5.35 inches of rain in Terrell County that morning. The temperature had fallen to 58 degrees by the time a worried Sheriff Cooksey went into the Cactus Café.[633] Pilar Rodriguez, Terrell County jailer and custodian, was there getting breakfast for a prisoner that they had in jail. "You stay here until the water recedes. You don't leave, it's too dangerous to go outside," Cooksey told Rodriquez.[634]

Pilar Rodriguez was born in Mexico about 1895. He was a light complexioned, blonde-headed and blue-eyed man who was also a lay minister at a Methodist Church. His light characteristics came from a biological father, a German doctor who never married his mother. His stepfather, Federico Rodriguez, and his mother Sebastiana moved him and his sister Maria to the United States where his father worked for the railroad.

Pilar Rodriguez went to school in Sanderson. He married Consuelo Villarreal in 1924 and they had two children, a little boy who died at birth, and a daughter named Ana Bertha.[635]

Rodriguez went to work at the Terrell County Courthouse in 1950. As a jailer, he regularly provided copies of the New Testament,[636] copies printed in Spanish that were provided by rancher Walter G. Downie,[637] to many of those in jail. According to the family, by 1965 he had great respect and admiration for the new Terrell County Sheriff Bill Cooksey. "Mr. Cooksey saved my father's life by telling him to stay there in that cafe the morning of the flood," said Bertha Marquez.[638]

But nearby, Jesus Marquez Jr., Bertha's husband, left the McKnight Motor Company in the wrecker he regularly drove and headed out around the moving water, heading for his house and his family on the east end of town.[639]

Marquez was born in 1927, two years before his wife. The couple met while she was in the third grade. He quit school when he was 13. He tried to get into the army when the war broke out but he had flat feet and they wouldn't take him. After Bertha completed the lower grades she was sent to the Lydia Patterson (private) School in El Paso. "I rode a train to get there. There were a lot of kids from Mexico learning to speak English there. Jesus and I wrote each other while I was away," said Bertha Marquez.[640]

After she returned to Sanderson, Bertha worked at the drug store; then took a job at a hardware store. The owner opened another store; a record (music) store where Bertha waited on what was soon a steady flow of customers, especially boys. Jesus worked at McKnight's. "We'd go out dancing and have a good time, but he really didn't like me working at the record store," said Bertha Marquez.[641]

She was a Methodist and he was Catholic but nevertheless their love persevered and they were married in December 1948. He was five-foot-eight and she was five-foot-three. They lived with her parents at first but Jesus soon bought the corner lot, a lot right on Highway 90 near the eastside bridge that spanned Sanderson Canyon, a place where the Marquez home set in 1965. He also bought a pink adobe house in the middle of the same block for his wife's parents. He and his wife Bertha had four children, a boy named Reymario and three girls—Belinda, Rosella and Lizbeth, at the time the water came raging through their neighborhood.[642]

Fifteen-year-old Rey was asleep in his grandparents' house when a floating end table hit him in the head and woke him up. He awoke his grandmother and his sister seven-year-old Rosella. Due to the rising water, he put Rosella up on top of a heavily built closet that was in the house. His grandmother took hold of the same closet and held on for dear life. Rey broke out a window, cutting his arm in the process and finally got out onto a floating sofa trying to get to his mother's house[643]

Bertha Marquez stood at the open back door and tried to reach for a car that was passing, floating close to the house. She was holding her youngest, Liz, to her bosom. The baby had not yet reached her third birthday. The oldest daughter, Belinda born in 1954, was clutching, holding onto her mother at the waist. Then with a surge in the current, Belinda was swept away and gone.[644] The mother's response was written in the book, The Sanderson Flood of 1965, Crisis In A Rural Texas Community, written by Russell Ashton Scogin and published by Sul Ross State University, Copyright 1995 by the Center for Big Bend Studies, SRSU, "I clutched my baby girl and went in deep rushing water all the way to the street to see if I could find her. The water was so clean and clear, you could see everything—gas tanks, poles and stuff. I never did see her, so I ran back in the house with my other little girl..... I was not hysterical. I just stood there and thought, "God take her soon. I don't know what is going to happen."[645]

Bertha stood on a bed, holding the baby high to protect her from the rising water. She heard the house creak and groan as though it might be going to explode. Then she heard a noise at the open door and she saw a hand; it was Belinda. The young girl was naked, her clothes had been ripped from her body by the force of the current. Her mother pulled her up onto the bed and wrapped her in a curtain that she pulled from a nearby window.[646]

Dudley Harrison had gone to his service station early that morning. The night man had called to tell him the air compressor was not working. "I went to the station before daylight, but I called Ed Kerr because of all the water. I told him we had a problem," said Harrison.[647]

Harrison was born in September 1929, when his parents, John and Wilma Harrison, lived at Rocksprings. They moved to a ranch south of Dryden later that same year. He graduated from Sanderson High School early, in 1946, and attended Sul Ross, Texas A&M and Texas Tech. "I finally came home and went into the ranching business on San Francisco Creek. I conned my parents into letting me get a Masters Degree from the University of Hard Knocks at Dryden," said Harrison.[648]

Harrison met his wife, Doris Cooke, while in the second grade. He proposed while they were in their senior year and they were married in 1950. "My father started paying on the ranch in the late 20's and Doris and I paid it off in 1966," said Harrison.[649]

The morning of the flood Harrison drove by to tell Judge Wilkinson that the water level was rising and that he might want to get out of his house, then he stopped by the Oasis Café and picked up his friend Charlie Shoemaker. They drove over to higher ground and away from the rising water that was starting to come in the doors. Finally they stopped north of Main Street, about a block north of where Joe Borrego lived.[650]

Joe Borrego worked at Dudley's Texaco. He'd called earlier that morning and told Harrison that his car would not start. Harrison related the following, "The water level was at my knees as I waded across Main Street. When I got to Joe's house, I hollered and he opened a window. He handed me a cat and a dog and I threw them up onto the roof. He handed me two kids and I put them up there too. Then Joe and his wife came out. By then the water was up to my chest and we all ended up on his roof. We watched as his car rose up, turned, inverted and floated on by us. Then a butane tank broke loose and started floating too."[651]

The water receded fairly quickly and Harrison and the others got down and headed toward safety. As they were nearly across Main Street, Harrison looked east, across the east-side bridge, across the debris of cars and muck that the flood had deposited there, and he saw a man carrying a child. It was Sheriff Bill Cooksey carrying the only surviving Johnson child in his arms.[652]

The Johnsons were a large family that had been staying in a motel just across the bridge. The boy's parents and his brothers and sisters were all lost to the flood. Harrison and Shoemaker took the youngster from Cooksey and transported him to a hospital in Fort Stockton.[653]

Aurora Galvan watched as a line of men used a long rope to pull survivors from the tragedy of the flood. The men were lined up one next to the other, moving one victim after another through the water and on to safety.[654]

Bertha Marquez gave the men her little Lizbeth first, but one of the men dropped her into the cesspool area of their backyard. With God's help another man quickly reached down and caught her, and though dirty from the muck, she was okay and moved on to safety. Belinda and Bertha were rescued next.[655]

Reymario was found alive some distance away. Though most of the grandparents' house was destroyed, Rosella was rescued after she was found on top of the surviving closet. Consuelo Rodriguez, the grandmother, was also saved though the men had to move a car that had her pinned against the frame of the closet. In all, 26 people died that day, including Bertha's husband, Jesus Marquez Jr. His body was never found.[656] "He tried to save one of his children, but he didn't make it, even though the child did," said Cliff Wilson.[657]

This has only been a tidbit of a few personal accounts from the Sanderson Flood. Volumes could be written just about the strength, sacrifice and tragedy that the people of Sanderson suffered through because of it.

Sanderson Times June 18, 1965. Copyright photo courtesy of J.A. Gilbreath, former editor/publisher of The Sanderson Times, and courtesy of Archives of the Big Bend, Bryan Wildenthal Memorial Library, Sul Ross State University, Alpine, Texas.

Jesus Marquez. His body was never found after the Sanderson Flood. Photo courtesy of Bertha Marquez.

Terrell County jailer and custodian Pilar Rodriguez. Photo courtesy of Bertha Marquez.

Two days after Bill Cooksey was shot, Pilar Rodriguez and little Liz, his granddaughter, went into the drugstore to buy the Sheriff a Get Well card. The little girl kept picking a blue card off the rack but the grandfather kept putting it back. She'd pick it again. Finally he bought the card and wrote something to the effect, 'Little Liz picked this card for you. Get well soon and get back to us. God Bless you.' It was a sympathy card.[658]

The same Saturday morning, the Cooksey children were finally able to visit their father in the hospital. "Daddy was so swollen and looked so bad," said Candace Cooksey Fulton. When the children left the room, they saw their mother talking to their Grandpa Mills, her dad, just down the hall.[659]

Mills was one of those Central Texas farmers who had made his way during the depression. Frugal was a noun that was incorporated into his very way of life. He always paid cash for everything, fought for our Country during World War I and he loved to sit on his front porch and whittle on a piece of wood.[660]

The kids saw their Grandpa Mills trying to hand a handful of dollar bills to their mother. They later learned that it was $500. Bernice Cooksey pushed it back and said, "Daddy I can't take your money."[661]

But the man gave her back the money, and as tears swelled into his eyes and ran down his cheeks, he said, "Honey, you've got to (take it). I don't know anything else I can do."[662]

Bernice Cooksey had also learned to be frugal herself; she'd had to since they were living on a lawman's salary. She was also fortunate that she didn't have to get a motel room while she was in Del Rio. She stayed with Red and Wanda Sue Mayfield. Wanda Sue was her sister's husband's sister.[663] While at the hospital, she fielded a number of calls from well-wishing friends and the media. One call was from newspaper reporter Ross McSwain who was checking on Bill's condition.[664]

While Sheriff Bill Cooksey laid in his hospital bed, law enforcement officers and their posses on both sides of the border searched for the man some had already dubbed the Caveman Bandit. "I took Rangers Gould Hardin and Alfred Allee Jr. riding along the river in my Jeep," said Odell 'Pinky' Carruthers.[665]

Carruthers' family had ranched in Terrell County since 1928. He knew the countryside like the back of his hand, especially since he ranched 130 sections himself that were south of Dryden and west of the Deaton place. Though he didn't know the Bandit, he did know many of the people who regularly crossed the border looking for work. "Most of those people were really hard working folks who didn't give us any problems," said Carruthers.[666]

The day Pinky Carruthers chauffeured the Rangers, they did see a Herder, a man who was watching after some sheep that were across the river. One of the Rangers reached for a gun but Carruthers told him it was just a man working his sheep.[667]

Val Verde County Sheriff Herman Richter told a reporter for the San Angelo Standard-Times that they had actually found twenty such sheep camps in and along the river, but the suspect still had not been located. He theorized that the man, Hernandez, was still in the United States hiding in extremely rough country along the river,[668] but Benny Ray Ross and Jimmy Merritt had a different idea.[669]

Jimmy Merritt spent part of that second day piloting his Piper Cub airplane slow and low to the ground around Dryden. Ross was riding shotgun. They looked along every draw and across every ridgeline. Of course, aviation gasoline was expensive so they didn't fly too long, but they did have the right idea.[670] The next day George Adams' house was burglarized at Dryden.[671]

CHAPTER SIXTEEN
For Every Action

After Bill Cooksey was shot, Terrell County might have been a good test for Sir Isaac Newton's law of physics that says that 'for every action, there is an equal and opposite reaction.' People had been concerned after Pelham Bradford was shot, but after the Sheriff was shot—fear immediately swept across their part of West Texas. The actions of Alfredo Hernandez, who some had dubbed the Caveman Bandit, caused more than its share of reaction.[672]

The Terrell County Commissioners Court met on Thursday, November 11, 1965. Seated were County Judge R.S. Wilkinson, Pct. 1 Commissioner F.M. Weigand, Pct. 2 Commissioner Roy Deaton, Pct. 3 Commissioner Sid Harkins and Pct. 4 Commissioner C.M. Turk. County Clerk Ruel Adams, County Attorney Jack Hayre and Deputy Sheriff Dalton Hogg were also present. At some point, after a briefing by Deputy Hogg, Sid Harkins made a motion, "that we pay the hospital bills of Sheriff Bill Cooksey." The motion was seconded by Turk and passed by the governing body.[673] (The bills would eventually total about $35,000.)[674]

Dalton Hogg told the court that he was keeping the Sheriff abreast of any developments and anything else that was going on in Terrell County. This was something the Deputy did until the Sheriff returned to work.[675]

While the initial search for Hernandez would go on for weeks, the legend of the Caveman Bandit started to develop right away. Highway Patrolman Buddy Burgess thought of the man as an Indian, with traits like those who had lived within the Chihuahuan Desert for hundreds of years before.[676] Cliff Wilson thought of him as a Coyote, the animal—not the person who helps deliver illegal aliens into this country.[677] The November 11 edition of the Del Rio News-Herald called him the Bug-

Eyed Bandit.[678] The Sanderson Times dubbed him the 'Cave Man'[679] and others used names common for such a person, names like outlaw, robber and bandit. And in some places he was called a Bad One.

It was the Friday before the opening day of deer season and a week and a day after the shooting of the Terrell County Sheriff. Frank Caraway, a San Angelo oilfield drilling contractor, and Mike, his 18 year old son, drove onto the J.V. Drisdale Ranch that was located along Ranch Road 189 southwest of Sonora and not too far from the intersection of Highway 163.[680] Measuring as the crow flies, the ranch was about 55 miles from Dryden and farther if you had to drive it.

Caraway had leased approximately 1,000 acres of the large ranch for deer hunting for several years. Drisdale, who was from a pioneer West Texas ranching family, had been a good host and the oilman was happy with the arrangements. That Friday the ranch foreman, Natividad Salazar, had a message for the hunters.[681]

Salazar related how the Sheriff had been shot, how people were scared and now carrying guns; and how they had taken all the food and blankets out of any caves and unoccupied living quarters on the ranch. Previously, it had been common for ranchers to leave food and other necessities in places where they could be found by those who came to this country looking for a job and/or a better way of life. It was a pretty standard operating procedure all up and down the border, not to mention that they made contact with good ranch-hands that way. But that all changed after Cooksey was shot. "We have a Bad One on the loose and we're going to flush him out," said Salazar who was armed himself.[682]

So the actions of Alfredo Hernandez, the man known as the Caveman Bandit, made it hard on those who crossed the Rio Grande in search of the pursuit of happiness and prosperity. "The majority of those men and women who crossed the river looking for work were pretty good well meaning people. The cowboys could ride and they put in a real days work. This was also during a time when they would take their hats off before they would talk to you. It was a way they showed respect and they rarely ever carried guns," said Texas Ranger Alfred Allee Jr.[683]

The other little communities up and down Highway 90 and along the railway were not immune to the fear. The neighbors started talking about little things they had thought were inconsequential before. They now paid more attention to what they were doing and what was going on around them. They honked their horns when they got home to let the guy know they were there, if he happened to be inside their house. They quit taking things for granted.

One example was Reggie and Reba Monroe who ranched thousands of acres about 30 miles north of Dryden. "My parents were really cautious afterwards. If we came home at night, they'd drive around the house just to make sure the guy wasn't there," said Marsha Monroe who was in Jr. High when Sheriff Cooksey was shot.[684]

Tom and Donna Smith bought the Texaco Service Station at Langtry not too many years before Cooksey was shot. They had a pretty steady flow of customers that included mostly neighbors and highway travelers. Luckily, they had not been a victim of Hernandez and thought he'd left them alone because the Border Patrol office was next door, but they did hear talk in their store. "We knew we had a Bad One out there because of what we heard he took. He didn't just take food; he took other things like hair tonic, shampoo, toothbrushes and toothpaste," said Donna Smith.[685]

Deputy Dalton Hogg heard similar stories. He also heard stories about holes that were found in the walls of some of the victim's houses; small round holes that appeared to be drilled in the bathrooms.[686] Was Hernandez a voyeur? Quite possibly, because during the initial search the tool used to drill the holes may have been found.[687]

The search for Hernandez expanded out over a much larger area as the days passed by. On November 14, 1965, the Del Rio News-Herald published a picture of Texas Ranger L.H. Purvis and Val Verde County Deputy Sheriff Samuel Perez. The men had searched a cave between Pumpville and Pandale. The man they were looking for was not there, but they dug up the floor of the cave and found an array of hidden stolen property. They also found a bit and brace, a manually operated drill and coloring books that belonged the Ted Luce's children. They found other things too.[688]

The newspaper caption read, 'Cave Yields Plunder From Burglaries.' The officers were shown holding boxes of jewelry. Quoting the story, 'suspended from a shovel are two face masks, a rag with eyeholes cut in it. Food, clothes, tools, flashlight and a book are displayed; some of the items identified as stolen from the Bradford home at Pumpville last July. The cave, about two miles from Pumpville, in a ravine, was well hidden in brush; all items recovered were buried in the dirt in the cave.'[689]

Cave Yields Plunder From Burglaries

Texas Ranger L.H. Purvis and Val Verde County Deputy Sheriff Samuel Perez are shown with stolen property they dug up in a cave near Pumpville. Copyright 1965 Del Rio News-Herald, Del Rio, Texas. Reprinted with permission.

The Bradfords knew that some of the things were theirs right away. One pair of pants had surely come from their store. They knew because it was a pair in which the waist and length sizes were switched on the tag. "Some books we hadn't seen in years were in with a bunch of U.S. News and World Report (magazines) and we were the only ones who had it in the entire country. Harvey Hall was the one who gave it to us each week after he read it," wrote Stella Bradford years later.[690]

Mrs. Bradford also wrote about losing a roast while she went to visit her friend Annie Lou White at their ranch. After getting back home that night, she found someone had come into their house and taken a roast out of their oven. But she was not the only person to lose food; food that some thought was surely taken by the Caveman Bandit.[691]

The Dryden Mercantile had become a gathering place for area residents since the Ten Eyck's had taken it over in 1960. The Kerr family, who had the Kerr Mercantile in Sanderson, actually owned the building but Ten Eyck owned and managed the business.[692]

Bill Ten Eyck was 34 when Bill Cooksey was shot. He was tall, about six-foot-four, and lean but not skinny. He had black hair, blue eyes and wore the big windshield type glasses with plastic rims. His daily dress was blue jeans, a simple western shirt, Brogans or loafers and a baseball cap.[693]

It was not uncommon to see him smoking a cigarette and chewing tobacco at the same time. He had a slow drawl way of talking probably partially due to his like for tobacco. "He'd talk with a mouth full of spit and might spit in a trashcan right in front of you," said Jess Ten Eyck, the youngest son who was five at the time.[694]

Bill Ten Eyck grew up in Bakersfield that was about halfway between Fort Stockton and Sheffield. He went into the Army and found himself in a place called Korea. He and his wife Mary Lois, who grew up in El Paso, met through mutual friends in Fort Stockton.[695]

Mary Lois was 34 in 1965. She was a quiet person who had brown hair and blue eyes. She wore glasses, glasses described by her son as "Catwoman-type glasses." She was pretty much the bookkeeper in those days. She'd also borne four children by then, Eddie (9 years of age), Gay (8), Jesse (5) and Paula (4). She also kept a close eye on the kids after the Sheriff was shot. "They wouldn't let us go off away from the house like they used to, they'd keep us close," said Jess Ten Eyck.[696]

Bill Ten Eyck took other measures too. He started carrying a borrowed .45 caliber revolver, a big old hog-leg type pistol that he sometimes tucked inside his waistband. He also had a borrowed 12-gauge pump shotgun and a personal 30:30 caliber rifle. But it was a burglary of their own house not too long after the Sheriff's shooting that increased the concern of both parents.[697]

The Ten Eyck's had taken the kids to Sanderson for a night on the town. They saw a show at the movie theater and stopped next door at Harvey's Café for supper. When they returned home the store's moneybox was missing from the house. "My parents thought the guy had been watching us, otherwise he wouldn't have known that we were gone," said Jess Ten Eyck.[698]

After the burglary, Ike Billings, a tall lanky rancher in his 30s, whose wife Barbara taught school in Sanderson, would stay in the house when the Ten Eyck's were away. Of course, Bill Ten Eyck was concerned that the Bandit would show up when they were there too, so he ran fishing line out away from his house. The fishing line ran out in different directions but was set high enough so a body would touch it if they passed by. The ends were all tied to cowbells back in his bedroom. He hoped to have a little edge on the Bandit if he came their way, especially since they didn't have a phone in their house. In fact, the only phone was a pay phone outside their store.[699]

The Dryden Mercantile was set within a large concrete wall building that had Mobil Oil logos on it. Entering the store a passerby would find a cash register and check out area to the left that was highlighted by a knife display. There was a meat market in the back and rows and rows of groceries in the middle. Along the right wall there were pants, shirts, cowboy hats and other clothing, along with all kinds of ranching supplies, things like horse shoes, pipe fittings, windmill leathers, leather tack and such.[700]

The storekeeper also sold ammunition, picks, shovels, crowbars, camping equipment and cast iron cookware. "Dad would always say we didn't make anything off of his prices on the cast iron cookware, but it always brought people through the doors," said Jess Ten Eyck.[701]

Behind the Post Office building that was attached to the west side of the building, there was a feed room full of livestock feed and salt blocks. It was through the two back feed room doors that the Ten Eyck's believed that Hernandez entered the store on several occasions, occasions when he basically took food and clothing. Between the house burglary and the store burglaries, Bill Ten Eyck became plenty upset about the Bandit. "We all felt violated," said the son.[702]

The Post Office, managed by Alma Jewel Littleton with help at times from Mary Lois Ten Eyck, probably had more than a little to do with the number of people who stopped by the store. They'd pick up their mail and just saunter next door to pick up a few things or just have a little conversation.[703]

In the wintertime, Ten Eyck would pull a big gas stove into the store and conversations would take place around it. The summertime found most people near the checkout counter or out front on the porch. The main topic, after the Sheriff was shot, was the Bandit, especially if rancher George Adams was around; his house was broken into twice before the dawn of 1966. It was just a common occurrence to have people in the store anytime it was open for business.[704]

Such was the case one afternoon when Benny Ray Ross, Woody Rutledge and Bill Ten Eyck were deep in conversation. Rutledge announced that he'd left a roast cooking on his stove and had to go check on it. He'd been just passing the time while it cooked. He marched the short distance up the hill to his house only to find the roast was gone, taken right in broad daylight from across open ground. "Rutledge ran back into the store, carrying a rifle and ranting and raving about the Bandit," said Ross.[705]

The three men took their guns and searched the area for the thief but they didn't find him or the roast.[706] " My dad and Benny Ray searched for the Bandit several times," said Jess Ten Eyck.[707]

The timeline on the food thefts is probably over a year but the last occurred when the Postmistress had gone home for lunch. Lewis Cash was out of town that day and Benny Ray Ross was helping Minnie Dee manage the Cactus Café. "We saw Alma Jewel (Littleton) from the window as she headed out the highway toward their place at noon. But it was just a few minutes later that we saw her driving real fast back into Dryden," said Ross.[708]

Mrs. Littleton had realized something was missing or out of place as soon as she opened the door. (Possibly a pie she'd left on the kitchen counter.) She was sure the guy was still in the house and hurried back into town. Of course her burglar was gone by the time a group of men got back there to check on it.[709] This incident put Benny Ray Ross in the law enforcement spotlight for a second time.

Highway Patrolman Malcolm Bollinger would tell Ross that Deputy Hogg suspected him of the Littleton burglary. Only it could not have been Ross because he was working at the café at the time. It was not the first time Ross had heard those words from Bollinger.[710]

Ross had also been the topic of discussion after one of the burglaries of George Adams' house, the time a pair of binoculars was stolen. These field glasses had a serial number on them and Adams had the number. Large footprints were in the dirt leading from the house; prints that matched the size of boots like those worn by Benny Ray Ross. "I've got him now," said Deputy Hogg.[711]

The Deputy gave the job of talking to Ross to Bollinger who already had a pretty good relationship with the teenager. Bollinger was in his late 30s, with gray streaks already starting to show in his black hair. His square jaw and dry wit matched well with the way he spoke in a slow drawl sort of way. His noticeable flat belly fit well on his five-foot eleven-inch frame.

The teenager denied any involvement in the theft,[712] so within a few days, Bollinger took Ross to the Midland office of the Texas Department of Public Safety where he underwent a polygraph examination, an examination where he ran an exceptionally clean, non-deceptive chart. He hadn't committed the theft.[713]

Benny Ray Ross was greatly disappointed that he was accused of the burglary. He still held Hogg responsible for the inaccuracy when he was interviewed nearly 40 years later.[714] He was not the only one who felt that way.

Law enforcement officials had given Alfredo Gallegos a pistol for self-protection right after Cooksey was shot. Within a few more weeks he was also taken to El Paso where he underwent a polygraph examination that was administered in Spanish.[715] Nearly forty years later, the question he asked, or should I say his daughter Christina asked on his behalf was, "Why did they polygraph my daddy? Was it because he was Mexican?"[716]

Even though neither man knew that the other had undergone a similar test, they each had a similar question about why the test had been administered. The following answer is what the author surmised based on many years of my own law enforcement experience.[717]

The shooting of Sheriff Cooksey put a lot of pressure on Deputy Hogg and the law enforcement officers who were doing everything they knew how to do to catch the Bandit. The pressure grew when the burglaries started to occur again just a few days after the shooting. It wasn't long before the officers were frustrated, what with all their effort and no results.[718]

Their frustration was evidenced by a story that ran in the San Angelo Standard-Times on Friday morning, November 19, 1965. The headlines read, 'It Would Take A Thousand Men A Hundred Years...' The smaller bold type said, 'Border Hunt Continues For Man Who Shot Terrell County Sheriff.' The reporter had interviewed Texas Ranger Arthur Hill, "it would take a hundred years to search all the caves, canyons and hiding places in the vast territory where the man is said to be hiding." The frustration grew even more after the Bandit was seen near the river by a ranch-hand named Isidro Blanco who was riding fence not too many miles from the Agua Verdes crossing.[719]

Alfredo Hernandez told Blanco that he was going to Mexico but Blanco never saw him cross the river. He was armed with a 30:30 rifle and two pistols. The information was relayed to law enforcement officers but a search provided negative results.[720]

Law enforcement officers are trained to follow the evidence. Good investigators actually eliminate people from being a suspect to a crime on a pretty regular basis. The polygraph is only a tool, a tool that is sometimes used to quickly eliminate suspects. The officers were doing anything they could, looking for any lead and for the answers to the burglaries. They wanted to catch the Caveman Bandit as bad as anyone ever wanted to catch anyone.[721] "There was no one who wanted to catch the Bandit anymore than Dalton," said Cooksey years later.[722]

Residents all over the area wanted the man caught too. Take for instance Joanne Bell who heard the dogs barking one night, not too long after the Sheriff was shot. "Bert was out of town with the railroad and those dogs were really acting up and the leaves were rustling in the backyard, so I gathered up my two girls and just sat there in bed—all night," said Bell.[723]

The Bell's lived on Cargile Street just up the hill from the Sheriff, but, of course, he was not there. There were caves up along the sides of the mountain and it was anyone's guess where Hernandez might be. "It was a real change since Sanderson wasn't the type of place where you locked your doors. People would actually go off on vacation and leave their house unlocked or keys in their cars," said Bell.[724]

Joanne Bell also missed Bernice Cooksey, her dear friend who she described as Sanderson's own Erma Bombeck. "She and Bill were special people who kinda' took everything in stride and didn't fall to pieces over things. During neighborhood get-togethers they were the best entertainment, they would joke and banter back and forth with each other," said Bell. The barking dogs really made her wish her friends were home.[725]

Bernice Cooksey was at the Val Verde Memorial Hospital when the Standard-Times reporter was interviewing people for a November 19th story. He asked about the Sheriff's condition. "He still has a tube in his lung," she told the reporter. The story also revealed that he was only breathing from the upper third of the lung that was punctured by the bullet, but had recovered from the wounds and surgery "real well," said Mrs. Cooksey.[726]

On December 12, 1965, Bill Cooksey was moved to the Methodist Hospital in San Antonio. Doctors were greatly concerned about the possibility of pneumonia. In the final analysis though, the pain from the sciatic nerve injury, the lung injury and the loss of his spleen would follow him for the rest of his life. (The Sheriff would always have a noticeable limp that was due to the sciatic nerve injury.)[727]

Sheriff Cooksey was discharged from the hospital just before Christmas. "We were at Grandpa and Grandma Mills in Mills County for Christmas," said Candace Cooksey Fulton.[728]

In some ways it was a wonderful Christmas. The kids had their daddy back and they had gifts, gifts made possible because Terrell County residents had taken up a love offering of around $2,000 for the Cooksey family. But the Sheriff was still in tremendous pain and his recuperation at his in-laws was not easy. It would be a while, a new year, before the kids heard their daddy whistle again.[729]

Along with the pain, Bill Cooksey had a growing desire to meet up with and take care of the man who had caused him to suffer. It would not be easy and he knew it. As he told Bill Scott, a reporter for the San Angelo Standard-Times, for a December 12, 1965 story, "This is not like hunting an ordinary human being.... He is an animal with human instincts (This is probably inversed in the newspaper story.) He can cover 30 to 40 miles of the roughest country at leisure in a day's time."[730]

"The modern day law enforcement officer is not set up to trail one of these boys.... He can live under conditions that would knock us out of commission in no time.... He is an exception, not the rule.... (but) There's not much criminal element among the Mexican aliens generally," said Cooksey.[731]

The reaction to the shooting of Sheriff Bill Cooksey hurt many good people, people on both sides of the border. It caused people to be more aware and cast a great suspicion and hardship on those Mexican aliens who crossed the border looking for work, a better way of life or both.[732]

In 1965, there were plenty of things going on outside of Terrell County. It had been a year of change in the United States. The Beatles and rock and roll music were making a name for themselves, muscle cars were ripping up the blacktop; the United States sent troops to Vietnam and the Sound of Music was the top grossing film of the year.[733]

Popular television shows that year were Hogan's Heroes, I Dream of Jeannie, The Andy Griffith Show, Bonanza, Gunsmoke and others. Sony produced the Betamax, a home video tape recorder;[734] the Cleveland Browns won the football championship[735] and Sports Illustrated raised more than a few eyebrows when it published a January 18, 1965 edition that included the photograph of a pretty girl in a bathing suit on the cover, with others wearing mesh net attire on the inside.[736] The cover of a U.S. News and World Report read, 'How Supreme Court Is Changing U.S.'[737]

Yet the year was definitely a time of tragedy for Terrell County. There was the Sanderson flood, the tornado at Dryden and the shooting of their Sheriff. Not to mention that officers had spent an untold number of hours looking for their Caveman Bandit and burglaries were on the rise again.

As the sun set for the last time that year, Bill Cooksey wanted to meet up with his assailant again. Of course, he knew that to do so—he had to get back on his feet first.

CHAPTER 17

D *alton Hogg was a good listener and never shirked from what he had to do. He wanted to find the Bandit as bad as anyone." Retired Customs Agent Cliff Wilson.*[738]

Alfredo Hernandez eluded officers from several agencies through the end of 1965. Texas Ranger L.H. Purvis had even borrowed dogs from the prison system to try to track down the guy, but the effort proved fruitless. "Dad thought the guy may have used garlic or something (else) to throw the dogs off," said Irion County Chief Deputy H.B. 'Butch' Purvis.[739] But as the New Year (1966) began, Dalton Hogg had faith that dogs could help him catch the man who had shot Bill Cooksey; he just didn't have the money to buy them.[740]

It was around the time Bill Cooksey returned to the hospital for leg surgery,[741] that Indio Calzada ended Hogg's dilemma. The Terrell County businessman and rancher, who gave money to charity on occasion, gave the deputy the money to buy two dogs.[742]

Bill Cooksey returned home on January 11th with his leg trussed up in a sling to keep its weight off the ground. "There was a strap that went from his shoulders down around his ankle; then a weight hung off the ankle, stretching the leg back. Every month or so they'd lengthen the strap and (I think) increase the weight until he got to where he only limped as he did for the rest of his life," said Candace Cooksey Fulton.[743]

At the end of the month, Texas Ranger Forest Gould Hardin retired.[744] Ranger Alfred Allee Jr, who had been transferred to Ozona, inherited Hardin's Terrell County responsibilities, responsibilities that included the hunt for the Caveman Bandit.[745]

Though the out-of-county officers had returned home, Dalton Hogg worked with the Border Patrol in hopes they could get a lead on the Bandit's whereabouts. The Immigration officers allowed cooperative illegal aliens to work on area ranches. The workers reported back that they were afraid of the man, that they thought he was loco.[746] "I'd have liked to have worked (undercover) for Roy Deaton as a cowboy; I thought we could have had a chance of catching the guy that way, but Deaton didn't allow it," said Border Patrol agent Ray Fitzgerald.[747]

The Border Patrol agents knew that ranchers regularly worked these people and got along better with local law enforcement. As Fitzgerald said nearly forty years later, "You might say there was a little bit of professional jealousy involved in the investigation. We didn't think that they really wanted our help."[748]

Roy Deaton had his own reasons for not allowing the undercover operation. His first priority was the safety of his family. He knew that the Caveman Bandit was very dangerous because he'd already shot Pelham Bradford and Bill Cooksey. He knew the man could kill him or his family at anytime.[749] But no matter what he thought, at first, he did play more than one part in this historical event.

One direct-contact meeting occurred one afternoon when Deaton, his wife and their son delivered flour tortillas over to the Gatlin Ranch headquarters ranch house. The food was for a group of 'ranch hands' that would arrive and work for him the next day. When the Deatons walked into the house they smelled goat cooking in the oven. "Dad told mother and me to go back to the pickup but to not get the gun or show any sign of aggression," said Roy Deaton, the son.[750]

The tall, gangly Roy Deaton, wearing his big cowboy hat, western shirt, jeans and boots, with a pair of leather gloves wrapped within the grasp of his right hand, walked out behind the house and hollered. He hollered again and Alfredo Hernandez stood up from behind a barrel they burned trash in occasionally. Deaton invited him to stay and eat. He also told him that he had a job for him—if he needed one. Then Deaton and his family drove away and left the man standing there.[751]

Another time Deaton's son and his best friend, Wally Welch whose parents were railroad folks, were out in the son's maroon top gray-bottomed 50-model Plymouth car. "We pushed it more than it ever started and that day we'd pushed it off into a swag, a gully that was on our place," said Roy 'Hoot' Deaton. But the car still didn't start.[752]

The boys had the hood up and were trying to identify the problem. And Hernandez, with his morral across his shoulder, walked right out into the road and across the bottom right beside them.[753] (If there was ever a time that a car needed to start…) It would be awhile before they saw him again, but they were not the only ones who would see him.

On March 19, 1966, The Sanderson Times reported that Texas Game Warden David Cook had been assigned to Terrell County.[754] What the newspaper didn't report was an incident that happened at Dryden about that same time.

The slim dark complexioned woman, with black hair that flowed down past her shoulders, walked out of the back of her house to take clothes off of their clothesline. The thirty-one-year-old mother of three stood five-foot five-inches tall, had brown eyes and was of Cherokee Indian, German and Dutch decent. Her name was Adrienne. She was married to Iva Rogers Vasquez's oldest son Virgil McElhaney.[755]

Virgil and Adrienne had returned to Dryden in November 1965. They'd previously been in Industria, Argentina working in the oilfields. They were both fluent in Spanish. Virgil was now working for Indio Calzada, welding the stock pens out west of Dryden. She was a housewife who took care of their kids. They lived in a house just north of the railroad tracks and away from the main population of Dryden. The house was near the water station that was formerly used by steam engine locomotives.[756]

On that particular day Adrienne was watching after her sister-in-law's two children and it was their clothes that were on the clothesline. It was just about dusk, as she removed clothespins from each garment, when she noticed a man standing about twenty-five yards away. "He had long hair and a beard and wore a dirty western hat. But he took the hat off and bowed, and asked if he could approach and talk to me," said Adrienne McElhaney.[757]

The polite man made her think of an Apache Indian. He told her he hadn't eaten in two days and asked if she'd make him two sandwiches. Speaking in Spanish, as he had, she told him no, to go on or that she would call the 'Chote,' the Border Patrol. And she said the man moved off, back out into the pasture.[758]

It wasn't too many days later that she returned home to find a bar of soap out in their yard near a water hose, as though the guy had taken a bath. Lunchmeat and a Bible, a Bible written in Spanish that had been a present from friends in Argentina, were missing from the house. "No one locked their houses back then and things did come up missing," said Adrienne.[759]

Then one morning, not too long before the kids were supposed to catch the school bus, Adrienne sent her oldest daughter, Naomi who was 11 at the time, down the railroad right-of-way to run some of Roy Deaton's sheep off of the railroad tracks. This was a pretty regular task for the youngster who kept the livestock from getting run over by the Sunset Limited, a fast passenger train that didn't slow down as it sped through town. (Other trains ran through the place pretty often but most were slower. Many carried military trucks and tanks that most people thought were destined for Vietnam.)[760]

The 5th grader had long brown hair that fell down to her waist and she carried 95 pounds on her slim 5-foot frame. As her mother watched her from the house, she thought of how her daughter ran like a deer, how she was a lot like a little Indian herself. Then the mother went about her chores as the girl ran the sheep back into the pasture north of the railroad tracks.[761]

In what seemed like just a minute, Naomi came running back to the house. She was breathing hard and all excited. "Momma, the sheep ran into some brush and a man ran out the other side," said the girl.[762]

After the kids caught the bus, Adrienne went down to the Chevron Station and told Joe Vasquez what had happened. Vasquez called Dalton Hogg in Sanderson.[763]

It wasn't long before law enforcement officers started gathering near the McElhaney house. Dalton Hogg and Malcolm Bollinger brought horses and the dogs they'd bought earlier, dogs they'd spent weeks learning how to track with. Texas Ranger Alfred Allee Jr. and others came to help them search for the Bandit. "The dogs found the camp and brought out a white piece of paper, the type of paper you wrap meat in when it is frozen," said Alfred Allee Jr.[764]

The girl had run the sheep right over one of Hernandez's camps; he had had a fire going and was cooking something when it happened. Other than the meat wrapper, the officers found a school photograph of a local girl and a sock full of quarters, quarters that were missing from Joe Vasquez's store. The dogs got after his trail several times but couldn't keep the scent long. They finally couldn't find it at all and he got away. Allee would later say, "The guy was pretty sharp."[765]

1966 cooking camp photograph taken by Texas Department of Public Safety, photography section, Austin, Texas. Photo courtesy of Candace Cooksey Fulton.

Joe Vasquez told the officers that he had been having some thefts and that the meat wrapper had come out of the freezer in his store. "Afterwards, Wayne Rogers, my 19 year old twin brother, used to sleep in the back of the store, but he was a really sound sleeper or the guy was just really cunning, or both, and he'd still break in and steal food," said Elaine Rogers O'Donnell, who had already married and gone prior to 1966.[766]

The search that morning and the dogs' noses had educated the law enforcement officers about the way Hernandez built his hiding places with tiny entrances front and back, something more like an animal would go through than something you'd think a man would. Afterwards, after they knew what to look for, they started finding others inside plots of brush and cactus.[767]

The camps never had visible trails that led to the entrance leading the officers to believe that the guy must have come in from a different direction each time. He didn't discard empty cans or other trash where they could be seen either; they learned he would wrap his trash in burlap and tie it to tree trunks. They found where he would defecate in the same place about 15 feet from where he ate, where he built and rebuilt fires. They found his pots and pans. "They found some of the camps on the Deaton Ranch south of Dryden," said Cliff Wilson.[768]

Nell Deaton, Roy's wife, liked to read, especially at night before she went to bed. She used to sit by a kitchen window and consume the words off of the pages. One night she got really spooked when she looked out the window and realized that somebody was standing there, watching her. "Roy, somebody was looking in the window at me, somebody was watching me," she told her husband.[769]

It was not too many days later, on Monday, April 18, 1966, that a guard light allowed Roy Deaton to catch sight of the Bandit. The shootings of Pelham Bradford and Bill Cooksey had caused Deaton to place a light fixture down at their barn, a light he could turn on from the house. Early that morning he saw the guy—standing right under it, holding what appeared to be a pair of binoculars (binoculars that were probably the ones missing out of the front of Deaton's pickup) and what appeared to be a lever action rifle.[770]

Deputy Hogg got the call and quickly loaded two horses that he kept behind his house into an open-top 14-foot stock trailer. He picked up Highway Patrolman Malcolm Bollinger and the bloodhounds, which were kept at Bollinger's house, and they were on their way headed out Highway 90 toward Dryden.[771]

Dalton Hogg had been in such a hurry to get out there that he'd put the horses in the back of the trailer and not in the front. This allowed the horses to sit back when he hit the breaks of his station wagon near the airport west of Dryden. This took weight off the rear wheels and the trailer started whipping, then it jack-knifed and the car and trailer rolled.[772] And as reported in the Sanderson Times on April 21, 1966, 'The car was demolished.'[773]

Elizabeth Murrah called Henry Beth Hogg at the Kerr Mercantile. "Don't get upset but Dalton has had a wreck."[774]

Dalton had been working on their house, so Henry Beth asked, "Did he fall off the house?"[775]

"No, he had a car wreck but he's up walking around," said Mrs. Murrah who had also summoned the ambulance.[776]

The Sanderson Times April 21, 1966. Copyright photo courtesy of J.A. Gilbreath, former editor/publisher of The Sanderson Times, and courtesy of Archives of the Big Bend, Bryan Wildenthal Memorial Library, Sul Ross State University, Alpine, Texas.

John Harrison, Dudley's dad, had already heard about the wreck and stopped by to see if he could give Henry Beth a ride to the hospital. She said, "No, I'll take my own car (which was parked across the street.)"[777]

When she started across the street, Henry Beth saw the ambulance headed her way. Dudley Harrison, the driver with Troy Druse in the passenger seat, stopped for just a second or two. Dalton was staring at his hand and he kept saying, "Where are you taking us?"[778] Of course, they were taking them to the hospital in Fort Stockton.

Henry Beth drove to the school and picked up Evelyn Bollinger. When they got to the hospital Dr. John Hundley told her that Dalton had a concussion. The deputy kept asking, "Mamma, where is Johnny, where is Johnny?" And she responded, "You know he's in Vietnam." The answer upset the deputy.[779]

The wreck crippled Johnny Hogg's 3-year old mare. It permanently bruised Charles Stegal's horse that he'd loaned Bollinger to use to hunt the Bandit. The hounds were okay, but the officers were hurt. Dalton did have a concussion and as the Sanderson Times reported, 'Bollinger had abrasions and a slight neck injury,'[780] but the injuries didn't keep the officers down long and their Sheriff had started to get around better too.

It was shortly after high school graduation 1966 that Bill Ten Eyck found things missing from his Dryden Mercantile store. Sheriff Cooksey and Deputy Hogg went to the scene and initially thought the thefts might have been high school kids out to celebrate the end of the educational experience. They thought this until Roy Deaton, who just happened to be in the store, found where someone had changed clothes and left his old clothes behind. They finally decided it might have just been the man who shot the Sheriff.[781]

Deaton had one unique way to see if the Bandit had been around his house. The rancher had an outside kitchen for his workers. He'd line up the cans of food and count them. He'd have them all pulled out to the front of the shelf. Then he'd put a few cans in behind those up front. He knew if the Bandit came by that he never took cans off the front, he only took those that were in the back.[782]

Two Texas Rangers followed up on a Roy Deaton tip that year too. Rangers H.L. Purvis and Alfred Allee Jr. left their vehicle a long way from where Deaton had seen the Bandit. They parked there around midnight and headed out on foot in hopes that Hernandez would not know they were on to him, in hopes of catching the man. They were well armed with pistols and Winchester 30:30 lever action carbines. They settled into their hiding places a few hours before daylight.[783]

It was one of those crystal clear nights when there was very little wind and sound carried over great distances. It was dark though the glow from the stars shown enough light to reveal a well-used trail not far from the men. "It was not too long before sunrise that we heard someone coming, someone that was whistling, and we got ready," said Allee.[784]

The Rangers were sure that the person making the sound had to be the Bandit; surely he was the man who had shot Bill Cooksey. The whistling was getting closer—and closer—and closer. Finally it sounded as though it was hardly twenty yards away. Then it stopped and there was nothing but silence.[785]

When the sun brought enough light for the men to see, they found a set of footprints that had stopped, seemingly walked backwards for a ways, then turned around and left. "Maybe the guy was like one of the old timers, he seized the moment, realized that something was not right and got away," said Allee.[786]

There was no doubt that Alfredo Hernandez had great survival instincts. Another example is the time when the occupants of an airplane saw a jackrabbit spook and run from something. The story is that it may have been a Border Patrol airplane, though Harvey Rogers, who owned Harvey's Café and Bill Hargus, who ran the Fort Stockton airport, both spent time in the air looking for the guy. Nonetheless, the pilot turned the plane around and swung low—only to see Hernandez standing straight up and motionless, covered with his painted hat that acted as camouflage from above. The only problem was there was no way to communicate with anyone to tell them that they had the guy located.[787]

It was that same summer when Benny Ray Ross was drafted and headed to boot camp. He would later find himself in a place called Vietnam.[788] Back at home, the search for the Caveman Bandit continued anytime there was even a hint that he might be someplace.

The experience of hunting the Caveman Bandit led the officers to believe several things. First they started to believe that he wore different size shoes to throw them off.[789] When they did get on to his trail with the dogs, they started to realize that he would immediately head toward a fence and cross it; or, if it was nearby, he'd head toward the railroad tracks and start down the right-of-way, leading the officers to believe that the creosote might mess up the dogs' noses. They may have been right (though a few tracking dog owners might disagree) because of what a teenager saw that summer.[790]

Brad Bradley was on horseback looking for a flock of Ted Luce's sheep on the Hamilton place not too far from Pumpville. The youngster rode up to the railroad right-of-way and noticed Hernandez near some old railroad ties that were stacked not far from the tracks. The man was kneeling and appeared to be using a knife to scrape chips of the creosote-soaked wood into a piece of cloth. (Later, Bradley asked Texas Ranger Tol Dawson what he thought the guy was doing. He'd responded with," Using creosote to throw the dogs off his scent.")[791]

There was another man who nearly had a face-to-face experience with the man too. It was Jack Deaton, the brother and ranching partner of Roy Deaton.

Jack Deaton had stopped over at their barn on the place they called Green Gables, a place that was south of Dryden off Bootlegger Road. He noticed feathers, dove feathers all over the floor when he walked into the barn to get some feed. He walked around to where a stove was and found a pot full of boiling water. He assumed the guy had been killing doves (that were attracted to the feed in the building) and cooking them in the boiling water.[792]

Deaton assumed the guy had run out back when he first drove up. Later though he realized the guy had probably just climbed up into the hayloft, was probably lying there the whole time with his hand on his pistol, right there in their barn. Of course, it was his brother Roy who had more than his share of direct contact with the guy.[793]

It was early August 1966 when Roy Deaton and a ranch hand saw Hernandez while they were in the Green Gables area themselves. The guy walked out into the road as they were riding by. Deaton asked the guy if he needed a job and he said no, that he was going to Mexico. Then he said, "You shouldn't have put those dogs on me!" which Deaton assumed meant the dogs that Dalton Hogg and Malcolm Bollinger had been using to try to catch the guy. Deaton went straight to his ranch house and called Sheriff Bill Cooksey.[794]

The bold black letters above the story in the August 11, 1966 edition of the Sanderson Times said, 'Cave Man Eludes 100-Man Hunt Last Weekend.' The first sentence underneath told the story—'Terrell County's elusive Cave Man was again successful in hiding from police officers last Thursday and Friday.' The story said that officers from all over West Texas, from all branches of county, state and national forces, using dogs, airplanes, jeeps and horses, were involved in the search.[795]

This was the only time that Roy Deaton had actually physically helped in the search for the man. It was he and Dalton Hogg who found his camp hidden in the middle of a very thick mesquite thicket. Once again Hernandez had escaped into parts unknown.[796]

Texas Department of Public Safety photograph of trail that led to the camp in the mesquite thicket. Photo courtesy of Candace Cooksey Fulton.

CHAPTER EIGHTEEN
You Can't Catch Him...

Felix Harrison parked and got out of his pickup behind the old Hamilton ranch house. He wanted to tell Ted Luce and his wife Shirley, who was Harrison's niece, that the Bandit had been seen around Dryden again. Luce still ranched the land around Pumpville but there had been a few changes since Pelham Bradford was shot.[797]

By August 1966 Pelham Bradford and his wife had retired and moved to Alpine. Their son John, a slim, sandy haired fellow who stood a little over six feet, and his wife Ella Ruth, who was a short but rather attractive blonde, now ran the store. The 23-year-old couple lived in a trailer house that they'd moved in between the store and the old Bradford house. Ella Ruth's sister Billie was visiting them the night that Harrison stopped by to warn the Pumpville residents.[798]

Ted Luce had taken off a week from his Del Rio cable company job so he, his wife, their two sons and a teenager named Kelly Goble could round up his sheep. "I'd just gotten back from selling the lambs when Felix stopped by to tell us about the Bandit," said Luce.[799]

It was August 5, 1966 when Harrison told them, "You know he'll be here at Pumpville soon."[800]

Luce had real concerns about the man who shot Bradford and Cooksey. He'd called Val Verde County Sheriff Herman Richter several times and told him they needed to catch the guy before he killed somebody. Deputy Calvin Wallen had driven through the area occasionally and Deputy Jim Boatright had even stayed in the store several times, but neither ever caught sight of, much less caught the Bandit.[801]

Harrison's warning caused Luce to make sure that his two rifles were loaded. One was an octagon-barreled Winchester rifle that his grandfather had given him when he was just a child. The other was a Winchester saddle-gun that he'd bought for himself when he was about 12. Both rifles were lever action 30:30 caliber firearms with open sights. Luce kept the octagon-barreled rifle in his room and gave the other to

Goble. Luce and his wranglers had had a long hot day, a day when the temperature had risen to just one degree shy of the century mark, so it was not too long after dark that they settled in for what they hoped would be a good night's sleep. And it was—until Shirley looked out the front bedroom window.[802]

"Ted, wake up! The guys behind the store, he's out there!" Shirley Luce said as she shook her husband about 11:30 p.m. that night.[803]

A guard light had been installed after the Bradford shooting and those in the Hamilton house could clearly see the back of the Pumpville store. "The Bandit was moving slowly across the back wall of the store, from right to left with what appeared to be a lever action rifle in his left hand. He appeared to be pushing on the store wall, or balancing himself against it, with the other. He wasn't 50 yards away," said Ted Luce.[804]

Everyone in the house was awake now. Teenager Kelly Goble wanted to shoot the guy but Luce and crew were all pretty scared—they knew the guy had already shot Pelham Bradford and Sheriff Cooksey. "If I'd have had a scoped rifle I might have done something but I was afraid the guy would shoot back at us and the walls of the old Hamilton place were paper thin," said Luce.[805]

All of a sudden the door to the trailer house flew open and Ella Ruth and her sister came out and started walking over to the back of the store. When Luce looked back toward where the Bandit had been, he was now out of sight.[806]

Luce went outside, yelling, "Get out of there, get out of there!" as he saw the two women talking near the back door. He would later learn that the sister, Billie, had thought she'd heard something inside the store.[807]

Ella Ruth was just opening the door and they hadn't heard his warning probably because of a strong wind that had the Hamilton house creaking and groaning that night. Boom! Luce fired a round off up into the air to get the women's attention. As the women hurried back to the trailer and as Luce got to the trailer side of the store, a piece of tin popped up on the roof. "I just knew I was shot. I was scared to death," said Luce.[808]

An armed John Bradford came out of the trailer. Luce yelled that the Bandit had been behind the store. They went around different ways and met up at the front. It wasn't until later that they realized that the guy probably slipped out the back while they were up front.[809]

The men called the Val Verde County Sheriff Herman Richter and Terrell County Deputy Dalton Hogg.[810] Of course, Pumpville lies in Val Verde County, but Sanderson in Terrell County, where Sheriff Cooksey and Hogg lived, was less than half the distance away. The lawmen also had a vested interest in catching the guy even if they didn't have any normal jurisdiction in Val Verde County.

Luce was at wits end by about 2 a.m. He hadn't seen any headlights on the horizon and he knew that he and the others would not sleep that night. Then he remembered that Texas Ranger Alfred Allee Jr. had been transferred to Ozona.[811]

Ted Luce had met the Ranger one afternoon while he drove through a Del Rio neighborhood. The Ranger was in a tussle with a guy beside an open car door. Luce had stopped to see if he could help. Allee handcuffed the one guy and told Luce to hang onto him, while he disappeared inside a house and finally came back with another man.[812]

Luce used the phone to call the Ranger in Ozona. He told him he needed his help but didn't know if he would show up because the Ranger said that Pumpville was out of his territory. Yet a few hours later Alfred Allee Jr. was drinking coffee and eating breakfast in the kitchen of the Hamilton ranch house. "I gave him hell about the deputies not catching the guy already. I told him that sooner or later the guy was going to kill somebody," said Luce.[813]

News of the incident had quickly spread across the area phone lines. By daylight law enforcement officers from both counties, highway patrolmen, Border Patrol agents and ranchers, ranchers who'd brought saddled horses for the lawmen and for themselves, were gathering outside the Pumpville store. Even the railroad detective, H.P. Boyd, was there and a Border Patrol pilot had one of their planes up in the air.[814]

At some point that morning, while Ted Luce and Felix Harrison leaned against Luce's old Dodge pickup talking to Dalton Hogg, Harrison blurted out, "You can't catch the Mexican from behind—you have to get in front of him."[815]

Ranger Allee, who was standing nearby, walked over and asked Harrison, "What did you say?" He listened while Harrison repeated himself, then turned away and walked over to talk to Sheriff Cooksey.[816]

The law enforcement officers did not find their quarry that day, but when they left Pumpville—they had an idea, they had a plan, a plan to bring the culprit to justice.[817]

The basic plan was simple; just stake out Dryden and Pumpville and wait until the guy returns and arrest him. The officers knew that the Bandit was armed, smart and had evaded them many times before. They knew it wouldn't be like in the movies, but they knew he did seem to move back and forth between those places...[818]

Sheriff Cooksey, Deputy Hogg and Ranger Allee knew that most of the things they'd found in the camps around Dryden had come out of Joe's Chevron Station. The best observation point that was close enough for the officers to see the front of the store from, to conceal themselves in and yet close enough to make an arrest from, was the deserted Purple Sage Café that was just across Highway 90 from the station. The men measured the distance from the café to the station.[819]

Over a period of time, Dalton Hogg took an array of shotguns out to the shooting range, a range that he, Border Patrolman Ken Epperson and others had built outside of Sanderson. The deputy patterned each gun to see what kind of impact they would have at the distance between the café and the station. He shot them into paper and studied the tightness and number of pellets with different shells.[820] In the final analysis it was Lewis Cash's Model 12 16-gauge Winchester, a hammerless pump shotgun and #3 buckshot shells that held the tightest pattern.[821]

The length of the shotgun's barrel is unknown but, according to the book, The Winchester Model Twelve, 1 of 1000 by George Madis, copyright 1982, the gun was produced in 26, 28 and 30 inch barrels with modified or full chokes. The gun held five shells in the magazine and the shells ejected out the right side.[822] Whatever the barrel length, it was Cash's gun that kept the tightest pattern at the distance across the highway right-of-way. However the gun was not their only concern.

Joe Vasquez had been having so many burglaries, losing so much inventory that he was in the process of changing the locks on the place. "But Sheriff Cooksey asked him not to, he asked him to put everything back like it was, that he'd take care of anything that was torn up," said stepson E.A. 'Junior' Rogers. Vasquez agreed to cooperate with their plan.[823]

The stakeout at Dryden could have started a few days earlier, but Bill Cooksey wanted to be there for the first night's surveillance and he had to take his daughter Billie Kay to San Angelo for eye surgery first. "Dr. Lamb operated on her at the old Clinic Hospital that was located on Beauregard Street. She had lazy eye," said Candace Cooksey Fulton.[824]

So when the Sheriff returned on August 19, 1966, Ranger Sergeant John Wood, Rangers Bud Newberry and Alfred Allee Jr. met with Cooksey and Dalton Hogg to discuss a permanent schedule of who would work the Dryden stakeout. The Sheriff was ready to get started so he and Texas Ranger Alfred Allee Jr. took their turn that very night.[825]

Temperatures were somewhat mild that day, having risen to only 94 degrees during the hottest part of the day, though they would fall into the low 70s by midnight. Of course the dust was back in the air after only a smidgen of rain fell on the 15th.[826] A slice of moon, what is known as a waxing crescent moon with only about 15% of it showing in the sky, set low and descending[827] as Lewis Cash left his café and drove out toward the airport in his pickup.[828]

Sheriff Cooksey and Ranger Allee were at the airport waiting for the ride that would take them to their hiding place. They were well aware that Hernandez probably watched a place for a good while before he broke into it. It wasn't long before they were hidden in the back of Cash's pickup and headed back to town.[829]

The lights were on at Cash's Cactus Café as he drove back down the highway beside it. A few customers' cars were parked outside. Across the street there were cars parked in front of Amelia Gallegos' Do Drop Inn. Just past the intersection at 349, the Dryden Mercantile was closed but Joe's Chevron, on the left, was brightly lit and open for business. Jodie, the Spanish goat that Joe Vasquez kept around for amusement, a goat that could drink and eat with the best of them, was milling around outside. Cash turned right and drove behind the closed and deserted Purple Sage Café that was across the highway.[830]

The officers slipped out of the pickup bed and made their way into the deserted café through a pair of French doors that led previous customers out the east side of the small building. By the time that Sheriff Cooksey took up a position near the front door that led out toward Highway 90 and Joe's Chevron, Lewis Cash was well on his way back to his own cafe. Ranger Allee settled in and watched through a broken glass wood framed window, one of two that let former customers look out toward the highway. Both officers were well armed.[831]

Each officer wore a holstered Smith and Wesson .357 caliber revolver. Sheriff Cooksey had Cash's Model 12 Winchester pump shotgun and Ranger Allee had his department issued 30:30 Winchester-carbine, and they had all the amenities they might need for a night's stay in the small building.[832]

The officers watched as cars drove up and down the highway, with a few occasionally stopping at Joe's for gas or other incidentals. Then they watched as Joe turned the lights off and closed the station. It was about 10 p.m., just after the moon had completely disappeared on the western horizon[833] that they watched as Joe and Jodie left and headed for the house that was up on the hill. They watched as Archie Stewart walked over to Jimmy Merritt's former house.[834]

Merritt had moved away after he and his wife had divorced. Archie and Jean Stewart, both in their 50s, had recently moved from Corpus Christi and moved into Merritt's house directly beside and west of the garage and the station. Jean was Iva Lee's sister and Joe's sister-in-law. Archie, the brother-in-law was helping Joe with the station.[835] It wasn't too long before their lights were out and everything was pretty dark around Joe's Chevron.

The officers' eyes adjusted to the darkness, then readjusted each time a car with bright headlights came down the highway, but it wasn't long before there wasn't much traffic along Highway 90.[836]

The officers could see Joe's garage next to where Archie Stewart lived. Right beside it, just a short distance to the east, they could see Joe's Chevron station and store. They could see the door that led into a parts room on the west side of the building; they knew this entrance would lead someone to another door that led into the store and grill-part of the business. They could see the front of the station and the front door underneath the canopy.[837]

The combination of a small light that was on inside the building and a good-sized front window gave the officers a little visibility to anything that might occur inside the place. Outside, a carport came off the building toward the highway. The gas pump island was underneath along with a metal-framed squeegee ringer that stood about six-feet high.

An icebox, with the letters I-C-E in big blue letters, was just east of the station's main door. The officers used binoculars to enhance their eyesight, to search for any hint that someone might be poking around the station that night. It was around midnight when Cooksey picked up some movement.[838]

The Sheriff realized that what he saw was a man's arm moving as he walked around the east side of the store and across the front. "The guy just strided up there like the wind blew him in," said Allee.[839]

The officers watched as Hernandez stopped at the door at the front of the parts room. He wasn't there except for just a second, then disappeared inside. Then they could see him inside the main building taking merchandise off the shelves in the store. Sheriff Cooksey went out the front door of the old café and started toward Joe's Chevron while Ranger Allee went out the French doors. This put the Ranger off to the right side of the Sheriff.[840]

As Allee wrote later in a report to Colonel Homer Garrison, Jr., the Director of the Texas Department of Public Safety, 'As we started to approach Joe's place, this subject came out of the café (store/café/station) about 12:15 a.m. At this time Sheriff Cooksey and myself, both in English (Cooksey) and Spanish (Allee) shouted at the subject. I told him I was a Ranger, to put up his hands and give up, at which time he opened fire on us.'[841]

One shot apparently just missed the Sheriff as it hit above the doorframe of the Purple Sage Café.[842] Another hit the ground about five feet to the right of the Ranger.[843] The officers returned fire, (Cooksey using the shotgun and Allee the carbine) and Hernandez immediately fell to the ground, but then he got back up and returned fire[844] as he yelled Gringo this and Gringo that toward the officers.[845] "I shot several times and missed him every time, but Bill was hitting him with that shotgun," said Allee.[846]

The guy fell down again but then got back up again. As Ross McSwain reported in the San Angelo Standard-Times, "He came out the front door, went down one side of the building, across the back and up the other side of the station," said Cooksey. "He emptied his pistol at us."[847]

The newspaper story included, 'Cooksey, armed with a shotgun, fired five times at the man. He then shot at him three times with his revolver. Allee fired three times with a 30-30 carbine. He said 17 shots were fired in less than a minute.'[848]

The investigation would reveal that 17 shots were fired that night. Hernandez fired six shots out of a Model 10 Military and Police style 38-caliber 5-inch barreled Smith and Wesson revolver. The officers had fired eleven times, but it was the last shot that ultimately put their quarry down.[849]

The gunfight had seen Hernandez fall and move several times and he was finally in front of the main part of the station. As he rose up from behind the squeegee ringer, he became a silhouette that was brought about by the light inside the station and the glass window that was behind him. Alfred Allee Jr. got a bead on the man and pulled the trigger, "The guy screamed like an animal, then whirled and ran around toward the back of the station, around the east side of the building," said Allee.[850]

"You okay Bill?" Allee hollered to the Sheriff.[851]

The Sheriff hollered back, "Yea, I'm okay."[852]

Another Bill, Bill Ten Eyck who was standing outside his own house, above and behind them, hollered back, "Yea, I'm okay."[853]

Paula Ten Eyck would later say she heard a splat, a thud as one of the Bandit's bullets went high and hit their house. "I still remember the sound of it. Everybody in the house was suddenly awake and mother yelled for us to stay away from the windows," said Jess Ten Eyck.[854]

The truth was that the shooting caused the whole little town to come awake. The lights came on in the Stewart's house, and everyone but the McElhaney's who lived north of the railroad tracks knew it was gunshots. "I heard the rat-tat-tat and just thought Joe was fixing somebody's flat tire, hitting the rim with a hammer," said Adrienne McElhaney.[855]

(Adrienne would tell Sheriff Cooksey a few weeks later, after Hernandez's picture was in the newspaper, that it was the same man who approached her when she taking clothes off the clothesline in her backyard.)[856]

Sheriff Cooksey and the Ranger slipped through the darkness and headed for the east side of the gas station. The Ranger put down his carbine, pulled his Model 19 Smith and Wesson .357-magnum revolver and turned on a flashlight that he held out away from his body. "I didn't want to make it easy for the guy (to see us)," said Allee.

Then as the officers started to move down the east side of the building, they heard someone yell, "He's over here!"[857]

Archie Stewart, the blonde-headed former oilfield toolpusher who stood just under six-feet and sported a belly that might make you think he drank a beer on occasion, wearing khaki clothes and a baseball cap and holding a flashlight, was standing away but not too far away from a stock trailer near the northwest corner of the service station. A pretty dark-headed woman, who wasn't much shorter than Archie, stood behind him. It was his wife Jean.[858]

Alfredo Hernandez was lying behind the stock trailer. He was covered in blood, blood mixed with chili and beans. (A similar mixture was on the walls of the front of the station and everyplace where the man moved during and after the shooting.)[859] The man had been lucky on several counts.

First, the Ranger's bullet had hit the frame of the squeegee ringer before it hit his jaw or the wound would have surely been fatal.[860] Secondly, his morral, his burlap knapsack was full of canned food, food that stopped most of the pellets from the Sheriff's shotgun. It had become a bulletproof vest of sorts.[861]

As the Sheriff and the Ranger approached they saw the small man writhing in agony, lying there covered in the result of the last few minutes. They saw George Adams binoculars around the man's neck, the same binoculars that Benny Ray Ross had once been accused of taking.[862] Then something came over Bill Cooksey.[863]

Bill Cooksey would tell D'Wayne Jernigan 6 years later, "You know I just couldn't wait to find and kill that SOB, I wanted him so bad. But when we shot him and he ran out back, when I got to him and leaned over him, all of a sudden something came over me—and I didn't want to kill him anymore. I forgave him."[864]

Bill Ten Eyck arrived at the scene and others started to gather as the officers moved the man out in front of the mechanic/tire shed part of Joe's business. Joe turned on the lights and lit the place up like they were open for business.[865] And Bill Cooksey used the telephone.

Dalton Hogg took the call. "They got him, they got the Bandit!" he told his wife Henry Beth after he hung up. She'd never seen her husband dress so fast as he got ready to take the ambulance to Dryden. He also called Roy Deaton who was fluent in Spanish and asked him to meet him there.[866]

Hernandez had fired all six cartridges from his .38 caliber revolver. He had one unspent round in his shirt pocket, a round that had been hit by a shotgun pellet that would later be identified as a W.J. Vaughan reload that was part of a coffee can full stolen years before, reloads that were thought to be used to shoot Bradford and Cooksey.[867]

The Ranger also found Bill Cooksey's wallet on the man. The wallet contained two addresses on small slips of paper and photographs of two women. He also found a small piece of tin in the morral. It was bent in such a way that the officers figured the guy used it to jimmy his way through locked doors.[868] The officers also found out why Bill Cooksey had not seen a gun on the man the day he was shot. Hernandez had a holster tied underneath his left arm. The black hat he was wearing, a straw hat he'd apparently painted, had a bullet hole right through the crown.[869]

It was about then when a gold-colored 4 door Chevrolet Biscayne drove right up to within 15 feet of Hernandez and the crowd. Bill Ten Eyck's wife was behind the steering wheel and their four kids were hanging out the windows. "What are you doing woman, get back, back up," Bill Ten Eyck told his wife who was trying to get a look at the man on the ground.[870]

"We saw the guy sprawled out there, he was moving around, writhing around, he kept twisting. His morral was lying there too. He looked so small, so different than what I had envisioned," said Jess Ten Eyck.[871]

Then another car carrying California license plates drove up into the station. Apparently the driver and his family thought it was open so they could get gas.[872] Instead they saw several armed people, a Sheriff and a Texas Ranger and the bad guy lying on the ground. West Texas—just like they had seen in the movies, something their family probably still talks about today.

Dalton Hogg and Roy Deaton, who'd brought along his son Roy 'Hoot' Deaton, arrived at about the same time. Amelia Gallegos, who was now part of the crowd, said to Dalton, "I didn't see them search him." So the deputy searched Hernandez again. He found a pocketknife in one of his pockets before they loaded him on the stretcher and put him in the ambulance. As they got into the station wagon, Dalton said to Roy Deaton and his son, "Well, I'm taking him over the same road as I took Cooksey, but just not as fast."[873]

As the ambulance left the scene, Bill Cooksey used the phone again to call Ross McSwain, his friend and reporter from the San Angelo Standard-Times. "He told me that A.Y. Allee Jr. had shot that boy and I ended up winning a writing award for the story (I wrote)," said McSwain.[874]

Sheriff Cooksey and Ranger Allee left Joe's Chevron and headed toward the hospital in Del Rio. They would learn later that the night's events had done a little damage to the service station. Their bullets had traveled through the walls and windows of the building and had entered the soda pop box and seven car batteries. One had even entered the lay-down freezer that Hernandez had stolen so much frozen meat out of. The bullet that entered the freezer was wedged inside between a few packages of meat.[875] The officers would also find that the man had dropped a sock full of bullets outside, in the back of the station, probably as he ran after being shot in the jaw.[876]

Medical personnel were working to stabilize Hernandez's vital signs when the Sheriff and the Ranger arrived at the hospital. Their suspect had been given a blood transfusion and would have died without medical treatment. As Texas Ranger A.Y. Allee Jr. wrote in his report, "We learned he had been shot once near the knee, once in the lower abdomen, once in the left side and once in the jaw. The doctor advised this subject needed to go to San Antonio for treatment…. Subject wrote on a piece of paper that his name was Alfredo Hernandez from San Luis Potosi, Mexico. Sheriff Cooksey and witnesses identified him as being the same one that shot Cooksey."[877]

It wasn't quite daylight when Sheriff Cooksey and Ranger Allee stepped outside the hospital doors and looked out toward a new day that was breaking on the horizon. They knew that Dalton Hogg would soon load the man back into the ambulance and take him to the Santa Rosa Hospital in San Antonio. They knew that except for the follow-up investigation that their pursuit of the Caveman Bandit was over.[878]

As the first rays of sunlight filtered into the eastern sky, the Ranger turned toward the Sheriff and said, "You know Bill, we've had hundreds of people out there looking for this guy and we didn't find him; but if this had been a hundred years ago, my grandfather (also a Texas Ranger) would have just saddled his horse, put his rifle in its scabbard and ridden off after him. And he would have brought him back."[879]

THE EPILOGUE

The arrest of Alfredo Hernandez led DPS fingerprint expert Billy R. Wier to a copy of the man's fingerprints that were already on file with his Texas Department of Public Safety. Within six days he'd already matched three of the man's prints to those found from three different crime scenes. Letters were prepared and mailed to the appropriate law enforcement agencies.[880]

Hernandez's fingerprints were found on a chili can label that was in a cave near Pumpville.[881] It was the same cave that contained stolen property from the robbery of the Post Office. Another fingerprint was obtained from a Dr. Pepper can that was found in the hidden-camp near Dryden,[882] and the last was found on a 6-volt, dry cell flashlight battery that Deputy Dalton Hogg found in the cave where Bill Cooksey was shot.[883]

Deputy Hogg had also submitted hair samples to the lab at the Texas Department of Public Safety. C.H. Beardsley, Supervisor of the Chemistry Section reported back on August 24, 1966, 'The examination has been completed and we wish to report that the hair is of human origin.'[884]

A few weeks later, on September 6, 1966, Joel Tisdale, Chief of the Texas Department of Public Safety Identification and Records Division, reported in a letter that the .38 caliber Smith and Wesson revolver (recovered from Alfredo Hernandez at Dryden), after examination by Fred R. Rymer from the firearms section, was, in their opinion, the same gun used in case number L-85372.[885] This writer presumes that the gun was matched to the Pelham Bradford shooting based on the following facts.[886]

The case number for the Cooksey shooting was L-88624[887] and the case number for the Hernandez arrest was L-88734.[888] The Bradford shooting was months before the Cooksey shooting, in another jurisdiction and the letter to Cooksey was carbon copied to Val Verde County Sheriff Herman Richter. Richter had jurisdiction in the Pelham Bradford shooting at Pumpville.

Rymer had also started a trace of ownership on the .38 caliber Military and Police model 10 Smith and Wesson revolver with serial number 96877.[889] A letter dated September 15, 1966 revealed that the gun was shipped from the factory to the Straus-Frank Company in San Antonio on December 31, 1947.[890] It was finally traced to the O.P. Couch Gun Shop in Kerrville, a business that had been closed for some time.[891]

One fact that ties the gun to both crimes is a memo sent from Sheriff Bill Cooksey to Kerr County Sheriff Leon F. Maples on October 17, 1966. In it he states, 'the gun in question was used to shoot me in November 1965 and used to shoot Pelham Bradford in July of 1965."[892] There is no direct evidence as to where Alfredo Hernandez came into possession of it.

Alfredo Amador Hernandez tried to escape while he was in the Santa Rosa Hospital.[893] Can you imagine the guy running down the hall in one of those open-back gowns and all those hoses hanging off of his body,[894] and just imagine his thoughts when he came to a window and realized that he was up several floors off the ground. He was subdued, but thereafter law enforcement officers from either Terrell or Uvalde Counties took their turn standing guard.[895] Terrell County had a $6,000 medical bill by the time he was returned to the Val Verde County jail.[896]

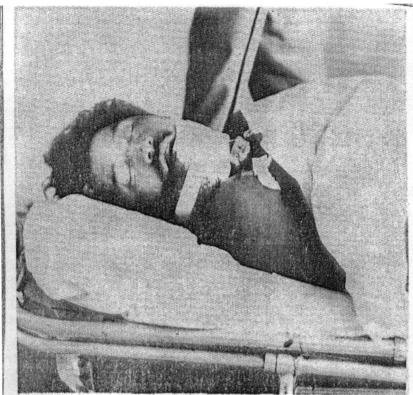

GUN BATTLE VICTIM — Alfredo Hernandez, 35-year-old Mexican alien wounded in a gun battle with a sheriff and Texas Ranger in Dryden in West Texas, is wheeled into Santa Rosa Hospital early Saturday. He remained in critical condition late Saturday.—Staff Photo by Joe Davenport.

Man Wounded
In Gun Battle

Sunday August 21, 1966 San Antonio Express and News photograph by photographer Joe Davenport. Copyright 1966 San Antonio Express-News. Reprinted with permission.

Terrell County Sheriff Bill Cooksey asked Customs agent Cliff Wilson to interview Hernandez when he was placed back in the Val Verde County Jail. He interviewed him in the jail-annex building with

Chief Deputy Calvin Wallen (Wilson's uncle), Bill Cooksey and others in the room. "I just remember him sitting there staring at the wall with this blank expression. When he did talk he only talked in general terms, not giving me anything until I talked about family and religion," said Wilson.[897]

Wilson felt Hernandez wasn't very educated and had possibly been belittled as a child. He told the officers that he had used the trains as transportation for years but that now they were much faster and hard to jump onto. Finally, he did confess to the Happy Hollow and Pumpville crimes and said he shot Bill Cooksey because he was scared he would be arrested. "And he did tell us about several caves that he had things hidden in, but he didn't see the country as we did and didn't know how to tell us where they were," said Wilson.[898]

As the interview wound down, Wilson saw tears come to the man's eyes when he asked him if there was anything that he wanted to get off his chest, something he wanted to tell them or a priest. The officers felt that he may have done something really bad in the past but Hernandez never said anything else.[899]

A few weeks later, the man known as the Caveman Bandit was escorted into Terrell County's Chihuahuan Desert in an attempt to recover some stolen property. He led the officers to a few hidden camps but nothing of importance was located, other than a few school photographs of local girls. At some point that day he did tell two assisting Acuna, Mexico police officers that he would return someday and take care of them and everyone else who had anything to do with putting him in jail.[900]

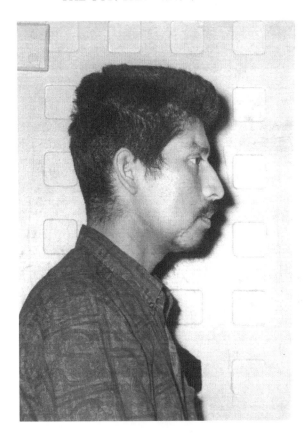

Photograph of Hernandez after he was returned to jail from hospital. Note the scar on his lower right jaw-line. Photo courtesy of Candace Cooksey Fulton.

It was around this same time that Border Patrol agent Glenn Weatherman and Chief of Police Vela from Acuna, Mexico went to Monterrey to interview Rosa, the registered prostitute whose home address and photograph were in Cooksey's stolen wallet when the man was arrested. "She was not what I would have expected. She was about 25, attractive with long dark hair. She said she hadn't seen Hernandez in about a year but we felt that they had much more than a casual relationship," said Weatherman.[901]

Rosa, whose last name was not used for privacy reasons, told the officers that Hernandez sent her money. As Weatherman wrote in his report, 'She stated the subject did not appear to be mentally deranged, that he did not use drugs or smoke marijuana. She said that, at times, he sent her money or left money with her to be sent to his mother, and she produced an envelope with the name (of his mother and her address).' The other address in the wallet belonged to a doctor who told the officers that he had treated the man about two years before for sexually transmitted diseases.[902]

Weatherman attempted to identify the second woman from the other picture in the wallet, even went to El Paso and other places along the border, but he was unsuccessful.[903]

Alfredo Amador Hernandez was indicted by a Terrell County Grand Jury in September 1966 for assault with intent to commit murder in the shooting of Sheriff Bill Cooksey.[904] He was re-indicted in October for Robbery by Assault in the shooting of Bill Cooksey.[905] He was indicted for the burglary of Joe Vasquez's house,[906] probably because the second photograph in Cooksey's wallet was Elaine Rogers' 8th grade school photo. "I was already married and gone by July 1965 and the guy must have taken the photograph when he stole food out of the house. Sheriff Cooksey gave the photo back to me after the guy went to prison," said Elaine Rogers O'Donnell.[907]

Worn 1963 photograph of Elaine Rogers that Sheriff Cooksey returned to her after Hernandez was sent to prison. This was the second photograph that Glenn Weatherman was not able to identify. Photo courtesy of Elaine Rogers O'Donnell.

There were two other Terrell County indictments. The first was the burglary of the home of Mrs. Ray Brotherton[908] and the other was for the burglary of George Adams' house.[909] He was indicted in Uvalde County for felony theft from the A.V. Rutherford home.[910] Bail was set at $2000 for each burglary by presiding Judge John F. Sutton. He denied bail in the robbery by assault case.[911]

On the 29th day of November 1966, Texas State District Judge John Sutton signed an order changing the venue of the Terrell County cases to Val Verde County.[912] He had also assigned Del Rio attorney Arturo C. Gonzalez to represent Alfredo Hernandez.[913]

During an interview on August 6, 2004, attorney Arturo C. Gonzalez said he did not remember representing the defendant,[914] however a search of the Val Verde County District Court records revealed he was paid $100 to represent the defendant.[915]

On January 27, 1967, Alfredo Amador Hernandez pled guilty and was sentenced to a charge of robbery by the use of a firearm. The order said he should be confined in the Texas Department of Corrections for a minimum of five years to a maximum of ninety-nine years. The court order was assessed and signed by District Judge Ray Thurmond. The other charges were dismissed against the man who ultimately would become somewhat of a legendary figure around Terrell County.[916]

Legends have a tendency to grow and change with time. This writer spent more than two years trying to get this story right. A few discrepancies were found in news reporting and in one statement, but it was truly amazing how the stories that Ben Ross and Alfredo Gallegos told, 39 years after the shooting of Bill Cooksey, were nearly identical accounts of what happened that day at that cave. Yet for those of us who were not there, the legend grows every time the story is told.

An example surfaced in August 2004 when I spent a week in Terrell County. I met and interviewed many wonderful and interesting people there. One person, in recounting the story about the night Hernandez was captured, said, "Deputy Dalton Hogg was just up the highway hiding in the brush the night the Bandit was caught."[917] Of course, Dalton Hogg was home in bed and he took the call and drove the ambulance to Dryden. And such it is with legends....

Dalton Hogg became the Terrell County Sheriff after Bill Cooksey resigned to pursue a teaching career. Copyright San Angelo Standard-Times, San Angelo, Texas. Reprinted with permission.

Sheriff Bill Cooksey and Texas Ranger Alfred Allee Jr. pose with their reward checks from the United States Post Office Department. Copyright photos from San Angelo Standard-Times, San Angelo, Texas. Reprinted with permission.

Sheriff Bill Cooksey and Texas Ranger Alfred Allee Jr. each received a $200 reward from the United States Post Office Department for the arrest of the man who shot the Postmaster at Pumpville.[918] A letter sent from the Texas Department of Corrections to Sheriff Cooksey showed that Hernandez's minimum release date from prison was June 22, 2026,[919] but Alfredo Hernandez came up for parole in 1977.

Although Bill Cooksey had resigned his position as Terrell County Sheriff by the time Hernanez came up for parole that year, he wrote a letter to then Texas Governor Dolph Briscoe stating, 'I must plead, however, for the hundreds of ranch families that live in the most isolated part of our State, located on the Mexican border, between Uvalde and Sanderson. Prior to this man's capture, these people lived in a state of constant fear for their families. If Mr. Hernandez were paroled and deported, deportation would be merely a formality to him. There is no doubt in my mind, that with his vast knowledge of the River Country, he would be back in operation within a matter of weeks."[920]

Hernandez was not paroled in 1977, but on February 6, 1984, Alfredo Hernandez was given an OUT OF COUNTRY CONDITIONAL PARDON by then Governor Mark White.[921] This recommendation came from the Texas Board of Pardons and Parole who credited Hernandez with forty years and six months on a ninety-nine year sentence.[922] He'd spent 17 years in prison.

This type of conditional pardon was common in cases where the defendant was not a United States citizen; otherwise he would have been paroled.[923] Hernandez was released into the custody of the United States Immigration Service and deported back into Mexico through Brownsville, Texas on December 06, 1984.[924]

This was about the same time that Jess Ten Eyck, who was now a grown man, was riding an ATV (all terrain vehicle) along a ridge south of Dryden. It was there that he noticed a good-sized rock sitting a little cockeyed in that part of the Chihuahuan Desert. He stopped and moved it. And he found a small cave...Inside the small cavern he found a few jars and a coffee can half full of .38 caliber cartridges. Were these the bullets that were taken out of W.J. Vaughan's house many years before? Most probably, but we'll never know for sure because they were sold a short time later in a garage sale.[925]

A few years later, in what was reportedly 1986, local residents were plenty spooked after a reported sighting of Hernandez near Dryden. A Texas Highway Department road crew identified the man from a prison release photograph after he'd approached them while they performed highway repairs. Residents were concerned that the man had returned to make good his threat. But the man, to date, has never been seen again. "No one seems to know whatever became of him. I guess he just rode off into the sunset...at least we hope he did," said J.D. Hogg.[926]

Of course, there are unconfirmed, unsubstantiated rumors that the man met a violent death either in the United States or in Mexico.[927] But this writer was unable to turn up any evidence that he is living or dead, though with my meager resources I did try to find him in Mexico, but to no avail.[928]

This writer first heard about Alfredo Hernandez when Bill Cooksey told a group of Odessa College law enforcement students, "I'd suggest you carry your off-duty gun where you carry your duty weapon, because someday you may suddenly need it, reach for it and it may not be there." Of course, those words, spoken by the former Terrell County Sheriff, inspired the title "The Gun That Wasn't There."[929]

It was a recruiting trip for the San Angelo Police Department that put me in the right place at the right time to learn about the Caveman Bandit. The year was 1989 and Cooksey was then the Department Chairman of Law Enforcement and Fire Technology at Odessa College.[930]

Bill and Bernice Cooksey were interviewed in their home in January 1990. At the end of a full day, Bill gave me his case file and said he had one request, "The book should not be about me; it should be about the Bandit and those special people who live in Terrell County."[931]

In April 1995, Bill Cooksey was airlifted from Brownwood to the Shannon Hospital in San Angelo. He had suffered a broken neck in a car wreck and was being treated by Dr. James R. Mull. The doctor asked him to move his leg but Cooksey said, "I can't move that leg. I got shot in 65." Dr. Mull stiffened and asked, "Hunting accident?" Cooksey said, "Yeah, I was hunting a man and he found me."[932]

Alfredo Hernandez, the man who shot Bill Cooksey, caused the Sheriff to limp for the rest of his life. Even though I never heard Cooksey complain about any pain or discomfort, I know it was there.[933] And as he told Ray Fitzgerald many years before, "You know, you just don't get over those gunshot wounds in real life—like they do on television."[934]

TRADE MARK—Terrell County Sheriff Bill Cooksey displays a mask used by a suspect who terrorized the Dryden area for more than a year with his daring burglaries. Cooksey said several of the masks were found which were all made in an identical manner. (Staff Photos)

MANHUNT---

Terrell County Sheriff Bill Cooksey. Copyright 1966 Odessa American, Odessa, Texas. Reprinted with permission.

SPECIAL NOTE TO LAW ENFORCEMENT OFFICERS

I'd like to think that Bill Cooksey was watching over my shoulder as I interviewed people, talked on the phone, researched the records and typed on the keyboard. This lawman and educator was a man I came to greatly respect and admire. I wish he could have read "The Gun That Wasn't There."

If there is a message that came out of our friendship, it was the words that he expressed over and over to anyone about to enter a law enforcement career, " Police officers should be both morally and ethically a cut above the norm; they should treat people as they would want to be treated; and, officers should wear their off-duty-gun where they carry their duty weapon, or, otherwise, they might reach for it someday and it might not be there."

ABOUT THE AUTHOR

Russell Smith was born in Uvalde, Texas to parents Dick and June Smith. He started writing poems and short stories long before he graduated from high school in 1969. He attended Southwest Texas Junior College, Howard College and Angelo State University; the majority of his classes dealt with criminal justice.

His law enforcement career began as a reserve deputy with the Tom Green County Sheriff's Department in 1977 and ended when he retired as the San Angelo Texas Police Chief in 1999. This experience spurred his professional writing career when he sold his first article to a police trade magazine in 1980.

Russell spent five years as an outdoor columnist for the San Angelo Standard-Times and several magazines. He received numerous awards for his writing and photography from the Texas Outdoor Writers' Association. He continues to do research for non-fiction books from his home in San Angelo where he and his wife reside.

ENDNOTES

[1] Bill Cooksey, former Terrell County Sheriff, interview by Russell Smith, January 6, 1990, Odessa, Texas; Alfred Allee Jr., retired Texas Ranger, interview by Russell Smith, February 4, 2004, Alpine, Texas; Odell 'Pinky' Carruthers, interview by Russell Smith, August 4, 2004, Sanderson, Texas.

[2] Bill Cooksey, former Terrell County Sheriff, interview by Russell Smith, January 6, 1990, Odessa, Texas.

[3] Uvalde Leader News, June 7, 1962; November 29, 1962; March 7, 1963; December 12, 1963; February 27, 1964; March 1, 1964; March 8, 1964.

[4] Del Rio News-Herald, July 12, 1965; November 5, 1965; November 7, 1965; November 14, 1965; undated August 1966.

[5] Sanderson Times, January 15, 1965; February 19, 1965; July 16, 1965; August 20, 1965; November 12, 1965; November 25, 1965; April 21, 1966; July 21, 1966; August 11, 1966; August 25, 1966; September 15, 1966; September 29, 1966; November 3, 1966; September 14, 1967.

[6] Odessa American, November 11, 1965; August 21, 1966; September 11, 1966.

[7] Corpus Christi Caller-Times, November 6, 1965.

[8] San Angelo Standard-Times, July 12, 1965; November 5, 1965; November 6, 1965; November 8, 1965; November 11, 1965; November 19, 1965; December 12, 1965; August 6, 1966; August 21, 1966; August 23, 1966.

[9] San Antonio Express-News, November 19, 1965; August 21, 1966.

[10] Daisy Diaz-Alemany, PhD, LPC, suggested title, Austin, Texas.

[11] Russell Smith, perception after all research, knowledge from career in law enforcement.

[12] Bill Cooksey, former Terrell County Sheriff, and wife Bernice, interview by Russell Smith, tape recording, January 6, 1990, Odessa, Texas.

[13] Ibid.

[14] Ibid.

[15] Ibid.

Cliff Wilson, retired U.S. Customs Agent, interview by Russell Smith, July 10, 2004, Uvalde, Texas.

[16] Texas Department of Corrections, Bureau of Records and Identification Document, Huntsville, Texas.

[17] Bill Cooksey, former Terrell County Sheriff, and wife Bernice, interview by Russell Smith, tape recording, January 6, 1990, Odessa, Texas.

[18] Ibid

Cliff Wilson, retired U.S. Customs Agent, interview by Russell Smith, July 10, 2004, Uvalde, Texas.

[19] Wanda M. Hunt, Chief, Freedom of Information Act section, U.S. Department of Justice, Federal Bureau of Prisons, letter to Russell Smith, August 24, 2004.

[20] Bill Cooksey, former Terrell County Sheriff, interview by Russell Smith, tape recording, January 6, 1990, Odessa, Texas.

[21] Bill Cooksey, interview by Russell Smith, January 6, 1990, Odessa, Texas; Alfred Allee Jr., retired Texas Ranger, interview by Russell Smith, February 4, 2004, Alpine, Texas.

[22] E.A. 'Junior' Rogers, phone interview by Russell Smith, May 2005, Kermit, Texas.

[23] Bill Cooksey, former Terrell County Sheriff, interview by Russell Smith, January 6, 1990, Odessa, Texas; J.D. Hogg, email to Russell Smith, fall 2004, El Paso.

[24] Bill Cooksey, former Terrell County Sheriff, interview by Russell Smith, January 6, 1990, Odessa, Texas; Dalton Hogg, Terrell County Deputy, statement given to Texas Ranger J.S. Nance, undated in Cooksey's file on case.

[25] Greg Magers, interview by Russell Smith, September 2004, Concan, Texas; Willard VanPelt, phone interview by Russell Smith, September 2004, Concan, Texas.

[26] Alfredo Gallegos, interview by Russell Smith, June 2004, Uvalde, Texas.

[27] Marcella and Felix Harrison, interview by Russell Smith, June 2004, Eldorado, Texas; Billy R. Wier, Latent Fingerprint Expert, Texas Department of Public Safety, letter to Bill Cooksey, August 24, 1966.

[28] Bill Cooksey, former Terrell County Sheriff, interview by Russell Smith, January 6, 1990, Odessa, Texas; Sanderson Times, September 15, 1966.

[29] Ibid; Wanda Hunt, Chief, Freedom of Information section, U.S. Department of Justice, Federal Bureau of Prisons, August 24, 2004.

[30] Bill Cooksey, former Terrell County Sheriff, interview by Russell Smith, January 6, 1990, Odessa, Texas.

[31] Glenn Weatherman, retired U.S. Border Patrol Agent, Investigator, Immigration and Naturalization Service, letter to Bill Cooksey, September, 27, 1966.

[32] Ibid.

[33] Bill Cooksey, former Terrell County Sheriff, interview by Russell Smith, January 6, 1990, Odessa, Texas; Adrienne McElhaney, phone interview by Russell Smith, fall 2004, Iraan, Texas; J.D. Hogg, email to Russell Smith, fall 2004, El Paso, Texas; San Angelo Standard-Times, August 21, 1966.

[34] Bill Cooksey, former Terrell County Sheriff, interview by Russell Smith, January 6, 1990, Odessa, Texas.

[35] Joaquin Jackson, retired Texas Ranger, phone interview by Russell Smith, spring 2004, Alpine, Texas.

[36] Bill Cooksey, former Terrell County Sheriff, interview by Russell Smith, January 6, 1990, Odessa, Texas; Sanderson Times, September 15,1966.

[37] City of Uvalde, Texas website, www.uvaldetx.com.

[38] Russell Smith, author, common knowledge, grew up in Uvalde.

[39] Uvalde Leader News, June 7, 1962.

[40] Bill Cooksey, former Terrell County Sheriff, interview by Russell Smith, January 6, 1990, Odessa, Texas; Adrienne McElhaney, phone interview by Russell Smith, fall 2004, Iraan, Texas; J.D. Hogg, email to Russell Smith, fall 2004, El Paso, Texas.

[41] Ibid.

[42] Bill Cooksey, former Terrell County Sheriff, interview by Russell Smith, January 6, 1990, Odessa, Texas; Donna Smith, interview by Russell Smith, August 4, 2004, Sanderson, Texas; Marcella and Felix Harrison, interview by Russell Smith, June 2004, Eldorado, Texas; Kenneth Kelley, retired Uvalde County Sheriff, interview by Russell Smith, August 27, 2004, Uvalde, Texas; W.J. Vaughan, interview by Russell Smith, August 27, 2004, Batesville, Texas; Adrienne McElhaney, phone interview by Russell Smith, fall 2004, Iraan, Texas; Blain Chriesman, interview by Russell Smith, August 2, 2004, Sanderson Texas.

[43] Bill Cooksey, former Terrell County Sheriff, interview by Russell Smith, January 6, 1990, Odessa, Texas; Ben Ross, interview by Russell Smith, late February 2004, Ozona, Texas.

[44] Bill Cooksey, former Terrell County Sheriff, interview by Russell Smith, January 6, 1990, Odessa, Texas; San Angelo Standard-Times, August 21, 1966; Johnie and Hudson Hillis, interview by Russell Smith, August 27, 2004, Uvalde, Texas.

[45] Roy Deaton, interview by Russell Smith, August 2, 2004, Sanderson, Texas.

[46] Glenn Weatherman, retired United States Border Patrol, Imimigration and Naturlization Service Investigator, letter to Bill Cooksey, September 27, 1966.

[47] Ibid.

[48] Del Rio News-Herald, November 14, 1965.

[49] Ibid.

[50] Johnie and Hudson Hillis, interview by Russell Smith, August 27, 2004; Mrs. Ray Rutherford, phone interview by Russell Smith, August 27, 2004.

[51] Ibid.

[52] Ibid.

[53] Ibid.

[54] Ibid.

[55] Ibid.

[56] Texas Parks and Wildlife website, www.tpwd.state.tx.us/park/garner/

[57] Johnie and Hudson Hillis, interview by Russell Smith, August 27, 2004, Uvalde, Texas; Mrs. Ray Rutherford, interview by Russell Smith, August 27, 2004, Uvalde, Texas.

[58] Ibid.

[59] Ibid; Alfred Allee Jr., retired Texas Ranger, interview by Russell Smith, February 4, 2004, Alpine, Texas.

[60] Ibid; Uvalde Leader News, March 7, 1963.

[61] Johnie and Hudson Hillis, interview by Russell Smith, August 27, 2004, Uvalde, Texas; Mrs. Ray Rutherford, phone interviews by Russell Smith, August 27, 2004, October 18, 2004, January 8, 2006.

[62] Ibid.

[63] Uvalde Leader News, March 7, 1963.

[64] Johnie and Hudson Hillis, interview by Russell Smith, August 27, 2004, Uvalde, Texas; Mrs. Ray Rutherford, interview by Russell Smith, August 27, 2004, Uvalde, Texas; Greg Magers, interview by Russell Smith, September 2004, Concan, Texas; Willard VanPelt, phone interview by Russell Smith, September/October 2004.

[65] Greg Magers, interview by Russell Smith, September 2004, Concan, Texas.

[66] Don Emsley, email to Russell Smith, September 2, 2004; letter dated September 30, 2004, Ennis, Texas.

[67] Ibid.

[68] Beaumont 'Beau' Watkins, former Uvalde County Sheriff, phone interview by Russell Smith, fall 2004, Uvalde, Texas; Raymond Custer, retired Game Warden, Texas Parks and Wildlife, interview by Russell Smith, summer 2004, January 2006, San Angelo, Texas.

[69] Don Emsley, email to Russell Smith, September 2, 2004, letter to Russell Smith, September 30, 2004; photocopied photographs, September 30, 2004, Ennis, Texas.

[70] Ibid.

[71] Johnie and Hudson Hillis, interview by Russell Smith, August 27, 2004, Uvalde, Texas; Mrs. Ray Rutherford, phone interviews by Russell Smith, August 27, 2004.

[72] Ibid.

[73] Ibid; Brad Bradley, interview by Russell Smith, February 2004; J.D. Hogg, phone interview and email, fall 2004, El Paso, Texas.

[74] Johnie and Hudson Hillis, interview by Russell Smith, August 27, 2004, Uvalde, Texas.

[75] Greg Magers, interview by Russell Smith, September 2004, Concan, Texas.

[76] Joaquin Jackson, retired Texas Ranger, interview by Russell Smith, May 18, 2006.

[77] Alfred Allee Jr., retired Texas Ranger, interview by Russell Smith, February 4, 2004, Alpine, Texas.

[78] www.wordiq.com/definition/1963_in_music

[79] Alfred Allee Jr., retired Texas Ranger, interview by Russell Smith, February 4, 2004, Alpine, Texas.

[80] Texas Ranger Hall of Fame website, www.texasranger.org.

[81] Russell Smith, knowledge from career in law enforcement; Alfred Allee Jr., retired Texas Ranger, interview by Russell Smith, February 4, 2004, Alpine, Texas.

[82] Alfred Allee personnel file, Texas Ranger Hall of Fame; Alfred Allee Jr., interview by Russell Smith, February 4, 2004, Alpine, Texas.

[83] Ibid.

[84] Ibid.

[85] Ibid.

[86] Alfred Allee Jr., retired Texas Ranger, interview by Russell Smith, February 4, 2004, Alpine, Texas.

[87] Texas Ranger Hall of Fame website, www.texasranger.org; Alfred Allee Jr., retired Texas Ranger, interview by Russell Smith, February 4, 2004, Alpine, Texas; Jerry Byrne, Texas Ranger, interview by Russell Smith, spring 2004, San Angelo, Texas.

[88] Alfred Allee Jr., retired Texas Ranger, interview by Russell Smith, February 4, 2004, Alpine, Texas; Levi Duncan personnel file, Texas Ranger Hall of Fame.

[89] Ibid.

[90] Alfred Allee Jr., retired Texas Ranger, interview by Russell Smith, February 4, 2004, Alpine, Texas; Alfred Allee Jr. personnel file, Texas Ranger Hall of Fame.

[91] Ibid.

[92] Alfred Allee Jr., retired Texas Ranger, interview by Russell Smith, summer 2005, San Angelo, Texas.

[93] San Angelo Standard-Times photograph of Alfred Allee Jr.; Alfred Allee Jr. personnel file, Texas Ranger Hall of Fame; Alfred Allee Jr., retired Texas Ranger, interview by Russell Smith, February 4, 2004, Alpine, Texas.

[94] Russell Smith, common mistake by citizen-victims, knowledge from career in law enforcement.

[95] Ibid.

[96] Alfred Allee Jr., retired Texas Ranger, interview by Russell Smith, February 4, 2004, Alpine, Texas.

[97] Russell Smith, knowledge from career in law enforcement.

[98] Russell Smith, knowledge from career in law enforcement, common police practice in evidence collection.

[99] Ibid.; Alfred Allee Jr., retired Texas Ranger, interview by Russell Smith, February 4, 2004, Alpine, Texas, fall 2005, San Angelo, Texas.

[100] Russell Smith, knowledge from career in law enforcement, gathering elimination prints is common police practice

[101] Ibid; Russell Smith, statement heard many times during law enforcement career

[102] Ibid.; assumption on part of author.

[103] Ibid.

[104] Russell Smith, knowledge from career in law enforcement.

[105] Alfred Allee Jr., retired Texas Ranger, interview with Russell Smith, February 4, 2004, Alpine, Texas; fall 2005, San Angelo, Texas.

[106] Ibid.

[107] Ibid.

[108] Bill Cooksey, former Terrell County Sheriff, interview by Russell Smith, January 6, 1990, Odessa, Texas.

[109] Juan Flores, Immigration and Customs Enforcement Special Agent, interview by Russell Smith, spring 2005, San Angelo, Texas.

[110] Glenn Weatherman, retired U.S. Border Patrol agent, Immigration and Naturalization Service investigator, letter to Bill Cooksey, September 27, 1966.

[111] AllRefer.com website, reference.allrefer.com, town spelled as Tamazunchale rather than as Tomezunchale as in Glenn Weatherman's letter.

[112] Glenn Weatherman, retired U.S. Border Patrol agent, Immigration and Naturalization Service investigator, letter to Bill Cooksey, September 27, 1966.

[113] Joaquin Jackson, retired Texas Ranger, phone interview by Russell Smith, spring 2004, Alpine, Texas.

[114] Ibid.

[115] Greg Magers, interview by Russell Smith, September 2004, Concan, Texas; Johnie and Hudson Hillis, interview by Russell Smith, August 27, Uvalde, Texas.

[116] Ibid.

[117] Greg Magers, interview by Russell Smith, September 2004, Concan, Texas.

[118] Ibid.

[119] Ibid.

[120] Ibid.

[121] Justice of the Peace A.A. Collins, Uvalde County Certificate of Death for Louise Magers, August 6, 1963; Greg Magers, interview by Russell Smith, September 2004, Concan, Texas.

[122] Ibid.

[123] Greg Magers, interview by Russell Smith, September 2004, Concan, Texas.

[124] Ibid.

[125] Russell Smith, personal knowledge; word IQ website, www.wordiq.com;

[126] Russell Smith, personal knowledge about this time in history, author grew up nearby in Uvalde.

[127] Ibid.

[128] Willard VanPelt, interview by Russell Smith, September 2004, Concan, Texas; Greg Magers, interview by Russell Smith, September 2004, Concan, Texas; The Uvalde Leader News, December 12, 1963.

[129] Willard VanPelt, interview by Russell Smith, September 2004, Concan, Texas; Greg Magers, interview by Russell Smith, September 2004, Concan, Texas; The Uvalde Leader News, December 12, 1963; The The Uvalde Leader News, December 15, 1963.

[130] The Uvalde Leader News, December 12, 1963.

[131] The Uvalde Leader News, December 12, 1963; Rushing Estes Funeral Home, Funeral Arrangements form for Ruth Niggli.

[132] A.A. Collins, Certificate of Death for Alice Ruth Niggli, December 13, 1963.

[133] Greg Magers, interview by Russell Smith, September 2004, Concan, Texas.

[134] Ibid.

[135] Ibid.

[136] Ibid.

[137] Ibid.

[138] Ibid.

[139] National Weather Service personnel, interviews by Russell Smith, spring/summer 2005, San Angelo, Texas.

[140] Ibid.

[141] Ibid.

[142] Ibid.

[143] Ibid.

[144] Ibid.

[145] Ibid.

[146] San Antonio Express-News, January 15, 1964.; National Weather Service personnel, interviews by Russell Smith, spring/summer 2005, San Angelo, Texas.

[147] Ibid.

[148] Greg Magers, interview by Russell Smith, September 2004, Concan, Texas.

[149] Ibid.

[150] Ibid.

[151] Ibid.

[152] Ibid.

[153] Willard VanPelt, interview by Russell Smith, September 2004, Concan, Texas; Greg Magers, interview by Russell Smith, September 2004, Concan, Texas.

[154] Johnie and Hudson Hillis, interview by Russell Smith, August 27, 2004, Uvalde, Texas; Mrs. Ray Rutherford, interview by Russell Smith, August 27, 2004, Uvalde, Texas; The Uvalde Leader News, February 27, 1964; Joaquin Jackson, phone interview by Russell Smith, spring 2004, Alpine, Texas.

[155] National Weather Service personnel, interviews by Russell Smith, spring/summer 2005, San Angelo, Texas; U.S. Naval Observatory website.

[156] Johnie and Hudson Hillis, interview by Russell Smith, August 27, 2004, Uvalde, Texas; Mrs. Ray Rutherford, interview by Russell Smith, August 27, 2004, Uvalde, Texas; The Uvalde Leader News, February 27, 1964; Joaquin Jackson, phone interview by Russell Smith, spring 2004, Alpine, Texas.

[157] Ibid.

[158] Ibid.

[159] Ibid.

[160] Ibid.

[161] Ibid.

[162] Ibid.

[163] Ibid.

[164] Ibid.

[165] Ibid.

[166] Ibid.

[167] Ibid.

[168] Alfredo Hernandez, Texas Department of Corrections, Bureau of Records and Identifications form.

[169] Joaquin Jackson, retired Texas Ranger, phone interview by Russell Smith, spring 2004, Alpine, Texas.

[170] Ibid.

[171] The Uvalde Leader News, February 27, 1964.

[172] Ibid.

[173] The Uvalde Leader News, February 27, 1964; Joaquin Jackson, retired Texas Ranger, (Purvis), phone interview by Russell Smith, spring 2004, Alpine, Texas.

[174] Mrs. Ray Rutherford, phone interview by Russell Smith, August 27, 2004, October 18, 2004, January 8, 2006.

[175] The Uvalde Leader News, February 27, 1964.

[176] Johnie and Hudson Hillis, interview by Russell Smith, August 27, 2004, Uvalde, Texas.

[177] The Uvalde Leader News, February 27, 1964; Johnie and Hudson Hillis, interview by Russell Smith, August 27, 2004, Uvalde, Texas.

[178] The Uvalde Leader News, February 27, 1964.

[179] Jo Mari Stark Bradley, phone interview by Russell Smith, December 2005, Del Rio, Texas.

[180] Willard VanPelt, phone interview by Russell Smith, September 2004, Concan, Texas.

[181] Ibid.

[182] The Uvalde Leader News, March 1, 1964.

[183] Willard VanPelt, phone interview by Russell Smith, September 2004, Concan, Texas.

[184] Ibid.

[185] Ibid.

[186] The Uvalde Leader News, March 1, 1964.

[187] The Uvalde Leaders News, March 8, 1964; Tom Hupp, retired Border Patrol agent, phone interview by Russell Smith, fall 2004, Uvalde, Texas.

[188] Tom Hupp, retired Border Patrol agent, phone interview by Russell Smith, fall 2004, Uvalde, Texas.

[189] Ibid.

[190] Willard VanPelt, phone interview by Russell Smith, September/ October 2004, Concan, Texas.

[191] Ibid.

[192] Ibid.

[193] Ibid.

[194] Ibid.

[195] Ibid.

[196] Ibid.

[197] Ibid.

[198] Greg Magers, interview by Russell Smith, September 2004, Concan, Texas.

[199] Ibid.

[200] Greg Magers, interview by Russell Smith, September 2004, Concan, Texas; Willard VanPelt, phone interview by Russell Smith, September/ October 2004, Concan, Texas.

[201] Ibid.

[202] Ibid.

[203] Ibid.

[204] Ibid.

[205] Ibid.

[206] Ibid.

[207] Ibid.

[208] Ibid.

[209] Ibid.

[210] Ibid.

[211] Ibid.

[212] Willard VanPelt, phone interview by Russell Smith, September/ October 2004.

[213] Kenneth Kelley, retired Uvalde County Sheriff, interviews by Russell Smith, August 27, 2004, November 14, 2005, Uvalde, Texas.

[214] Ibid.

[215] Russell Smith, personal knowledge of Kelley's character and demeanor.

[216] Kenneth Kelley, retired Uvalde County Sheriff, interviews by Russell Smith, August 27, 2004, November 14, 2005, Uvalde, Texas.

[217] Ibid.

[218] Ted Luce, interviews by Russell Smith, March 2005, Del Rio, Texas.

[219] Ibid.

[220] Ibid.

[221] Ibid.

[222] TexasEscapes.com website.

[223] Ted Luce, interviews by Russell Smith, March 2005, Del Rio, Texas; Marcella and Felix Harrison, interview by Russell Smith, June 2004, Eldorado, Texas; TexasEscapes.com website.

[224] Ibid.

[225] Ted Luce, interviews by Russell Smith, March 2005, Del Rio, Texas; Ted Luce, painting on the wall of Luce's home, March 2005, Del Rio, Texas.

[226] Ted Luce, interviews by Russell Smith, March 2005, Del Rio, Texas.

[227] Marcella and Felix Harrison, interview by Russell Smith, June 2004, Eldorado, Texas; Ted Luce, interviews by Russell Smith, March 2005, Del Rio, Texas.

[228] Ted Luce, interviews by Russell Smith, March 2005, Del Rio, Texas.

[229] Ibid.

[230] Ibid.

[231] Ibid.

[232] Ibid.

[233] Ibid.

[234] Ibid.

[235] Ibid.

[236] Ibid.

[237] Ibid.

[238] Ibid.

[239] Ibid.

[240] Ibid.

[241] Ibid.

[242] Ibid.

[243] Ibid.

[244] Russell Smith, perception after all interviews and research.

[245] Ted Luce, interviews by Russell Smith, March 2005, Del Rio, Texas.

[246] Ibid.

[247] Ibid.

[248] Ibid.

[249] Ibid.

[250] Ibid.

[251] Ibid.

[252] Ibid.

[253] Ibid.

[254] Ted Luce, interviews by Russell Smith, March 2005, Del Rio, Texas; Brad Bradley, interview by Russell Smith, February 2004, San Angelo, Texas, phone call to Del Rio, March 30, 2005.

[255] Brad Bradley, interview by Russell Smith, February 2004, San Angelo, Texas, phone call to Del Rio, March 30, 2005.

[256] Ibid.

[257] Ibid.

[258] Ibid.

[259] Ibid.

[260] Ibid.

[261] The Handbook of Texas Online, TSHA Online, www.tsha.utexas.edu.; TexasEscapes.com website, www.texasescapes.com; Desert USA website, www.desertusa.com; Ellis Helmers, interview by Russell Smith, August 1, 2004, Sanderson, Texas.

[262] Russell Smith, perception based on all interviews and research.

[263] Lee Miller, wildlife biologist, Texas Parks and Wildlife, interview by Russell Smith, December 15, 2004, San Angelo, Texas.

[264] Bill Cooksey, former Terrell County Sheriff, interview by Russell Smith, January 6, 1990, Odessa, Texas.

[265] Cliff Wilson, interview by Russell Smith, July 10, 2004, Uvalde, Texas.

[266] Donna Smith, interview by Russell Smith, August 4, 2004.

[267] Desert USA website, www.desertusa.com; Russell Smith, common knowledge.

[268] Chihuahuan Desert Research Institute, Fort Davis, Texas, website: www.cdri.org.

[269] Ibid.

[270] Ibid.

[271] Ibid.

[272] Glenn Weatherman, retired U.S. Border Patrol agent, interview by Russell Smith, August 7, 2004; letter to Bill Cooksey, September 27, 1966.

[273] Estella Rose, four page single-spaced typewritten letter, undated, copy provided to Russell Smith by Marcella Harrison, June 2004, Eldorado, Texas.

[274] Marcella and Felix Harrison, interview by Russell Smith, June 2004, Eldorado, Texas; Estella Rose, four page single-spaced typewritten letter, undated, copy provided to Russell Smith by Marcella Harrison, June 2004, Eldorado, Texas.

[275] Ibid.

[276] Ibid.

[277] Ibid.

[278] Ibid.

[279] Ibid.

[280] Ibid.

[281] Ibid.

[282] Ibid.

[283] Marcella and Felix Harrison, interview by Russell Smith, June 2004, Eldorado, Texas; photograph of house provided by Harrison's.

[284] Ibid.

[285] Marcella and Felix Harrison, interview by Russell Smith, June 2004, Eldorado, Texas; Estella Rose, four page single-spaced typewritten letter, undated, copy provided to Russell Smith by Marcella Harrison, June 2004, Eldorado, Texas.

[286] Ibid.

[287] Ibid.

[288] Ibid.

[289] Ibid.

[290] Ibid.

[291] Ibid.

[292] Ibid.

[293] Ibid.

[294] Ibid.

[295] Ibid.

[296] Ibid.

[297] Ibid.

[298] Ibid.

[299] Ibid.

[300] Ibid.

[301] Ibid.

[302] Ibid.

[303] Ibid.

[304] Ibid.

[305] Ibid.

[306] Ibid.

[307] Ibid.

[308] Ibid.

[309] Ibid.

[310] Ibid.

[311] Ibid.

[312] Ibid.

[313] Ibid.

[314] Ibid.

[315] Ibid.

[316] Ibid.

[317] Ibid.

[318] Ibid.

[319] Ibid.

[320] Ibid.

[321] Ibid.

[322] Ibid.

[323] Ibid.

[324] Ibid.

[325] W.J. Vaughan, interview by Russell Smith, August 27, 2004, Batesville, Texas.

[326] Ibid.

[327] Ibid.

[328] Ibid.

[329] Ibid.

[330] Ibid.

[331] Ibid.

[332] Ibid.

[333] Ibid.

[334] Marcella and Felix Harrison, interview by Russell Smith, June 2004, Eldorado, Texas; Estella Rose, four page single-spaced typewritten letter, undated, copy provided to Russell Smith by Marcella Harrison, June 2004, Eldorado, Texas.

[335] Ibid.

[336] Marcella and Felix Harrison, interview by Russell Smith, June 2004, Eldorado, Texas.

[337] Ibid.

[338] Leland K. 'Buddy' Burgess, Kinney County Sheriff, interview by Russell Smith, August 5, 2004, Kinney County Sheriff's Department, Brackettville, Texas.

[339] Ibid.

[340] Ibid.

[341] Ibid.

[342] Ibid.

[343] Ibid.

[344] Ibid.

[345] Marcella and Felix Harrison, interview by Russell Smith, June 2004, Eldorado, Texas; Estella Rose, four page single-spaced typewritten letter, undated, copy provided to Russell Smith by Marcella Harrison, June 2004, Eldorado, Texas.

[346] Leland K. 'Buddy' Burgess, Kinney County Sheriff, interview by Russell Smith, August 5, 2004, Bracketville, Texas.

[347] W.J. Vaughan, interview by Russell Smith, August 27, 2004, Batesvilles, Texas.

[348] San Angelo Standard-Times, July 12, 1965.

[349] Bill Cooksey, former Terrell County Sheriff, interview by Russell Smith, January 6, 1990.

[350] San Angelo Standard-Times, July 12, 1965.

[351] Jerry Richter, interview by Russell Smith, August 6, 2004, Del Rio, Texas.

[352] Del Rio News-Herald, July 12, 1965.

[353] H.B. 'Butch' Purvis, Irion County Chief Deputy, phone interview by Russell Smith, fall 2004, Mertzon, Texas; L.H. Purvis personnel file, Texas Ranger Hall of Fame.

[354] Ibid.

[355] The Sanderson Times, July 16, 1965.

[356] Ibid.

[357] Alfredo Gallegos, interview by Russell Smith, Saturday, June 2004, Uvalde, Texas.

[358] Bill Cooksey, former Terrell County Sheriff, interview by Russell Smith, January 6, 1990.

[359] Ben Ross, interview by Russell Smith, late February 2004, Ozona, Texas, interview and tour of Dryden by Russell Smith, September 26, 2004, letters and map, March 1, 2004; June 23, 2004; April 26, 2005; June 25, 2005; July 22, 2005. .

[360] Ibid.

[361] Ibid.

[362] Ibid.

[363] Ibid.

[364] Ibid.

[365] Ibid.

[366] Ibid.

[367] Ibid.

[368] Ibid.

[369] Ibid.

[370] Ibid.

[371] Ibid.

[372] Ibid.

[373] Ibid.

[374] Elaine Rogers O'Donnell, phone interview by Russell Smith, May 11, 2005, emails May 12, 2005, October 20, 2005, Marfa, Texas; Adrienne McElhaney, phone interviews by Russell Smith, fall 2004, May 2005, Iraan, Texas; E.A. 'Junior' Rogers, phone interview by Russell Smith, May 2005, Kermit, Texas.

[375] Ibid.

[376] Ibid.

[377] Ben Ross, interview by Russell Smith, late February 2004, Ozona, Texas, interview and tour of Dryden by Russell Smith, September 26, 2004, letters and map, March 1, 2004; June 23, 2004; April 26, 2005; June 25, 2005; July 22, 2005.

[378] Ben Ross, interview by Russell Smith, late February 2004, Ozona, Texas, interview and tour of Dryden by Russell Smith, September 26, 2004, letters and map, March 1, 2004; June 23, 2004; April 26, 2005; June 25, 2005; July 22, 2005; Joanne Carruthers Bell, interview by Russell Smith, June 22-23, 2004, San Angelo, Texas.

[379] Ibid.

[380] Ibid.

[381] Ibid.

[382] Ben Ross, interview by Russell Smith, late February 2004, Ozona, Texas, interview and tour of Dryden by Russell Smith, September 26, 2004, letters and map, March 1, 2004; June 23, 2004; April 26, 2005; June 25, 2005; July 22, 2005.

[383] Ibid.

[384] Ibid.

[385] Ibid.

[386] Ben Ross, interview by Russell Smith, late February 2004, Ozona, Texas, interview and tour of Dryden by Russell Smith, September 26, 2004, letters and map, March 1, 2004; June 23, 2004; April 26, 2005; June 25, 2005; July 22, 2005; Cliff Wilson, retired U.S. Customs agent, interview by Russell Smith, July 10, 2004, Uvalde, Texas; Bill Cooksey, former Terrell County Sheriff, interview by Russell Smith, January 6, 1990, Odessa, Texas.

[387] Ibid.

[388] Ibid.

[389] Cliff Wilson, retired U.S. Customs agent, interview by Russell Smith, July 10, 2004, Uvalde, Texas.

[390] Ibid.

[391] Ibid.

[392] Ibid.

[393] Ibid.

[394] Bill Cooksey, former Terrell County Sheriff, and wife Bernice, interview by Russell Smith, January 6, 1990, Odessa, Texas.

[395] Ibid.

[396] Ibid.

[397] Ibid.

[398] Ibid.

[399] Ibid.

[400] Ibid.

[401] Ibid.

[402] Ibid.

[403] Ibid.

[404] Ibid.

[405] Cliff Wilson, retired U.S. Customs agent, interview by Russell Smith, July 10, 2004, Uvalde, Texas.

[406] Cliff Wilson, retired U.S. Customs agent, interview by Russell Smith, July 10, 2004, Uvalde, Texas; Bill Cooksey, former Terrell County Sheriff, and wife Bernice, interview by Russell Smith, January 6, 1990, Odessa, Texas.

[407] Bill Cooksey, former Terrell County Sheriff, and wife Bernice, interview by Russell Smith, January 6, 1990, Odessa, Texas.

[408] Joanne Carruthers Bell, interviews by Russell Smith, June 22-23, 2004, San Angelo, Texas.

[409] Ibid.

[410] Bill Cooksey, former Terrell County Sheriff, and wife Bernice, interview by Russell Smith, January 6, 1990, Odessa, Texas.

[411] Ibid.

[412] Ibid.

[413] Ibid.

[414] Ibid.

[415] Joanne Carruthers Bell, interviews by Russell Smith, June 22-23, 2004, San Angelo, Texas.

[416] Ibid.

[417] Bill Cooksey, former Terrell County Sheriff, and wife Bernice, interview by Russell Smith, January 6, 1990, Odessa, Texas.

[418] Ibid.

[419] Ibid.

[420] Ibid.

[421] Ibid.

[422] Henry Beth Hogg, interviews by Russell Smith, August 1-3, 2004, October 15, 2005, Sanderson, Texas.

[423] Ibid.

[424] Ibid.

[425] Ibid.

[426] Ibid.

[427] Ibid.

[428] Ibid.

[429] Ibid.

[430] Ibid.

[431] Ibid.

[432] Ibid.

[433] Ibid.

[434] Bill Cooksey, former Terrell County Sheriff, and wife Bernice, interview by Russell Smith, January 6, 1990, Odessa, Texas.

[435] The Sanderson Times, July 20, 1062, Bill Cooksey, former Terrell County Sheriff, and wife Bernice, interview by Russell Smith, January 6, 1990, Odessa, Texas.

[436] Bill Cooksey, former Terrell County Sheriff, and wife Bernice, interview by Russell Smith, January 6, 1990, Odessa, Texas.

[437] Ibid.

[438] Cliff Wilson, retired U.S. Customs agent, interview by Russell Smith, July 10, 2004, Uvalde, Texas.

[439] Ibid.

[440] Ibid.

[441] Ibid.

[442] Ibid.

[443] Ibid.

[444] Ibid.

[445] Ibid.

[446] Ibid.

[447] Ibid.

[448] Ibid.

[449] Ibid.

[450] Ibid.

[451] Ibid.

[452] Bill Cooksey, former Terrell County Sheriff, and wife Bernice, interview by Russell Smith, January 6, 1990, Odessa, Texas; The Sanderson Times, March 2, 1962; March 9, 1962.

[453] Ibid.

[454] Ibid.

[455] The Sanderson Times, February 28, 1964; Bill Cooksey, former Terrell County Sheriff, and wife Bernice, interview by Russell Smith, January 6, 1990, Odessa, Texas.

[456] Candace Fulton Cooksey, interview and emails by Russell Smith, 2004-2005, Brownwood, Texas, interview by Russell Smith, July 2005, San Angelo, Texas.

[457] Bill Cooksey, former Terrell County Sheriff, and wife Bernice, interview by Russell Smith, January 6, 1990, Odessa, Texas; Candace Fulton Cooksey, interview and emails by Russell Smith, 2004-2005, Brownwood, Texas, interview by Russell Smith, July 2005, San Angelo, Texas; The Sanderson Times, July 6, 1962.

[458] Bill Cooksey, former Terrell County Sheriff, and wife Bernice, interview by Russell Smith, January 6, 1990, Odessa, Texas; The Sanderson Times, Janaury 17, 1964.

[459] Bill Cooksey, former Terrell County Sheriff, and wife Bernice, interview by Russell Smith, January 6, 1990, Odessa, Texas; The Sanderson Times, July 27, 1962; December 7, 1962; November 29, 1963; February 21, 1964; February 28, 1964; April 24, 1964; August 14, 1964; January 5, 1965; February 19, 1965; June 18, 1965; July 16, 1965; July 30, 1965.

[460] Bill Cooksey, former Terrell County Sheriff, and wife Bernice, interview by Russell Smith, January 6, 1990, Odessa, Texas; Ben Ross, interview by Russell Smith, late February 2004, Ozona, Texas, interview and tour of Dryden by Russell Smith, September 26, 2004; Donna Rogers, phone interview by Russell Smith, August 1, 2004, Dryden, Texas; The Sanderson Times, August 20, 1965; September 23, 1965.

[461] Bill Cooksey, former Terrell County Sheriff, and wife Bernice, interview by Russell Smith, January 6, 1990, Odessa, Texas

[462] Ibid.

[463] Bill Cooksey, former Terrell County Sheriff, and wife Bernice, interview by Russell Smith, January 6, 1990, Odessa, Texas; Joanne Carruthers Bell, interview by Russell Smith, June 22-23, 2004, San Angelo, Texas; Alfredo Gallegos, interview and letter by Russell Smith, June 2004, Uvalde, Texas.

[464] Alfredo Gallegos, interview and letter by Russell Smith, June 2004, Uvalde, Texas.

[465] Ibid.

[466] Ibid.

[467] Ibid.

[468] Ibid.

[469] Ibid.

[470] Ibid.

[471] Alfredo Gallegos, interview and letter by Russell Smith, June 2004, Uvalde, Texas; Ben Ross, interview by Russell Smith, late February

2004, Ozona, Texas; Joe Gonzalez, Polygraph Examiner, El Paso Police Department, polygraph report addressed to Dalton Hogg, Terrell County Deputy Sheriff, December, 21, 1965, El Paso, Texas.

[472] Alfredo Gallegos, interview and letter by Russell Smith, June 2004, Uvalde, Texas.

[473] Bill Cooksey, former Terrell County Sheriff, interview January 6, 1990, Odessa, Texas.

[474] Bill Cooksey, former Terrell County Sheriff, interview by Russell Smith, January 6, 1990, Odessa, Texas;

Terrell Cooksey, email to Russell Smith, March 1, 2005, Austin, Texas.

[475] Bill Cooksey, former Terrell County Sheriff, interview by Russell Smith, January 6, 1990, Odessa, Texas.

[476] Ibid.

[477] Ibid.

[478] Ben Ross, interview by Russell Smith, late February 2004, Ozona, Texas; Joanne Carruthers Bell, interview by Russell Smith, June 22-23, 2004, San Angelo, Texas; Bill Cooksey, former Terrell County Sheriff, interview by Russell Smith, January 6, 1990, Odessa, Texas.

[479] Ibid.

[480] Bill Cooksey, former Terrell County Sheriff, interview by Russell Smith, January 6, 1990, Odessa, Texas; Ben Ross, interview by Russell Smith, late February 2004, Ozona, Texas; Alfredo Gallegos, interview by Russell Smith, letter, June 2004, Uvalde, Texas; Joe Gonzalez, Polygraph Examiner, El Paso Police Department, polygraph report addressed to Dalton Hogg, Terrell County Deputy Sheriff, December 21, 1965, El Paso, Texas.

[481] Ibid.

[482] Ben Ross, interview by Russell Smith, September 26, 2004, Dryden, Texas.

[483] Ben Ross, interview by Russell Smith, late February 2004, Ozona, Texas.

[484] Alfredo Gallegos, interview by Russell Smith, June 2004, Uvalde, Texas.

[485] Bill Cooksey, former Terrell County Sheriff, interview by Russell Smith, January 6, 1990; Ben Ross, interview by Russell Smith, late February 2004, Ozona, Texas; Alfredo Gallegos, interview by Russell Smith, June 2004, Uvalde, Texas.

[486] National Weather Service personnel, interviews by Russell Smith, spring/summer 2005, San Angelo, Texas.

[487] Cliff Wilson, interview by Russell Smith, July 10, 2004, Uvalde, Texas.

[488] Russell Smith, perception based on Alfredo Gallegos interview, June 2004, Uvalde, Texas.

[489] Bill Cooksey, former Terrell County Sheriff, interview by Russell Smith, January 6, 1990; Ben Ross, interview by Russell Smith, late February 2004, Ozona, Texas; Alfredo Gallegos, interview by Russell Smith, June 2004, Uvalde, Texas.

[490] Ibid.

[491] Ibid.

[492] Ibid.

[493] Ibid.

[494] Ibid.

[495] Joe Gonzalez, Polygraph Examiner, El Paso Police Department, polygraph report addressed to Dalton Hogg, Terrell County Deputy Sheriff, December 21, 1965, El Paso, Texas.

[496] Ibid.

[497] Bill Cooksey, former Terrell County Sheriff, interview by Russell Smith, January 6, 1990.

[498] Bill Cooksey, former Terrell County Sheriff, interview by Russell Smith, January 6, 1990; Ben Ross, interview by Russell Smith, late February 2004, Ozona, Texas; Alfredo Gallegos, interview by Russell Smith, June 2004, Uvalde, Texas.

[499] Bill Cooksey, former Terrell County Sheriff, interview by Russell Smith, January 6, 1990.

[500] Johnny K. Burkhalter, Ph.D., interview by Russell Smith, spring 2005; Russell Smith, similar personal experience, fall 1979.

[501] Ibid; Lewis Cash, statement made to Texas Rangers J.S. Nance and Arthur Hill, November 11, 1965, Dryden, Texas.

[502] Ben Ross, interview by Russell Smith, late February 2004, Ozona, Texas; Alfredo Gallegos, interview by Russell Smith, June 2004, Uvalde, Texas.

[503] Lewis Cash, statement given to Texas Rangers J.S. Nance and Arthur Hill, November 11, 1965, Dryden, Texas.

[504] Bill Cooksey, former Terrell County Sheriff, interview by Russell Smith, January 6, 1990; Ben Ross, interview by Russell Smith, late February 2004, Ozona, Texas; Alfredo Gallegos, interview by Russell Smith, June 2004, Uvalde, Texas.

[505] Bill Cooksey, former Terrell County Sheriff, interview by Russell Smith, January 6, 1990; Ben Ross, interview by Russell Smith, late February 2004, Ozona, Texas; Alfredo Gallegos, interview by Russell Smith, June 2004, Uvalde, Texas; Lewis Cash, statement made to Texas Rangers J.S. Nance and Arthur Hill, November 11, 1965, Dryden, Texas.

[506] Ibid.

[507] Ibid.

[508] Ibid.

[509] Ibid.

[510] Ibid.

[511] Ibid.

[512] Chihuahuan Desert Research Institute website, www.cdri.org; Ellis Helmers, retired County Agent, interview by Russell Smith, August 1, 2004, Sanderson, Texas.

[513] Bill Cooksey, former Terrell County Sheriff, interview by Russell Smith, January 6, 1990, Odessa, Texas; Ben Ross, interview by Russell Smith, late February 2004, Ozona, Texas; Alfredo Gallegos, interview by Russell Smith, letter, June 2004, Uvalde, Texas; Lewis Cash, statement made to Texas Rangers J.S. Nance and Arthur Hill, November 11, 1965, Dryden, Texas

[514] Ibid.

[515] Bill Cooksey, former Terrell County Sheriff, interview by Russell Smith, January 6, 1990; Candace Cooksey Fulton, interview by Russell Smith, emails 2004-2005, Brownwood, Texas, interview by Russell Smith, July 2005, San Angelo, Texas.

[516] Ben Ross, interview by Russell Smith, late February 2004, Ozona, Texas.

[517] Ibid; Dalton Hogg, statement given to Texas Ranger J.S. Nance, November 1965.

[518] Lewis Cash, statement made to Texas Rangers J.S. Nance and Arthur Hill, November 11, 1965, Dryden, Texas; Dalton Hogg, statement given to Texas Ranger J.S. Nance, November 1965.

[519] Bill Cooksey, former Terrell County Sheriff, interview by Russell Smith, January 6, 1990, Odessa, Texas; Ben Ross, interview by Russell Smith, late February 2004, Ozona, Texas.

[520] Ben Ross, interview by Russell Smith, late February 2004, Ozona, Texas.

[521] Ibid.

[522] Alfredo Gallegos, interview by Russell Smith, June 2004, Uvalde, Texas.

[523] Gene Kline, retired U.S. Border Patrol, interview by Russell Smith, August 3, 2004, Sanderson, Texas.

[524] Alfredo Gallegos, interview by Russell Smith, June 2004, Uvalde, Texas.

[525] Ibid.

[526] Ibid.

[527] Ibid.

[528] Henry Beth Hogg, interviews by Russell Smith, August 1-3, 2004, Sanderson, Texas.

[529] Ibid.

[530] Candace Cooksey Fulton, interview by Russell Smith, emails, 2004-2005, Brownwood, Texas.

[531] Ibid.

[532] Mary Beth Hogg, interviews by Russell Smith, August 1-3, 2004, Sanderson, Texas.

[533] Dalton Hogg, statement given to Texas Ranger J.S. Nance, November 1965.

[534] Ibid.

[535] Ben Ross, interview by Russell Smith, late February 2004, Ozona, Texas.

[536] Dr. Hi Newby, phone interview by Russell Smith, winter 2004, Arlington, Texas.

[537] Ibid.

[538] Ibid.

[539] Candace Cooksey Fulton, interviews by Russell Smith, emails, 2004-2005, Brownwood, Texas.

[540] Ibid.

[541] Ibid.

[542] Ibid.

[543] Bernice Cooksey, interview by Russell Smith, January 6, 1990; Candace Cooksey Fulton, interview by Russell Smith, emails, 2004-2005, Brownwood, Texas.

[544] Candace Cooksey Fulton, interviews by Russell Smith, emails, 2004-2005, Brownwood, Texas.

[545] Ibid.

[546] Dalton Hogg, statement given to Texas Ranger J.S. Nance, November 1965.

[547] Bill Cooksey, former Terrell County Sheriff, interview by Russell Smith, January 6, 1990, Odessa, Texas; Henry Beth Hogg, interviews by Russell Smith, August 1-3, 2004, Sanderson, Texas.

[548] Ben Ross, interview by Russell Smith, late February 2004, Ozona, Texas; Bill Cooksey, former Terrell County Sheriff, interview by Russell Smith, January 6, 1990, Odessa, Texas; Henry Beth Hogg, interviews by Russell Smith, August 1-3, 2004, Sanderson, Texas; Dr. Hi Newby, phone interview by Russell Smith, winter 2004, Arlington, Texas.

[549] Ibid.

[550] Dr. Hi Newby, phone interview by Russell Smith, winter 2004, Arlington, Texas.

[551] Ben Ross, interview by Russell Smith, late February 2004, Ozona, Texas, J.D. Hogg, phone interview by Russell Smith, email, fall 2004, El Paso, Texas.

[552] Ray Fitzgerald, retired U.S. Border Patrol, phone interview by Russell Smith, September 2004, Van Horn, Texas.

[553] Ibid.

[554] Ibid.

[555] Ben Ross, interview by Russell Smith, late February 2004, Ozona, Texas.

[556] Texas Ranger Arthur Hill's personnel file, Texas Ranger Hall of Fame.

[557] Ben Ross, interview by Russell Smith, late February 2004, Ozona, Texas.

[558] Ferrell Humphrey, relative of Hinkle Boyd, interview by Russell Smith, January 2, 2006, San Angelo, Texas; Kathy Hinds, relative of Hinkle Boyd, interview by Russell Smith, December 5, 2005, San Angelo, Texas.

[559] Bernice Cooksey Wiley, letter to Russell Smith, January, 2006, interview by Russell Smith, January 6, 1990, Odessa, Texas; Candace Cooksey Fulton, interviews by Russell Smith, emails, 2004-2005, Brownwood, Texas.

[560] Del Rio News-Herald, November 5, 1965; San Angelo Standard-Times, November 5, 1965.

[561] San Angelo Standard-Times, November 5, 1965; Del Rio News-Herald, November 5, 1965.

[562] Russell Smith, career in law enforcement, Tom Green County, San Angelo, Texas; Federal Bureau of Investigation, statistics, www.fbi.gov.

[563] Blain Chriesman, interview by Russell Smith, August 2, 2004, Sanderson, Texas.

[564] Ibid.

[565] Odell 'Pinky' Carruthers, interview by Russell Smith, August 4, 2004, Sanderson, Texas; Marcella and Felix Harrison, interview by Russell Smith, June 2004, Eldorado, Texas; Ray Fitzgerald, retired U.S. Border Patrol agent, phone interview by Russell Smith, September 2004, Van Horn, Texas.

[566] J.D. Hogg, phone interview by Russell Smith, emails, fall 2004, El Paso, Texas; Henry Beth Hogg, interviews by Russell Smith, August 1-3, 2004, Sanderson, Texas.

[567] Bill Cooksey, former Terrell County Sheriff, interview by Russell Smith, January 6, 1990; Ray Fitzgerald, retired U.S. Border Patrol agent, phone interview by Russell Smith, September 2004, Van Horn, Texas, San Angelo Standard-Times, November 5, 1965.

[568] Forest Gould Hardin personnel file, Texas Ranger Hall of Fame.

[569] Alfred Young Allee Jr., interview by Russell Smith, February 4, 2004, Alpine, Texas; H.B. 'Butch' Purvis, Irion County Chief Deputy, phone interview by Russell Smith fall 2004, Mertzon, Texas; San Angelo Standard -Times November 5, 1965.

[570] Ben Ross, interview by Russell Smith, late February 2004, Ozona, Texas; Alfred Allee Jr., retired Texas Ranger, interview by Russell Smith, February 4, 2004, Alpine, Texas; Bill Cooksey's file, typed reports by Rangers Hill and Nance.

[571] Phillip Cooper, phone interview by Russell Smith, August 2004; Donna Cooper Mikeska, interview by Russell Smith, August 2004, San Angelo, Texas; Raymond Cooper, interview by Russell Smith, August

2004; G.W. 'Grabb' Davis, Tom Green County Sheriff's Department investigator, interview by Russell Smith, fall 2004, summer 2005, San Angelo, Texas.

[572] Ibid.

[573] Ibid.

[574] Ibid.

[575] Ibid.

[576] Ibid.

[577] Ray Fitzgerald, retired U.S. Border Patrol, phone interview by Russell Smith, September 2004, Van Horn, Texas.

[578] Phillip Cooper, phone interview by Russell Smith, August 15, 2004.

[579] Bill Cooksey, former Terrell County Sheriff, interview by Russell Smith, January 6, 1990; Ray Fitzgerald, retired U.S. Border Patrol agent, phone interview by Russell Smith, September 2004, Van Horn, Texas.

[580] Ibid.

[581] Ellis Helmers, retired County Extension Agent, interview by Russell Smith, August 1, 2004, Sanderson, Texas.

[582] Russell Smith, observation of pear cactus, September 26, 2004, Dryden, Texas; Jennifer Baur, Chihuahuan Desert Research Institute, email to Russell Smith, June 30, 2005.

[583] University of Texas at El Paso museum website, http://museum.utep.edu/chih/gardens/plants.

[584] Jennifer Baur, Chihuahuan Desert Research Institute, email to Russell Smith, June 30, 2005.

[585] Ray Fitzgerald, retired U.S. Border Patrol agent, phone interview by Russell Smith, September 2004, Van Horn, Texas.

[586] Ibid.

[587] Del Rio News-Herald, November 5 & 7, 1965.

[588] Richard Perez, phone interview by Russell Smith, summer 2005, San Antonio, Texas; Tino Flores,
phone interview by Russell Smith, summer 2005, Del Rio, Texas; Samuel Perez certificate of death, City of Del Rio, Texas.

[589] Samuel Perez photograph, observed and photographed with permission from Sheriff D'Wayne Jernigan, Val Verde County Sheriff's Office, Del Rio, Texas, August 6, 2004; Richard Perez, phone interview by Russell

Smith, summer 2004, San Antonio, Texas; Tino Flores, phone interview by Russell Smith, summer 2005, Del Rio, Texas.

590 Richard Perez, phone interview by Russell Smith, summer 2004, San Antonio, Texas; Tino Flores, phone interview by Russell Smith, summer 2005, Del Rio, Texas.

591 Ibid.

592 Del Rio News-Herald, November 5 & 7, 1965.

593 Phillip Cooper, phone interview by Russell Smith, August 15, 2004, Sonora, Texas.

594 Cliff Wilson, retired U.S. Customs Agent, interview by Russell Smith, July 10, 2004, Uvalde, Texas.

595 Ibid.

596 Blain Chriesman, interview by Russell Smith, August 2, 2004, Sanderson, Texas.

597 Cliff Wilson, retired U.S. Customs Agent, interview by Russell Smith, July 10, 2004, Uvalde, Texas.

598 Roy 'Hoot' Deaton, interview by Russell Smith, August 2, 2004, Sanderson, Texas.

599 Ibid.

600 Ibid.

601 Ibid.

602 Ibid.

603 Ray Fitzgerald, retired U.S. Border Patrol Agent, phone interview by Russell Smith, September 2004, Van Horn, Texas.

604 Henry Beth Hogg, interviews by Russell Smith, August 1-3, 2004, Sanderson, Texas.

605 Alfred Allee Jr., retired Texas Ranger, interview by Russell Smith, February 4, 2004, Alpine, Texas; Ben Ross, interview by Russell Smith, late February 2004, Ozona, Texas; Cliff Wilson, retired U.S. Customs Agent, interview by Russell Smith, July 10, 2004, Uvalde, Texas.

606 U.S. Naval Observatory, Astronomical Applications Department website: http://aa.usno.navy.mil/cgi-bin/aa_pap.pl

607 Corpus Christi Caller-Times, November 6, 1965

608 Russell Smith, knowledge and experience, career in law enforcement

609 Ross McSwain, interview by Russell Smith, March 9, 2003, San Angelo, Texas.

[610] Ibid.

[611] Ibid.

[612] Bill Cooksey, former Terrell County Sheriff, and wife Bernice, interview by Russell Smith, January 6, 1990.

[613] Ibid.

[614] Ibid.

[615] Ibid.

[616] Clifton Record, April 12, 1956, provided by Bosque County Historical Commission, Meridian, Texas.

[617] Clifton Record, April 12, 1956, provided by Bosque County Historical Commission, Meridian, Texas; Bill Cooksey, former Terrell County Sheriff, interview by Russell Smith, January 6, 1990, Odessa, Texas.

[618] Ibid.

[619] Ibid.

[620] Ibid.

[621] Ibid.

[622] Bill Cooksey, former Terrell County Sheriff, and wife Bernice, interview by Russell Smith, January 6, 1990; Candace Cooksey Fulton, interview by Russell Smith, emails, 2004-2005, Brownwood, Texas.

[623] Ibid.

[624] Bobby Berrie, retired San Angelo police officer, interview by Russell Smith, San Angelo, Texas.

[625] Candace Cooksey Fulton, interview by Russell Smith, emails, 2004-2005, Brownwood, Texas.

[626] Bill Cooksey, former Terrell County Sheriff, and wife Bernice, interview by Russell Smith, January 6, 1990.

[627] Corpus Christi Caller-Times, November 6, 1965.

[628] Ross McSwain, interview by Russell Smith, March 9, 2003, San Angelo, Texas.

[629] Corpus Christi Caller-Times, November 6, 1965.

[630] Aurora Galvan, interview by Russell Smith, August 1, 2004, Sanderson, Texas.

[631] Ibid.

[632] Dudley Harrison, interview by Russell Smith, August 3, 2004, Sanderson, Texas.

[633] National Weather Service personnel, interviews by Russell Smith, spring/summer 2005, San Angelo, Texas.

[634] Bertha Marquez, interview by Russell Smith, August 1, 2004, Sanderson, Texas; Lizbeth Marquez Castellano, interview by Russell Smith, August 1, 2004, Sanderson, Texas.

[635] Ibid.

[636] Marcella and Felix Harrison, interview by Russell Smith, June 2004, Eldorado, Texas; Bertha Marquez, interview by Russell Smith, August 1, 2004, Sanderson, Texas; Lizbeth Marquez Castellano, interview by Russell Smith, August 1, 2004, Sanderson, Texas.

[637] Terrell County Texas Its Past Its People,

[638] Bertha Marquez, interview by Russell Smith, August 1, 2004, Sanderson, Texas; Lizbeth Marquez Castellano, interview by Russell Smith, August 1, 2004, Sanderson, Texas.

[639] Ibid.

[640] Ibid.

[641] Ibid.

[642] Ibid.

[643] Ibid.

[644] Ibid.

[645] The Sanderson Flood of 1965, Crisis In A Rural Texas Community, written by Russell Ashton Scogin, Edited by Earl H. Elam, published by Sul Ross State University, Copyright 1995, Center for Big Bend Studies, Sul Ross State University, Alpine, Texas.

[646] Bertha Marquez, interview by Russell Smith, August 1, 2004, Sanderson, Texas; Lizbeth Marquez Castellano, interview by Russell Smith, August 1, 2004, Sanderson, Texas.

[647] Dudley Harrison, interview by Russell Smith, August 3, 2004, Sanderson, Texas.

[648] Ibid.

[649] Ibid.

[650] Ibid.

[651] Ibid.

[652] Ibid.

[653] Ibid.

[654] Aurora Galvan, interview by Russell Smith, August 1, 2004, Sanderson, Texas.

[655] Bertha Marquez, interview by Russell Smith, August 1, 2004, Sanderson, Texas; Lizbeth Marquez Castellano, interview by Russell Smith, August 1, 2004, Sanderson, Texas.

656 Ibid.

657 Cliff Wilson, retired U.S. Customs Agent, interview by Russell Smith, July 10, 2004, Uvalde, Texas.

658 Bertha Marquez, interview by Russell Smith, August 1, 2004, Sanderson, Texas; Lizbeth Marquez Castellano, interview by Russell Smith, August 1, 2004, Sanderson, Texas.

659 Candace Cooksey Fulton, interview by Russell Smith, emails, 2004-2005, Brownwood, Texas.

660 Ibid.

661 Ibid.

662 Ibid.

663 Ibid.

664 Bernice Cooksey, interview by Russell Smith, January 9, 1990, Odessa, Texas; Ross McSwain, interview by Russell Smith, March 9, 2003, San Angelo, Texas.

665 Odell 'Pinky' Carruthers, interview by Russell Smith, August 4, 2004, Sanderson, Texas.

666 Ibid.

667 Ibid.

668 San Angelo Standard-Times, Monday, November 8, 1965.

669 Ben Ross, interview by Russell Smith, late February 2004, Ozona, Texas.

670 Ibid.

671 George Adams, victim, Terrell County Grand Jury, August 1966 Indictment, Alfredo Hernandez suspect, date of offense November 7, 1965.

672 Bill Cooksey, former Terrell County Sheriff, interview by Russell Smith, January 6, 1990, Odessa, Texas; Ben Ross, interview by Russell Smith, late February 2004, Ozona, Texas; Henry Beth Hogg, interviews by Russell Smith, August 1-3, 2004, Sanderson, Texas; Greg Toomey, article Two Dollars For Luck, On Patrol, non-profit publication, July 1979, San Antonio.

673 Terrell County Commissioners' Court, Regular Meeting, Minutes, November 11, 1965.

674 Ben Ross, interview by Russell Smith, late February 2004, Ozona, Texas; Candace Cooksey Fulton, email to Russell Smith, March 17, 2004.

[675] Bill Cooksey, former Terrell County Sheriff, interview by Russell Smith, January 6, 1990, Ozona, Texas.

[676] Leland K. 'Buddy' Burgess, Kinney County Sheriff, interview by Russell Smith, August 5, 2004, Brackettville, Texas.

[677] Cliff Wilson, interview by Russell Smith, July 10, 2004, Uvalde, Texas.

[678] Del Rio News-Herald, November 11, 1965.

[679] The Sanderson Times, November 25, 1965.

[680] Mike Caraway, interview by Russell Smith, summer 2004, San Angelo, Texas.

[681] Ibid.

[682] Ibid.

[683] Alfred Allee Jr., retired Texas Ranger, interview by Russell Smith, February 4, 2004, Alpine, Texas.

[684] Marsha Monroe, interview by Russell Smith, October 15, 2005, Sanderson, Texas.

[685] Donna Smith, interview by Russell Smith, August 4, 2004, Sanderson, Texas.

[686] Henry Beth Hogg, interview by Russell Smith, August 1-3, 2004, Sanderson, Texas.

[687] Del Rio News-Herald, November 14, 1965.

[688] Del Rio News-Herald, November 14, 1965; Ted Luce, interviews by Russell Smith, March 2005, Del Rio, Texas.

[689] Ibid.

[690] Estella Bradford, 4 page single-spaced typed letter to children; Marcella and Felix Harrison, interview by Russell Smith, June 2004, Eldorado, Texas.

[691] Estella Bradford, 4 page single-spaced typed letter to children.

[692] Jess Ten Eyck, phone interview by Russell Smith, May 22-23, 2005, Bandera, Texas.

[693] Ibid.

[694] Ibid.

[695] Ibid.

[696] Ibid.

[697] Ibid.

[698] Ibid.

[699] Ibid.

[700] Ibid.

[701] Ibid.

[702] Ibid.

[703] Joanne Carruthers Bell, interview by Russell Smith, June 22-23, 2004, San Angelo, Texas;

Jess Ten Eyck, phone interview by Russell Smith, May 22-23, 2005, Bandera, Texas; Ben Ross, interview by Russell Smith, late February 2004, Ozona, Texas; Bill Cooksey, former Terrell County Sheriff, interview by Russell Smith, January 6, 1990, Odessa, Texas.

[704] Jess Ten Eyck, phone interview by Russell Smith, May 22-23, 2005, Bandera, Texas.

[705] Ben Ross, interview by Russell Smith, late February 2004, Ozona, Texas.

[706] Ibid.

[707] Jess Ten Eyck, phone interview by Russell Smith, May 22-23, 2005, Bandera, Texas.

[708] Ben Ross, interview by Russell Smith, late February 2004, Ozona, Texas.

[709] Ibid.

[710] Ibid.

[711] J.D. Hogg, phone interview by Russell Smith, email, fall 2004, August 22, 2005, El Paso, Texas.

[712] Ben Ross, interview by Russell Smith, late February 2004, Ozona, Texas.

[713] Ben Ross, interview by Russell Smith, late February 2004, Ozona, Texas; J.D. Hogg, email to Russell Smith, fall 2004, El Paso, Texas.

[714] Ben Ross, interview by Russell Smith, late February 2004, Ozona, Texas.

[715] Joe Gonzalez, Polygraph Examiner, El Paso Police Department, polygraph report addressed to Dalton Hogg, Terrell County Deputy Sheriff, December 21, 1965.

[716] Alfredo Gallegos, interview by Russell Smith with translation by daughter Christina Gallegos, June 2004, Uvalde, Texas.

[717] Russell Smith, knowledge and experience, career in law enforcement, Tom Green County, San Angelo, Texas.

[718] Ibid.

[719] San Angelo Standard-Times, November 19, 1965.

[720] Ibid.

[721] Russell Smith, knowledge and experience, career in law enforcement, Tom Green County, San Angelo, Texas.

[722] Bill Cooksey, former Terrell County Sheriff, interview by Russell Smith, January 6, 1990, Odessa, Texas.

[723] Joanne Carruthers Bell, interview by Russell Smith, June 22-23, 2004, San Angelo, Texas.

[724] Ibid.

[725] Ibid.

[726] San Angelo Standard-Times, November 19, 1965.

[727] Candace Cooksey Fulton, interview by Russell Smith, emails, 2004-2005, Brownwood, Texas.

[728] Ibid.

[729] Ibid.

[730] San Angelo Standard Times, December 12, 1965.

[731] Ibid.

[732] Ray Fitzgerald, phone interview by Russell Smith, September 2004, Van Horn, Texas.

[733] WordIQ.com website; www.wordiq.com.

[734] Ibid.

[735] Sports Illustrated; January 4, 1965.

[736] Sports Illustrated, January 18, 1964.

[737] U.S. News and World Report, January 18, 1965.

[738] Cliff Wilson, retired U.S. Customs Agent, interview by Russell Smith, July 10, 2004, Uvalde, Texas.

[739] H.B. 'Butch' Purvis, Irion County Chief Deputy, phone interview by Russell Smith, fall 2004, Mertzon, Texas.

[740] Henry Beth Hogg, interviews by Russell Smith, August 1-3, 2004, Sanderson, Texas.

[741] Candace Cooksey Fulton, interview by Russell Smith, emails, 2004-2005, Brownwood, Texas.

[742] Henry Beth Hogg, interviews by Russell Smith, August 1-3, 2004, Sanderson, Texas

[743] Candace Cooksey Fulton, interview by Russell Smith, emails, 2004-2005, Brownwood, Texas.

[744] Forest Gould Hardin personnel file, Texas Ranger Hall of Fame.

[745] Alfred Allee Jr., retired Texas Ranger, interview by Russell Smith, February 4, 2004, Alpine, Texas.

[746] J.D. Hogg, phone interview by Russell Smith, email, fall 2004, El Paso, Texas.

[747] Ray Fitzgerald, retired U.S. Border Patrol agent, phone interview by Russell Smith, September 2004, Van Horn, Texas.

[748] Ibid.

[749] Roy 'Hoot' Deaton, interview by Russell Smith, August 2, 2004, Sanderson, Texas.

[750] Ibid.

[751] Ibid.

[752] Ibid.

[753] Ibid.

[754] The Sanderson Times, March 19, 1966.

[755] Adrienne McElhaney, phone interviews by Russell Smith, fall 2004, May 2005, Iraan, Texas.

[756] Ibid.

[757] Ibid.

[758] Ibid.

[759] Ibid.

[760] Ibid.

[761] Ibid.

[762] Ibid.

[763] Ibid.

[764] Adrienne McElhaney, phone interviews by Russell Smith, fall 2004, May 2005, Iraan, Texas; Alfred Allee Jr., retired Texas Ranger, interview by Russell Smith, February 4, 2004, Alpine, Texas.

[765] Ibid.

[766] Elaine Rogers O'Donnell, phone interview by Russell Smith, May 11, 2005, Marfa, Texas.

[767] Bill Cooksey, former Terrell County Sheriff, interview by Russell Smith, January 6, 1990, Odessa, Texas; J.D. Hogg, phone interview by Russell Smith, email, fall 2004, El Paso, Texas.

[768] Cliff Wilson, retired U.S. Customs Agent, interview by Russell Smith, July 10, 2004, Uvalde, Texas.

[769] Roy 'Hoot' Deaton, interview by Russell Smith, August 2, 2004, Sanderson, Texas.

[770] Ibid.

[771] J.D. Hogg, phone interview by Russell Smith, email, fall 2004, El Paso, Texas; Joe Brown, phone interview by Russell Smith, August 15, 2004.

[772] Ibid.

[773] The Sanderson Times, April 21, 1966.

[774] Henry Beth Hogg, interviews by Russell Smith, August 1-3, 2004, Sanderson, Texas.

[775] Ibid.

[776] Ibid.

[777] Ibid.

[778] Ibid.

[779] Ibid.

[780] The Sanderson Times, April 21, 1966; J.D. Hogg, phone interview by Russell Smith, email, fall 2004, El Paso, Texas.

[781] Jack Deaton, interview by Russell Smith, October 15, 2005, Sanderson, Texas.

[782] Ibid.

[783] Alfred Allee Jr., retired Texas Ranger, interview by Russell Smith, February 4, 2004, Alpine, Texas.

[784] Ibid.

[785] Ibid.

[786] Ibid.

[787] J.D. Hogg, phone interview by Russell Smith, email, fall 2004, El Paso, Texas.

[788] Ben Ross, interview by Russell Smith, late February 2004, Ozona, Texas.

[789] Bill Cooksey, former Terrell County Sheriff, interview by Russell Smith, January 6, 1990, Odessa, Texas; J.D. Hogg, phone interview by Russell Smith, email, fall 2004, El Paso, Texas.

[790] J.D. Hogg, phone interview by Russell Smith, email, fall 2004, El Paso, Texas; Brad Bradley, interview by Russell Smith, February 2004, San Angelo, Texas; Johnie and Hudson Hillis, interview by Russell Smith, August 27, 2004, Uvalde, Texas.

[791] Brad Bradley, interview by Russell Smith, February 2004, San Angelo, Texas, March 30, 2005, Del Rio, Texas.

[792] Jack Deaton, interview by Russell Smith, October 15, 2005.

[793] Ibid.

[794] Ibid.

[795] The Sanderson Times, August 11, 1966.

[796] Jack Deaton, interview by Russell Smith, October 15, 2005.

[797] Ted Luce, interview by Russell Smith, March 2005, Del Rio, Texas.

[798] Marcella and Felix Harrison, interview by Russell Smith, June 2004, Eldorado, Texas, emails 2004-2005.

[799] Ted Luce, interview by Russell Smith, March 2005, Del Rio, Texas.

[800] Ibid.

[801] Ibid.

[802] Ibid.

[803] Ibid.

[804] Ibid.

[805] Ibid.

[806] Ibid.

[807] Ibid.

[808] Ibid.

[809] Ibid.

[810] Ibid.

[811] Ibid.

[812] Ibid.

[813] Ibid.

[814] Marcella and Felix Harrison, interview by Russell Smith, June 2004, Eldorado, Texas; Ted Luce, interview by Russell Smith, March 2005, Del Rio, Texas; Alfred Allee Jr., retired Texas Ranger, interview by Russell Smith, February 4, 2004, Alpine, Texas, April 2005, San Angelo, Texas.

[815] Ibid.

[816] Ibid.

[817] Alfred Allee Jr., retired Texas Ranger, interview by Russell Smith, February 4, 2005, Alpine, Texas, March 2005, San Angelo, Texas; Bill Cooksey, former Terrell County Sheriff, interview by Russell Smith, January 6, 1990, Odessa, Texas; J.D. Hogg, phone interview by Russell Smith, email, fall 2004, August 22, 2005, El Paso, Texas.

[818] Ibid.

[819] Ibid.

[820] J.D. Hogg, phone interview by Russell Smith, email, fall 2004, August 22, 2005, El Paso, Texas.

[821] Ben Ross, interview by Russell Smith, late February 2004, Ozona, Texas; Ben Ross, interview/tour by Russell Smith, September 26, 2004, Dryden, Texas.

[822] The Winchester Model 12, 1 of 1000, by George Madis, copyright 1982, reviewed by Russell Smith, September 2005, Cabelas Gun Library, Buda, Texas.

[823] E.A. 'Junior' Rogers, phone interview by Russell Smith, May 2005, Kermit, Texas.

[824] Candace Cooksey Fulton, interview and email by Russell Smith, July 2005, San Angelo, Texas.

[825] Alfred Allee Jr., Texas Ranger, letter to Colonel Homer Garrison, Jr,, Director, Texas Department of Public Safety, dated August 25, 1966.

[826] National Weather Service personnel, interviews by Russell Smith, spring/summer 2005, San Angelo, Texas.

[827] U.S. Naval Observatory, Astronomical Applications Department website, http://aa.usno.navy.mil.

[828] J.D. Hogg, phone interview by Russell Smith, email, fall 2004, El Paso, Texas; Alfred Allee Jr., retired Texas Ranger, interview by Russell Smith, February 4, 2004, Alpine, Texas, Summer 2005, San Angelo, Texas.

[829] Ibid.

[830] Russell Smith, perception of just another night in Dryden, Texas.

[831] Bill Cooksey, former Terrell County Sheriff, interview by Russell Smith, January 6, 1990, Odessa, Texas; Alfred Allee Jr., retired Texas Ranger, interview by Russell Smith, February 4, 2004, Alpine, Texas.

[832] Ibid.

[833] U.S. Naval Observatory, Astronomical Applications Department website, http://aa.usno.navy.mil.

[834] Ibid.

[835] E.A. 'Junior' Rogers, phone interview by Russell Smith, May 2005, Kermit, Texas; Elaine Rogers O'Donnell, phone interview by Russell Smith, May 11, 2005, Marfa, Texas; Adrienne McElhaney, phone interviews by Russell Smith, fall 2004 and May 2005, Iraan, Texas.

[836] Bill Cooksey, former Terrell County Sheriff, interview by Russell Smith, January 6, 1990, Odessa, Texas; Alfred Allee Jr., retired Texas Ranger, interview by Russell Smith, February 4, 2004, Alpine, Texas.

[837] Ibid.

[838] Ibid.

[839] Ibid.

[840] Ibid.

[841] Alfred Allee Jr., Texas Ranger, letter to Colonel Homer Garrison, Jr,, Director, Texas Department of Public Safety, dated August 25, 1966.

[842] Ben Ross, interview and tour of Dryden by Russell Smith, September 26, 2004, Dryden, Texas.

[843] Alfred Allee Jr., retired Texas Ranger, interview by Russell Smith, February 4, 2004, Alpine, Texas.

[844] Bill Cooksey, former Terrell County Sheriff, interview by Russell Smith, January 6, 1990, Odessa, Texas; Alfred Allee Jr., retired Texas Ranger, interview by Russell Smith, February 4, 2004, Alpine, Texas.

[845] Joe Brown, interview by Russell Smith, August 15, 2004, phone call to his West Texas residence.

[846] Alfred Allee Jr., retired Texas Ranger, interview by Russell Smith, February 4, 2004, Alpine, Texas.

[847] San Angelo Standard-Times, August 21, 1966.

[848] Ibid.

[849] Alfred Allee Jr., Texas Ranger, letter to Colonel Homer Garrison, Jr,, Director, Texas Department of Public Safety, dated August 25, 1966, San Angelo Standard-Times, August 21, 1966; Joel Tisdale, Texas Department of Public Safety, letter to Straus-Frank Company, September 22, 1966.

[850] Bill Cooksey, former Terrell County Sheriff, interview by Russell Smith, January 6, 1990, Odessa, Texas; Alfred Allee Jr., retired Texas Ranger, interview by Russell Smith, February 4, 2004, Alpine, Texas.

[851] Jess Ten Eyck, phone interview by Russell Smith, May 22-23, 2005, Bandera, Texas.

[852] Ibid.

[853] Ibid.

[854] Ibid.

[855] Adrienne McElhaney, phone interviews by Russell Smith, fall 2004, May 2005, Iraan, Texas.

[856] Ibid.

[857] Bill Cooksey, former Terrell County Sheriff, interview by Russell Smith, January 6, 1990, Odessa, Texas; Alfred Allee Jr., retired Texas Ranger, interview by Russell Smith, February 4, 2004, Alpine, Texas.

[858] E.A. 'Junior' Rogers, phone interview by Russell Smith, May 2005, Kermit, Texas; Bill Cooksey, former Terrell County Sheriff, interview by Russell Smith, January 6, 1990, Odessa, Texas; Alfred Allee Jr., retired Texas Ranger, interview by Russell Smith, February 4, 2004, Alpine, Texas.

[859] Ibid.

[860] Jess Ten Eyck, interview by Russell Smith, May 22-23, 2005, Bandera, Texas, E.A.'Junior' Rogers, phone interview by Russell Smith, May 2005, Kermit, Texas; Alfred Allee Jr., retired Texas Ranger, interview by Russell Smith, February 4, 2004, Alpine, Texas.

[861] Bill Cooksey, former Terrell County Sheriff, interview by Russell Smith, January 6, 1990, Odessa, Texas; Alfred Allee Jr., retired Texas Ranger, interview by Russell Smith, February 4, 2004, Alpine, Texas.

[862] J.D. Hogg, phone interview by Russell Smith, email, fall 2004, August 22, 2005, El Paso, Texas; Bill Cooksey, former Terrell County Sheriff, interview by Russell Smith, January 6, 1990, Odessa, Texas; Alfred Allee Jr., retired Texas Ranger, interview by Russell Smith, February 4, 2004, Alpine, Texas; Joe Brown, interview by Russell Smith, August 15, 2004, phone call to his West Texas residence.

[863] A. D'Wayne Jernigan, Val Verde County Sheriff, interview by Russell Smith, August 6, 2004, Del Rio, Texas.

[864] Ibid.

[865] Jess Ten Eyck, phone interview by Russell Smith, May 22-23, 2005, Bandera, Texas.

[866] Henry Beth Hogg, interviews by Russell Smith, August 1-3, 2004, Sanderson, Texas.

[867] W.J. Vaughan, interview by Russell Smith, August 27, 2004, Batesville, Texas.

[868] J.D. Hogg, phone interview by Russell Smith, fall 2004, El Paso, Texas; Henry Beth Hogg, interviews by Russell Smith, August 1-3, 2004, Sanderson, Texas; Bill Cooksey, former Terrell County Sheriff, interview by Russell Smith, January 6, 1990, Odessa, Texas; Alfred Allee Jr., retired Texas Ranger, interview by Russell Smith, February 4, 2004, Alpine, Texas.

[869] Bill Cooksey, former Terrell County Sheriff, interview by Russell Smith, January 6, 1990, Odessa, Texas; Odessa American, photograph, January 21, 1973, Odessa, Texas.

[870] Jess Ten Eyck, phone interview by Russell Smith, May 22-23, 2005, Bandera, Texas.

[871] Ibid.

[872] Ibid.

[873] Henry Beth Hogg, interviews by Russell Smith, August 1-3, 2004, Sanderson, Texas; Roy 'Hoot' Deaton, interview by Russell Smith, August 2, 2004, Sanderson, Texas.

[874] Ross McSwain, interview by Russell Smith, March 9, 2003, San Angelo, Texas.

[875] E.A. 'Junior' Rogers, phone interview by Russell Smith, May 2005, Kermit, Texas.

[876] Alfred Allee Jr., retired Texas Ranger, interview by Russell Smith, February 4, 2004, Alpine, Texas.

[877] Ibid.

[878] Bill Cooksey, former Terrell County Sheriff, interview by Russell Smith, January 6, 1990, Odessa, Texas.

[879] Ibid.

[880] Billy R. Wier, Latent Fingerprint Expert, Texas Department of Public Safety, Letter to Sheriff Herman Richter, August 24, 1966, Letters to Sheriff Bill Cooksey, August 24, 1966 and August 25, 1966.

[881] Billy R. Wier, Latent Fingerprint Expert, Texas Department of Public Safety, Letter to Sheriff Herman Richter, August 24, 1966.

[882] Billy R. Wier, Latent Fingerprint Expert, Texas Department of Public Safety, Letter to Sheriff Bill Cooksey, August 24, 1966.

[883] Billy R. Wier, Latent Fingerprint Expert, Texas Department of Public Safety, Letter to Sheriff Bill Cooksey, August 25, 1966.

[884] C.H. Beardsley, Chemistry Section Supervisor, Texas Department of Public Safety, Letter to Sheriff Bill Cooksey, August 24, 1966.

[885] Joel Tisdale, Chief, Identification and Records Division, Texas Department of Public Safety, Letter to Sheriff Bill Cooksey, September 6, 1966; Fred R. Rymer, Supervisor, Firearms Section, Texas Department of Public Safety, Letter to Bill Cooksey, September 6, 1966.

[886] Joel Tisdale, Chief, Identification and Records Division, Texas Department of Public Safety, Letter to Sheriff Bill Cooksey, September 6, 1966.

[887] J.D. Chastain, Laboratory Manager, Texas Department of Public Safety, Letter to Sheriff Bill Cooksey, July 1, 1969; Billy R. Wier, Latent

Fingerprint Expert, Texas Department of Public Safety, Letter to Sheriff Bill Cooksey, August 24, 1966.

[888] Fred R. Rymer, Supervisor, Firearms Section, Texas Department of Public Safety, Letter to Sheriff Bill Cooksey, September 6, 1966.

[889] Fred R. Rymer, Supervisor, Firearms Section, Texas Department of Public Safety, undated letter/memo to Smith and Wesson, Inc., P.O. Box 520, Springfield, Massachusetts, 01101.

[890] H.E. Steins, Service Manager, Smith and Wesson, Inc., Letter to Fred R. Rymer, September 15, 1966.

[891] Fred R. Rymer, Supervisor, Firearms Section, Texas Department of Public Safety, Letter to Bill Cooksey, October, 7, 1966.

[892] Bill Cooksey, Terrell County Sheriff's Department, Memo to Sheriff Leon Maples, Kerr County Sheriff's Department, October 17, 1966.

[893] Bill Cooksey, former Terrell County Sheriff, interview by Russell Smith, January 6, 1990, Odessa, Texas; Kenneth Kelley, retired Uvalde County Sheriff, interview by Russell Smith, August 27, 2004.

[894] J.D. Hogg, interview by Russell Smith, email, fall 2004, El Paso, Texas.

[895] Bill Cooksey, former Terrell County Sheriff, interview by Russell Smith, January 6, 1990, Odessa, Texas; Kenneth Kelley, retired Uvalde County Sheriff, interview by Russell Smith, August 27, 2004.

[896] Alfred Allee Jr., retired Texas Ranger, interview by Russell Smith, February 4, 2004, Alpine, Texas.

[897] Cliff Wilson, retired U.S. Customs agent, interview by Russell Smith, July 10, 2004, Uvalde, Texas.

[898] Ibid.

[899] Ibid.

[900] Ibid.

[901] Glenn Weatherman, retired U.S. Border Patrol agent, interview by Russell Smith, Augsut 7, 2004, Rochelle, Texas.

[902] Ibid.

[903] Ibid.

[904] Indictment #431, Terrell County District Clerk record, September 1966.

[905] Indictment #433, Terrell County District Court record, October 1966.

[906] Indictment # 434, Terrell County District Court record, October 1966.

[907] Elaine Rogers O'Donnell, phone interview by Russell Smith, May 11, 2005, Marfa, Texas.

[908] Indictment # 435, Terrell County District Court record, October 1966.

[909] Indictment # 436, Terrell County District Court record, October 1966.

[910] Indictment #4184, Uvalde County District Court record, witnessed by A.V. Rutherford, Alfred Allee, Jack Mercer, February 9, 1967.

[911] John F. Sutton, District Judge, Order Setting Bail, October 31, 1966.

[912] John F. Sutton, District Judge, Order Changing Venue, Terrell County District Court record, November 29, 1966.

[913] John F. Sutton, District Judge, Order Appointing Attorney, Terrell County District Court record, 63rd Judicial District, October 31, 1966.

[914] Arturo C. Gonzalez, interview by Russell Smith, August 6, 2004, Del Rio, Texas.

[915] Roger Thurmond, District Judge, order authorizing payment of $100 to Arturo C. Gonzalez, January 27, 1967.

[916] Roger Thurmond, District Judge, Sentencing document, Val Verde County District Court record, January 27, 1967.

[917] Russell Smith, name withheld but listed in research.

[918] H.B. Montague, Chief Inspector, Post Office Department, Chief Postal Inspector, Washington, D.C., letter to Sheriff Bill Cooksey, July 21, 1967.

[919] Henry B. Small, Bureau of Records and Identification, Texas Department of Corrections, Huntsville, Texas, letter to Terrell County Sheriff's Office, August 29, 1967.

[920] Bill C. Cooksey, Instructor, Law Enforcement and Security Training Division, Texas A&M University, College Station, letter to Governor Briscoe, March 21, 1977.

[921] Mark White, Governor of Texas, Proclamation by the Governor of the State of Texas, No. 84-00220, February 6, 1984; Texas Department of Corrections release notice, March 21, 1984.

[922] Mark White, Governor of Texas, Proclamation by the Governor of the State of Texas, No. 84-00220, February 6, 1984.

[923] Texas Board of Pardons and Paroles website, www.tdcj.state.tx.us/bpp/exec_clem.html.

924 Texas Department of Corrections release notice, March 21, 1984; Bill Cooksey, former Terrell County Sheriff, interview by Russell Smith, January 6, 1990, Odessa, Texas.

925 Jess Ten Eyck, phone interview by Russell Smith, May 22-23, 2005, Bandera, Texas.

926 J.D. Hogg, phone interview by Russell Smith, email, fall 2004, August 22, 2005, El Paso, Texas;

Joe Brown, interview by Russell Smith, August 15, 2004, phone call to his West Texas residence;

Jerry Byrne, Texas Ranger, interview by Russell Smith, summer 2004; Henry Beth Hogg, interviews by Russell Smith, August 1-3, 2004, October 15, 2005, Sanderson, Texas; Jess Ten Eyck, phone interview by Russell Smith, May 22-23, 2005, Bandera, Texas.

927 Joe Brown, interview by Russell Smith, August 15, 2004, phone call to his West Texas residence, Jess Ten Eyck, phone interview by Russell Smith, May 22-23, 2005, Bandera, Texas; Jerry Byrne, Texas Ranger, interview by Russell Smith, summer 2004.

928 Russell Smith, requested U.S. Border Patrol investigation file, U.S. Department of Homeland Security, U.S. Citizenship and Immigration Services, received 166 pages but only five with documentation and seven with partial, 154 pages were withheld because of what was listed as an unwarranted invasion of personal privacy; letters were sent to the address that were in Bill Cooksey's wallet when Alfredo Hernandez was arrested and to the address that Rosa, the girlfriend, listed for Hernadnez's mother; Emails were sent to the United States Embassy and to the Mexican Consulate, all attempts were unsuccessful in locating Hernandez; Enrique Cadena, retired Captain, State Judicial Police, interview by Russell Smith and Manny Perez (retired U.S. Border Patrol), August 5, 2004, Acuna, Mexico.

929 Russell Smith, personal knowledge and where book idea came from, 1989, Odessa, Texas; Daisy Diaz-Alemany, PhD, LPC, suggested title to Russell Smith, Labor Day weekend, 2004, Austin, Texas.

930 Ibid.

931 Bill Cooksey, former Terrell County Sheriff, interview by Russell Smith, January 6, 1990, Odessa, Texas.

[932] Candace Cooksey Fulton, interview by Russell Smith, emails, 2004-2005, Brownwood, Texas, interview by Russell Smith, July 2005, San Angelo, Texas.

[933] Russell Smith, personal knowledge and relationship with Bill Cooksey.

[934] Ray Fitzgerald, retired U.S. Border Patrol, phone interview by Russell Smith, September 2004, Van Horn, Texas.

INDEX